The Mountain Reader

THE MOUNTAIN READER

Edited by John A. Murray

THE LYONS PRESS

Printed in the United States of America

Designed by Compset, Inc.

The Library of Congress Cataloging-in-Publication Data is available on file.

For Natalya

$\mathscr{C}$ONTENTS

$\mathcal{F}$OREWORD

When I first heard the news last year that the frozen, mummified body of lost explorer George Leigh Mallory had been found near the summit of Mount Everest, a chill went up and down my spine. Like other mountaineering buffs, I had long wondered about the circumstances of Mallory's and climbing partner Andrew Irvine's heroic 1924 attempt to ascend the world's tallest peak. And while the question of whether they reached the summit remains shrouded in mystery, I believe our modern society will forever be indebted to these explorers for their quest and for Mallory's response when asked why he wanted to climb Mount Everest: "Because it is there."

Along with affirming the human desire to explore the unknown, Mallory's simple but profound observation underscores the vital role that mountains play in the human imagination. Today, even though much of the planet's landscape has been altered or destroyed, the great mountain ranges of the world continue to tower over us, lifting our spirits and mocking the human pretension to master all of nature.

Just as great climbers draw their strength from the challenge of difficult-to-scale peaks, I believe that nature lovers have much to gain from experiences in the hills and mountains that surround us. It is from these heights that we can better appreciate the tapestry of life playing out in both small and grand scales, from the sight and feel of delicate lichens and wildflowers to the views of eagles soaring overhead and the sound of bull elks bugling in mountain valleys during the fall mating season.

Indeed, it was these sounds that greeted me last fall when I paused to rest while hiking in Colorado's Mount Zirkel Wilderness.

This unexpected concert, combined with the experience of seeing golden aspen trees, a variety of songbirds, and pristine high-country lakes, filled me with both gratitude for the majesty of these mountains and resolve to work harder to protect the great places wherever they may be found.

A focus of that resolve was not too far from me at the time. For it is nearby in the 7,500-foot-elevation Yampa and Elk River Valleys that The Nature Conservancy is working closely with local ranchers to help prevent the subdivision and development of large landhold-ings and to encourage ranching practices that lead to the protection of biologically rich riparian habitats.

This kind of positive and creative action to protect mountains as well as other ecosystems has been a hallmark of The Nature Conser-vancy throughout our fifty-year history. Our work in American moun-tain areas extends from Maine's rocky coast to Hawaii's lush volcanic peaks. In New York's Adirondack Park, for example, we are protecting some 240,000 forested, wetland, riverine, and shoreline acres, and over one hundred globally rare species. Farther south in the central Appalachians—in the Clinch River Valley of eastern Tennessee and western Virginia—we are focusing on critical habitat for one of the world's most unheralded hot spots of aquatic (fish and mussel) biodi-versity. And back in the northern Rockies, in the heart of Idaho's spectacular Snake River Canyon, we are fighting to protect native grassland species from an invasion of the noxious yellowstar thistle and other aggressive weeds.

Similarly, our international program is aiming high in its con-servation activities. We are working with our partner organizations abroad to protect unique mountain ecosystems, such as Jamaica's Blue and John Crow Mountains; the coastal mountains of Colombia's Sierra Nevada de Santa Marta National Park that soar to 19,000 feet above sea level within twenty-five miles of the ocean; and the peaks that stretch through the rugged northwest corner of China's Yunnan Province.

Just as explorers and conservationists are compelled to take on the challenge of the mountain environment, so are great writers. In this *Mountain Reader* we have assembled an outstanding collection of works from a superb cast of writers whose prose aspires to match the grandeur of our highest peaks. I trust you will enjoy the thoughtful words of such giants of conservation as John Muir, Aldo Leopold, and William O. Douglas. No doubt you will also relish the powerful compositions of Rick Bass, Barbara Kingsolver, Jon Krakauer, and other leading lights of contemporary letters.

So please sit back and prepare to spend some quality time in the magnificent and often mythical upper regions of our world. I hope this collection will raise not only your spirits, but your appreciation for our common natural heritage as well.

John C. Sawhill
President and Chief Executive Officer
The Nature Conservancy
Spring 2000

PREFACE

This series of nature anthologies, published in collaboration with The Nature Conservancy, is dedicated to bringing readers the finest nature writing from the past and present. Each book is devoted to a single environmental subject and alternates classic selections with contemporary writings. The first volume is dedicated to rivers. The second celebrates the beauty and majesty of the seacoasts. This third volume focuses on the literature of mountains. Future volumes in the series will explore writings about forests, endangered species, wetlands, lakes, deserts, grasslands, urban nature, and oceans.

As always, I am committed to featuring the work of undiscovered and emerging writers as well as the work of well-established and mature authors. If you have or know of superb writings on nature, please send them to me at: P.O. Box 102345, Denver, CO 80250. I am particularly interested in writing from the following groups: (1) writers known only locally or regionally but with potential for national acclaim, (2) writers from the Midwest, Northeast, and Deep South, (3) women writers and writers from ethnic groups offering alternative perspectives on nature, and (4) writers with experiences abroad. I promise to respond to each submission. Working together—readers and editor—we can build anthologies in the future that will hold both literary excellence and thematic and stylistic diversity as the standard.

I have many thanks to give. First, the writers and their publishers have been extremely cooperative and I thank them all; no anthology is possible without such quick and enthusiastic assistance. My editor, Lilly Golden, has been wonderfully helpful; all authors should be blessed with such warm, energetic, and perspicacious guidance. I must, too, thank my readers. Over the five years during which I edited the Sierra Club nature writing annuals, you constantly brightened my days with postcards, letters, and phone calls. Finally, I must give thanks to the Murray family for their love and support, and especially my nine-year-old son, Naoki.

—J.A.M.
Denver, Colorado

ℐNTRODUCTION

Delightful, in a way,
to miss seeing Mount Fuji
in the fog and rain.
> —Basho, *The Narrow Road to the Deep North* (1698)

i.

As I looked I could see great mountains with rocks and forests on them.
I could see all colors of light flashing out of the mountains toward the four
quarters. Then they took me on top of a high mountain where I could see
all over the earth.
> —Black Elk, Oglala Sioux holy man, *Black Elk Speaks* (1932)

𝓔very September I drive up from the city—the sky cloudless, the mule deer at ease in the sage, the equinoctial sun bright and warm—and hike for a few days in Rocky Mountain National Park. I usually stay at the Moraine Park campground the first couple of nights. Then I move to Longs Peak campground. Each morning I take a different trail into the range, beginning an hour before sunrise. I like to hike eight or nine miles before turning back, and the park has many wonderful trails to accommodate long walks. It is a grand time of year, with the aspen leaves as luminous as lamps and the umber-maned elk bugling and the moon coming full toward the end of the month. The summer crowds are gone and there is a Virgilian peace on the land, a quality of spent fertility and loss, and yet also a sense of contentment, of fruition and completion.

The spruce grouse whirr among the boughs and the water ouzels sing along the creeks and in the clearings a few last purple asters and yellow paintbrushes bloom. Every so often you see a moose, or perhaps

1

a coyote. There is the fragrance of small berries ripening, and of fallen leaves turning to earth in quiet places. Sometimes an iridescent green hummingbird buzzes near, attracted by the red of your bandanna, and you recall the lines from *The Tempest* when Ariel, the invisible woodland spirit, plays a tune on his pipe:

> Be not afeard: this place is full of noises,
> Sounds and sweet airs that give delight and hurt not.
> Sometimes a thousand twangling instruments
> Will hum about mine ears; and sometimes voices
> That, if I then had waked after long sleep,
> Will make me sleep again; and then, in dreaming,
> The clouds methought would open and show riches
> Ready to drop upon me, that, when I waked
> I cried to dream again.

Above it all is that massive granite pyramid identified on the maps as Longs Peak (14,255 feet), a heavy solid rock painted here and there with dirty banks of snow and soaring one mile into the dark blue Colorado sky.

I climbed the peak once, stood there in the cold wind of early morning and looked down at the lower ridges and canyons still wrapped in shadow. Far to the east was the prairie, flat as the sea that once covered it. All around were mountains. I recalled Dante's lines, in his ascent of Mount Purgatory with Virgil: "This mountain is such that ever at the beginning below it is toilsome, but the higher one goes the less it wearies."

At the summit of a mountain one becomes for a moment as weightless as the shadow of a passing cloud.

Over the years I have come to regard Longs Peak probably much as the Japanese artist Hokusai (*One Hundred Views of Mount Fuji*, 1833) considered Mount Fuji. However far I range as a naturalist across the four seasons—from the Georgia seacoast to Big Sur, from the Alaskan tundra to the Arizona cactus country—I am always drawn to Longs Peak each fall. I have photographed the lovely crag from vantages well known and little known, from the trout pools of the St. Vrain River to the talus slide below the diamond, from the rolling tundra of Trail Ridge Road to the spruce-filled bottom of Forest Canyon, from Mills Lake with its wind-flagged bonsai to the old burn near Beaver Meadows. Once I photographed the mountain from downtown Denver, framed inside the steel and concrete canyon of Fifteenth Street. Another time I shot it from the old buffalo prairie east of town, my tripod set among prickly pear cactus and yucca. I think that, like Hokusai, I will be ninety years old and still climbing the high ridges for a better view of the peak, still waiting for the skies to share some new quality of light, still opening and closing the aperture and trying to capture something of its beauty.

I love the mountain best when the sun is about to rise and the sky is moving from violet-green toward cerulean blue and the whole landscape is filled with expectancy and invitation, when the meadow birds are singing and the game is moving toward water. Put a full moon behind it, setting into Glacier Ridge, and an elk bugling off in the timber, and I am about as close to Dante's paradise as you can get on earth.

Although the mountain is silent, it has often spoken to me in the quiet way of mountains. It has reminded me of how short life is, and how long death is. It has demonstrated what is noble and enduring in wild nature and what is valuable and unperishable in the human spirit. It has illustrated the necessity of establishing lofty but achievable goals. It has taught me humility and good humor. It has shown me that I must always be strong and that to remain strong I must stay deeply rooted to the earth. When I have fallen short of virtue, I have found purity again in its springs. Grief and loss have been healed among its fire-charred trees.

Implicit in every aspect of the mountain, and my attachment to it, has been all that is evoked by the word *freedom*. Finally, the mountain has underscored to me the importance of love—not just love of family and friends, but love of culture and country, ideals and ideas, truth and beauty, forgiveness and compassion.

The importance of love comes to you most when you are alone.

It occurs to me, in reflecting upon these twenty-two mountain essays, that every person should have such a mountain, an elevated feature on the local landscape to which they go for periodic inspiration and renewal. If people could only take the calm and strength of the peaks back with them to the valleys, the world would be a much more peaceful and happy place. The authors in this book write of their respective mountains in this spirit of hope and faith and generosity. They represent all parts of the country—east and west, south and north. Their selections range over three continents and 250 years. They include essays by a noted mountain climber (John Krakauer), a former Supreme Court justice (William O. Douglas), and a Pulitzer-prize-winning novelist (A. B. Guthrie). The selections vary widely in length, from a handful of pages, to several dozen pages reminding us that their sources of inspiration can vary also, from a salience on the order of David Petersen's Baboquivari to peaks with the stature of Clarence King's Sierra Nevadas. The styles are as diverse as their authors, or as the mountains about which the authors write. Leopold employed a minimalist style, an essential language stripped of modifiers. Thoreau wrote in the full-blown nineteenth-century style, with sentences and paragraphs of considerable length and complexity. Most of the others fall somewhere between these two outer boundaries. No matter length, style, or point of view, all of these essays celebrate their authors' passion for mountains. For each author, though in subtly different ways, mountains awaken wonder and powerfully inspire the imagination.

ii.

Something hidden. Go and find it.
Go and look behind the Ranges—
Something lost behind the Ranges.
Lost and waiting for you. Go!
      —Rudyard Kipling, "The Explorer"

Three themes pervade the diverse mountain essays gathered together in this book. They are communion, renewal, and liberation. All three are common in nature writing but are particularly evident in this collection, with its emphasis on such a spiritually moving subject. By far the most prevalent theme is the first, communion, which involves the intimate sharing of the human spirit with the natural world. This theme pervades the essay by Isabella Byrd on her first ascending Longs Peak. After mounting the summit her hiking companion exclaims, "I believe there is a God!" and Byrd states that she "felt as if, Parsee-like, I must worship." She recalls a line from the scripture: "The most high dwelleth not in temples made with hands." After descending from the heights Byrd concludes that she "would not now exchange my memories of its perfect beauty and extraordinary sublimity for any other experience of mountaineering in any part of the world." Like so many afterward (the editor of this anthology included), Byrd was forever changed by her moment alone on the summit of Longs Peak and her brief union with the eternal and immutable spirit of nature.

Elsewhere, the naturalist Aldo Leopold, one of the seminal conservationists of the twentieth century, climbs a mountain in southwestern New Mexico and is treated to a moving epiphany. While on a high ridge, he and his forest service coworkers (this was in Leopold's youth) shoot a Mexican gray wolf. After watching the animal die, Leopold realizes the tragic error of his ways and resolves to devote his life to the preservation of nature: "I realized then, and have known ever since, that there was something new to me in those eyes [the wolf's eyes]—something known only to her and to the mountain." Leopold had come to understand that the mountains needed the wolves to keep the deer population in check, and that, once the wolves were removed, the deer would overpopulate the range.

A second theme found in these essays is renewal, the rejuvenation of the fatigued spirit through contact with the regenerative forces of wild nature. Although present to a certain extent in all the essays, this theme is especially evident in two selections. The essay by Supreme Court Justice William O. Douglas comes to mind first, as he refers in the topic sentence to the fact that the White Mountains of New Hampshire and he are "old friends." His close relationship with the mountains goes back to his youth, when he would come up from New Haven to camp, fish, and hike. In the last paragraphs of the essay Douglas argues persuasively for the permanent preservation of the White Mountains as a sanctuary not only for himself, but for future generations: "The sacred precincts should be locked and barred against all machines and against all encroachments by civilization."

Montanan A. B. Guthrie, who wrote the Oscar-nominated screenplay for the classic western film *Shane*, writes in a similar spirit of his beloved Rocky Mountain Front. This area north of Great Falls, which is where Guthrie grew up, provided the writer-naturalist with a lifelong source of renewal, a strong sustaining force that helped him through the many seasons of life. "At the age of 86, living on the Front, I have come to feel a part of what has gone before, kin to dinosaur and buffalo and departed Indians that lived here . . . [and] as I am part and brother of what went before, so I am related to the living creatures that inhabit the Front." For Guthrie "good medicine [lay] all around" and nearby Ear Mountain was a personal "vision site."

The theme of liberation—which involves the sense of being disencumbered and quite literally freed from some internal or external burden—is particularly evident in the selection by Henry David Thoreau. The bard of Concord achieves a series of penetrating insights at the summit of the famous peak in Maine, as he leaves the last vestiges of civilization behind:

> Here was no man's garden, but the unhandselled globe. It was not lawn, nor pasture, nor mead, nor woodland, nor lea, nor arable, nor waste land. It was the fresh and natural surface of the planet Earth, as it was made forever and ever.

Never before or after during his brief life was Thoreau so far removed from the New England society he loved so much to dissect, or, it would seem, quite so happy.

Rick Bass, a kindred philosophical spirit, writes just as passionately of "some mountains in northern Utah" that he calls "the most majestic mountains in America—the wildest, freest, coldest, oldest, windiest, mountain wildflowerest, mule deerest mountains there are." Bass describes them as "magic mountains" where, so filled with joy, he often begins to "laugh almost uncontrollably." Bass's delight in the simple pleasures of mountaineering echoes John Muir's writings on the Sierra Nevada a century earlier. Like Bass, Muir fell deeply in love with the western mountains in his twenties, and lived near them all his life. Muir writes of his "first hour of freedom" on a Sierra mountaintop, and of an otherworldly panorama:

> How truly glorious the landscape circled around this noble summit!—giant mountains, valleys innumerable, glaciers and meadows, rivers and lakes, with the wide blue sky bent tenderly over them all.

The writings of all these authors collectively make it clear that mountains are as much a part of our inner landscape as they are geographic features on the surface of the earth. They lift our eyes and our spirits toward the sun and moon and stars. They are places of otherworldly revelation as well as sanctuaries for physical recreation. Once they were occupied only by the likes of Zeus and Hera, Apollo and Athena. Now we can climb into the high and lonely places where wisdom resides and visions are found and passing clouds leave beads of water on outstretched fingertips.

Introduction

No matter how sophisticated you may be, a large granite mountain cannot be denied—it speaks in silence to the very core of your being.
—Ansel Adams, Autobiography

It is late August as I write this—the first light dusting of snow in the high country, a scattering of yellow leaves in the aspen groves, a certain restlessness in the animal kingdom. Soon I will pack the car and make the autumnal trip to Rocky Mountain National Park. For more than three decades now I have called Colorado home, primarily because of the mountains. The winters are not as severe as up north, there are three hundred days of sunshine annually, and the state offers a kind of biblical anthology of peaks and crags, passes and tarns, arêtes and horns, cirques and headwalls, glaciers and moraines, cliffs and canyons, cataracts and waterfalls, hogbacks and flatirons, buttes and mesas. There are peaks in Colorado, like the Spanish Peaks near Walsenburg, that evoke the volcanoes of Japan, and others, such as the Maroon Bells north of Aspen, that are as striking as anything in the Canadian Rockies. The southern mountains of the state around Ouray and Silverton—the heart of the San Juan Range—are often referred to as "Little Switzerland." With three quarters of the nation's land above 10,000 feet, and three hundred peaks over 13,000 feet, Colorado is the place to live if you love mountains.

One often searches for something to carry away from a summit. Once, on a mountain in northern Colorado, I came upon the empty body and outstretched wings of a golden eagle. A few years later, I found the sun-bleached skull and horns of a fourteen-year-old bighorn ram. Not long after that I discovered a ten-thousand-year-old vision-quest site in Rocky Mountain National Park, an undisturbed rock bunker later excavated by park archaeologists. I have spent much time in the western peaks, wandering around far from anything resembling a trail, looking for whatever treasures and treats persistent curiosity and random chance might reveal. Sometimes you find nothing. In fact, most times you find nothing. But about once every decade, hiking steadily each summer, you happen upon the unexpected. The older I become the less inclined I am to search for *things,* in the sense of material objects, on these mountain walks, and the more interested I have become in establishing facts, distinguishing subtle but significant differences, identifying truths, finding connections, apprehending patterns.

This book, with its twenty-two essays, is not unlike a mountain range. To extend the metaphor, it can be thought of as a range with twenty-two peaks. You, the reader, can wander through these essays much as you would a series of mountains, looking for things in them that you can bring back with you, into your life. Five years, ten years, from now, the world will be a different place. New faces will have replaced the familiar. Old stories will have been told again. Nothing will have changed, but everything will have changed. You will have progressed farther on the journey, moving closer to the place from which you came. But the mountains will remain, and the words in this book will be unchanged. All the things of this world will come and go like the leaves on the trees or the clouds in the sky, but the mountains will endure. Be like the mountains, and you will last, too.

*K*TAADN

Henry David Thoreau

*I*n the night I dreamed of trout-fishing; and, when at length I awoke, it seemed a fable that this painted fish swam there so near my couch, and rose to our hooks the last evening, and I doubted if I had not dreamed it all. So I arose before dawn to test its truth, while my companions were still sleeping. There stood Ktaadn with distinct and cloudless outline in the moonlight; and the rippling of the rapids was the only sound to break the stillness. Standing on the shore, I once more cast my line into the stream, and I found the dream to be real and the fable true. The speckled trout and silvery roach, like flying-fish, sped swiftly through the moonlight air, describing bright arcs on the dark side of Ktaadn, until moonlight, now fading into daylight, brought satiety to my mind, and the minds of my companions, who had joined me.

By six o'clock, having mounted our packs and a good blanketful of trout, ready dressed, and swung up such baggage and provision as we wished to leave behind upon the tops of saplings, to be out of the reach of bears, we started for the summit of the mountain, distant, as Uncle George said the boatmen called it, about four miles, but as I judged, and as it proved, nearer fourteen. He had never been any nearer the mountain than this, and there was not the slightest trace of man to guide us farther in this direction. At first, pushing a few rods up the Aboljacknagesic, or "open-land stream," we fastened our batteau to a tree, and traveled up the north side, through burnt lands, now partially overgrown with young aspens and other shrubbery; but soon, recrossing this stream, where it was about fifty or sixty feet wide, upon a jam of logs and rocks,—and you could cross it by this means almost anywhere,—we struck at once for the highest peak, over a mile or more of comparatively open land, still very gradually ascending the while. Here it fell to my lot, as the oldest mountain-climber, to take the lead. So, scanning the woody side of the mountain, which lay still at an indefinite distance, stretched out some seven or eight miles in length before us, we determined to steer directly for the base of the highest peak, leaving a large slide, by which, as I have since learned, some of our predecessors ascended, on our left. This course would lead us parallel to a dark seam in the forest, which marked the bed of a torrent, and over a slight spur, which extended southward from the main mountain, from whose bare summit we could get an outlook over the country, and climb directly up the peak, which would then be close at hand. Seen from this point, a bare ridge at the extremity of the open land, Ktaadn presented a different aspect from any mountain I have seen, there being a greater proportion of naked rock rising abruptly from the forest; and we looked up at this blue barrier as if it were some fragment of a wall which anciently bounded the earth in that direction. Setting the compass for a northeast course, which was the bearing of the southern base of the highest peak, we were soon buried in the woods.

We soon began to meet with traces of bears and moose, and those of rabbits were everywhere visible. The tracks of moose, more or less recent, to speak literally, covered every square rod on the sides of the mountain; and these animals are probably more numerous there now than ever before, being driven into this wilderness, from all sides, by the settlements. The track of a full-grown moose is like that of a cow, or larger, and of the young, like that of a calf. Sometimes we found ourselves traveling in faint paths, which they had made, like cowpaths in the woods, only far more indistinct, being rather openings, affording imperfect vistas through the dense underwood, than trodden paths; and everywhere the twigs had been browsed by them, clipped as smoothly as if by a knife. The bark of trees was stripped up by them to the height of eight or nine feet, in long, narrow strips, an inch wide, still showing the distinct marks of their teeth. We expected nothing less than to meet a herd of them every moment, and our Nimrod held his shooting-iron in readiness; but we did not go out of our way to look for them, and, though numerous, they are so wary that the unskillful hunter might range the forest a long time before he could get sight of one. They are sometimes dangerous to encounter, and will not turn out for the hunter, but furiously rush upon him and trample him to death, unless he is lucky enough to avoid them by dodging round a tree. The largest are nearly as large as a horse, and weigh sometimes one thousand pounds; and it is said that they can step over a five-foot gate in their ordinary walk. They are described as exceedingly awkward-looking animals, with their long legs and short bodies, making a ludicrous figure when in full run, but making great headway, nevertheless. It seemed a mystery to us how they could thread these woods, which it required all our suppleness to accomplish,—climbing, stooping, and winding, alternately. They are said to drop their long and branching horns, which usually spread five or six feet, on their backs, and make their way easily by the weight of their bodies. Our boatmen said, but I know not with how much truth, that their horns are apt to be gnawed away by vermin while they sleep. Their flesh, which is more like beef than venison, is common in Bangor market.

We had proceeded on thus seven or eight miles, till about noon, with frequent pauses to refresh the weary ones, crossing a considerable mountain stream, which we conjectured to be Murch Brook, at whose mouth we had camped, all the time in woods, without having once seen the summit, and rising very gradually, when the boatmen beginning to despair a little, and fearing that we were leaving the mountain on one side of us, for they had not entire faith in the compass, McCauslin climbed a tree, from the top of which he could see the peak, when it appeared that we had not swerved from a right line, the compass down below still ranging with his arm, which pointed to the summit. By the side of a cool mountain rill, amid the woods, where the water began to partake of the purity and transparency of the air, we stopped to cook some of our fishes, which we had brought thus far in order to save our hard bread and pork, in the use of which we had put ourselves on short allowance. We soon had a fire blazing, and stood around it, under the damp and sombre forest of firs and birches, each with a sharpened stick, three or four feet in length, upon which he had spitted his trout, or roach, previously well gashed and salted, our sticks, radiating like the spokes of a wheel from one centre, and each crowding his particular fish into the most desirable exposure, not with the truest regard always to his neighbor's rights. Thus we regaled ourselves, drinking meanwhile at the spring, till one man's pack, at least, was considerably lightened, when we again took up our line of march.

At length we reached an elevation sufficiently bare to afford a view of the summit, still distant and blue, almost as if retreating from us. A torrent, which proved to be the same we had crossed, was seen tumbling down in front, literally from out of the clouds. But this glimpse at our whereabouts was soon lost, and we were buried in the woods again. The wood was chiefly yellow birch, spruce, fir, mountain-ash, or round-wood, as the Maine people call it, and moose-wood. It was the worst kind of traveling; sometimes like the densest scrub-oak patches with us. The cornel, or bunch-berries, were very abundant, as well as Solomon's seal and mooseberries. Blueberries were distributed along our whole route; and in one place the bushes were drooping with the weight of the fruit, still as fresh as ever. It was the 7th of September. Such patches afforded a grateful repast, and served to bait the third party forward. When any lagged behind, the cry of "blueberries" was most effectual to bring them up. Even at this elevation we passed through a moose-yard, formed by a large flat rock, four or five rods square, where they tread down the snow in winter. At length, fearing that if we held the direct course to the summit, we should not find any water near our camping-ground, we gradually swerved to the west, till, at four o'clock, we struck again in the torrent which I have mentioned, and here, in view of the summit, the weary party decided to camp that night.

While my companions were seeking a suitable spot for this purpose, I improved the little daylight that was left in climbing the mountain alone. We were in a deep and narrow ravine, sloping up to the clouds, at an angle of nearly forty-five degrees, and hemmed in by walls of rock, which were at first covered with low trees, then with impenetrable thickets of scraggy birches and spruce-trees, and with moss, but at last bare of all vegetation but lichens, and almost continually draped in clouds. Following at the course of the torrent which occupied this,—and I mean to lay some emphasis on this word *up*,— pulling myself up by the side of perpendicular falls of twenty or thirty feet, by the roots of firs and birches, and then, perhaps, walking a level rod or two in the thin stream, for it took up the whole road, ascending by huge steps, as it were, a giant's stairway, down which a river flowed, I had soon cleared the trees, and paused on the successive shelves, to look back over the country. The torrent was from fifteen to thirty feet wide, without a tributary, and seemingly not diminishing in breadth as I advanced; but still it came rushing and roaring down, with a copious tide, over and amidst masses of bare rock, from the very clouds, as though a waterspout had just burst over the mountain. Leaving this at last, I began to work my way, scarcely less arduous than Satan's anciently through Chaos, up the nearest, though not the highest peak, at first scrambling on all fours over the tops of ancient black spruce-trees (*Abies nigra*), old as the flood, from two to ten or twelve feet in height, their tops flat and spreading, and their foliage blue, and nipped with cold, as if for centuries they had ceased growing upward against the bleak sky, the solid cold. I walked some good rods erect upon the tops of these trees, which were overgrown with moss and mountain-cranberries. It seemed that in the course of time they had filled up the intervals between the huge rocks, and the cold wind had uniformly leveled all over. Here the principle of vegetation was hard put to it. There was apparently a belt of this kind running quite round the mountain, though, perhaps, nowhere so remarkable as here. Once slumping through, I looked down ten feet, into a dark and cavernous region, and saw the stem of a spruce, on whose top I stood, as on a mass of coarse basket-work, fully nine inches in diameter at the ground. These holes were bears' dens, and the bears were even then at home. This was the sort of garden I made my way *over*, for an eighth of a mile, at the risk, it is true, of treading on some of the plants, not seeing any path *through* it,—certainly the most treacherous and porous country I ever traveled.

"Nigh foundered on he fares, Treading the crude consistence, half on foot, Half flying."

But nothing could exceed the toughness of the twigs,—not one snapped under my weight, for they had slowly grown. Having slumped, scrambled, rolled, bounced, and walked, by turns, over this scraggy country, I arrived upon a side-hill, or rather side-mountain, where rocks, gray, silent rocks, were the flocks and herds that pastured, chewing a rocky cud at sunset. They looked at me with hard gray eyes, without a bleat or a low. This brought me to the skirt of a cloud, and bounded my walk that night. But I had already seen that Maine country when I turned about, waving, flowing, rippling, down below.

When I returned to my companions, they had selected a camping-ground on the torrent's edge, and were resting on the ground; one was on the sick list, rolled in a blanket, on a damp shelf of rock. It was a savage and dreary scenery enough; so wildly rough, that they looked long to find a level and open space for the tent. We could not well camp higher, for want of fuel; and the trees here seemed so evergreen and sappy, that we almost doubted if they would acknowledge the influence of fire; but fire prevailed at last, and blazed here, too, like a good citizen of the world. Even at this height we met with frequent traces of moose, as well as of bears. As here was no cedar, we made our bed of coarser feathered spruce; but at any rate the feathers were plucked from the live tree. It was, perhaps, even a more grand and desolate place for a night's lodging than the summit would have been, being in the neighborhood of those wild trees, and of the torrent. Some more aerial and finer-spirited winds rushed and roared through the ravine all night, from time to time arousing our fire, and dispersing the embers about. It was as if we lay in the very nest of a young whirlwind. At midnight, one of my bed-fellows, being startled in his dreams by the sudden blazing up to its top of a fir-tree, whose green boughs were dried by the heat, sprang up, with a cry, from his bed, thinking the world on fire, and drew the whole camp after him.

In the morning, after whetting our appetite on some raw pork, a wafer of hard bread, and a dipper of condensed cloud or waterspout, we all together began to make our way up the falls, which I have described; this time choosing the right hand, or highest peak, which was not the one I had approached before. But soon my companions were lost to my sight behind the mountain ridge in my rear, which still seemed ever retreating before me, and I climbed alone over huge rocks, loosely poised, a mile or more, still edging toward the clouds; for though the day was clear elsewhere, the summit was concealed by mist. The mountain seemed a vast aggregation of loose rocks, as if some time it had rained rocks, and they lay as they fell on the mountain sides, nowhere fairly at rest, but leaning on each other, all rocking-stones, with cavities between, but scarcely any soil or smoother shelf. They were the raw materials of a planet dropped from an unseen quarry, which the vast chemistry of nature would anon work up, or work down, into the smiling and verdant plains and valleys of earth. This was an undone extremity of the globe; as in lignite, we see coal in the process of formation.

At length I entered within the skirts of the cloud which seemed forever drifting over the summit, and yet would never be gone, but was generated out of that pure air as fast as it flowed away; and when, a quarter of a mile farther, I reached the summit of the ridge, which those who have seen it in clearer weather say is about five miles long, and contains a thousand acres of table-land, I was deep within the hostile ranks of clouds, and all objects were obscured by them. Now the wind would blow me out a yard of clear sunlight, wherein I stood; then a gray, dawning light was all it could accomplish, the cloud-line ever rising and falling with the wind's intensity. Sometimes it seemed as if the summit would be cleared in a few moments, and smile in sunshine; but what was gained on one side was lost on another. It was like sitting in a chimney and waiting for the smoke to blow away. It was, in fact, a cloud factory,—these were the cloud-works, and the wind turned them off done from the cool, bare rocks. Occasionally, when the windy columns broke in to me, I caught sight of a dark, damp crag to the right or left; the mist driving ceaselessly between it and me. It reminded me of the creations of the old epic and dramatic poets, of Atlas, Vulcan, the Cyclops, and Prometheus. Such was Caucasus and the rock where Prometheus was bound. Æschylus had no doubt visited such scenery as this. It was vast, Titanic, and such as man never inhabits. Some part of the beholder, even some vital part, seems to escape through the loose grating of his ribs as he ascends. He is more lone than you can imagine. There is less of substantial thought and fair understanding in him than in the plains where men inhabit. His reason is dispersed and shadowy, more thin and subtile, like the air. Vast, Titanic, inhuman Nature has got him at disadvantage, caught him alone, and pilfers him of some of his divine faculty. She does not smile on him as in the plains. She seems to say sternly, Why came ye here before your time. This ground is not prepared for you. Is it not enough that I smile in the valleys? I have never made this soil for thy feet, this air for thy breathing, these rocks for thy neighbors. I cannot pity nor fondle thee here, but forever relentlessly drive thee hence to where I *am* kind. Why seek me where I have not called thee, and then complain because you find me but a stepmother? Shouldst thou freeze or starve, or shudder thy life away, here is no shrine, nor altar, nor any access to my ear.

"Chaos and ancient Night, I come no spy
With purpose to explore or to disturb
The secrets of your realm, but . . .
      . . . . . as my way
Lies through your spacious empire up to light."

The tops of mountains are among the unfinished parts of the globe, whither it is a slight insult to the gods to climb and pry into their secrets, and try their effect on our humanity. Only daring and insolent men, perchance, go there. Simple races, as savages, do not climb mountains,—their tops are sacred and mysterious tracts never visited by them. Pomola is always angry with those who climb to the summit of Ktaadn.

According to Jackson, who, in his capacity of geological surveyor of the State, has accurately measured it,—the altitude of Ktaadn is 5300 feet, or a little more than one mile above the level of the sea,—and he adds, "It is then evidently the highest point in the State of Maine, and is the most abrupt granite mountain in New England." The peculiarities of that spacious table-land on which I was standing, as well as the remarkable semi-circular precipice or basin on the eastern side, were all concealed by the mist. I had brought my whole pack to the top, not knowing but I should have to make my descent to the river, and possibly to the settled portion of the State alone, and by some other route, and wishing to have a complete outfit with me. But at length, fearing that my companions would be anxious to reach the river before night, and knowing that the clouds might rest on the mountain for days, I was compelled to descend. Occasionally, as I came down, the wind would blow me a vista open, through which I could see the country eastward, boundless forests, and lakes, and streams, gleaming in the sun, some of them emptying into the East Branch. There were also new mountains in sight in that direction. Now and then some small bird of the sparrow family would flit away before me, unable to command its course, like a fragment of the gray rock blown off by the wind.

I found my companions where I had left them, on the side of the peak, gathering the mountain-cranberries, which filled every crevice between the rocks, together with blueberries, which had a spicier flavor the higher up they grew, but were not the less agreeable to our palates. When the country is settled, and roads are made, these cranberries will perhaps become an article of commerce. From this elevation, just on the skirts of the clouds, we could overlook the country, west and south, for a hundred miles. There it was, the State of Maine, which we had seen on the map, but not much like that,—immeasurable forest for the sun to shine on, that eastern *stuff* we hear of in Massachusetts. No clearing, no house. It did not look as if a solitary traveler had cut so much as a walking-stick there. Countless lakes,—

Moosehead in the southwest, forty miles long by ten wide, like a gleaming silver platter at the end of the table; Chesuncook, eighteen long by three wide, without an island; Millinocket, on the south, with its hundred islands; and a hundred others without a name; and mountains, also, whose names, for the most part, are known only to the Indians. The forest looked like a firm grass sward, and the effect of these lakes in its midst has been well compared, by one who has since visited this same spot, to that of a "mirror broken into a thousand fragments, and wildly scattered over the grass, reflecting the full blaze of the sun." It was a large farm for somebody, when cleared. According to the Gazetteer, which was printed before the boundary question was settled, this single Penobscot County, in which we were, was larger than the whole State of Vermont, with its fourteen counties; and this was only a part of the wild lands of Maine. We are concerned now, however, about natural, not political limits. We were about eighty miles, as the bird flies, from Bangor, or one hundred and fifteen, as we had ridden, and walked, and paddled. We had to console ourselves with the reflection that this view was probably as good as that from the peak, as far as it went; and what were a mountain without its attendant clouds and mists? Like ourselves, neither Bailey nor Jackson had obtained a clear view from the summit.

Setting out on our return to the river, still at an early hour in the day, we decided to follow the course of the torrent, which we supposed to be Murch Brook, as long as it would not lead us too far out of our way. We thus traveled about four miles in the very torrent itself, continually crossing and recrossing it, leaping from rock to rock, and jumping with the stream down falls of seven or eight feet, or sometimes sliding down on our backs in a thin sheet of water. This ravine had been the scene of an extraordinary freshet in the spring, apparently accompanied by a slide from the mountain. It must have been filled with a stream of stones and water, at least twenty feet above the present level of the torrent. For a rod or two, on either side of its channel, the trees were barked and splintered up to their tops, the birches bent over, twisted, and sometimes finely split, like a stable-broom; some, a foot in diameter, snapped off, and whole clumps of trees bent over with the weight of rocks piled on them. In one place we noticed a rock, two or three feet in diameter, lodged nearly twenty feet high in the crotch of a tree. For the whole four miles, we saw but one rill emptying in, and the volumes of water did not seem to be increased from the first. We traveled thus very rapidly with a downward impetus, and grew remarkably expert at leaping from rock to rock, for leap we must, and leap we did, whether there was any rock at the right distance or not. It was a pleasant picture when the foremost turned about and looked up the winding ravine, walled in with rocks and the green forest, to see, at intervals of a rod or two, a red-shirted or green-jacketed mountaineer against the white torrent, leaping down the channel with this pack on his back, or pausing upon a convenient rock in the midst of the torrent to mend a rent in his clothes, or unstrap the dipper at his belt to take a draught of the water. At one place we were startled by seeing, on a little sandy shelf by the side of the stream, the fresh print of a man's foot, and for a moment realized how Robinson Crusoe felt in a similar case; but at last we remembered that we had struck this stream on our way up, though we could not have told where, and one had descended into the ravine for a drink. The cool air above and the continual bathing of our bodies in mountain water, alternate foot, sitz, douche, and plunge baths, made this walk exceedingly refreshing, and we had traveled only a mile or two, after leaving the torrent, before every thread of our clothes was as dry as usual, owing perhaps to a peculiar quality in the atmosphere.

After leaving the torrent, being in doubt about our course, Tom threw down his pack at the foot of the loftiest spruce-tree at hand, and shinned up the bare trunk some twenty feet, and then climbed through the green tower, lost to our sight, until he held the topmost spray in his hand.[1] McCauslin, in his younger days, had marched through the wilderness with a body of troops, under General Somebody, and with one other man did all the scouting and spying service. The General's word was, "Throw down the top of that tree," and there was no tree in the Maine woods so high that it did not lose its top in such a case. I have heard a story of two men being lost once in these woods, nearer to the settlements than this, who climbed the loftiest

---

[1]"The spruce-tree," says Springer in '51, "is generally selected, principally for the superior facilities which its numerous limbs afford the climber. To gain the first limbs of this tree, which are from twenty to forty feet from the ground, a smaller tree is undercut and lodged against it, clambering up which the top of the spruce is reached. In some cases, when a very elevated position is desired, the spruce-tree is lodged against the trunk of some lofty pine, up which we ascend to a height twice that of the surrounding forest."

To indicate the direction of pines, one throws down a branch, and a man on the ground takes the bearing.

pine they could find, some six feet in diameter at the ground, from whose top they discovered a solitary clearing and its smoke. When at this height, some two hundred feet from the ground, one of them became dizzy, and fainted in his companion's arms, and the latter had to accomplish the descent with him, alternately fainting and reviving, as best he could. To Tom we cried, Where away does the summit bear? where the burnt lands? The last he could only conjecture; he descried, however, a little meadow and pond, lying probably in our course, which we concluded to steer for. On reaching this secluded meadow, we found fresh tracks of moose on the shore of the pond, and the water was still unsettled as if they had fled before us. A little farther, in a dense thicket, we seemed to be still on their trail. It was a small meadow, of a few acres, on the mountain side, concealed by the forest, and perhaps never seen by a white man before, where one would think that the moose might browse and bathe, and rest in peace. Pursuing this course, we soon reached the open land, which went sloping down some miles toward the Penobscot.

Perhaps I most fully realized that this was primeval, untamed, and forever untamable *Nature*, or whatever else men call it, while coming down this part of the mountain. We were passing over "Burnt Lands," burnt by lightning, perchance, though they showed no recent marks of fire, hardly so much as a charred stump, but looked rather like a natural pasture for the moose and deer, exceedingly wild and desolate, with occasional strips of timber crossing them, and low poplars springing up, and patches of blueberries here and there. I found myself traversing them familiarly, like some pasture run to waste, or partially reclaimed by man; but when I reflected what man, what brother or sister or kinsman of our race made it and claimed it, I expected the proprietor to rise up and dispute my passage. It is difficult to conceive of a region uninhabited by man. We habitually presume his presence and influence everywhere. And yet we have not seen pure Nature, unless we have seen her thus vast and drear and inhuman, though in the midst of cities. Nature was here something savage and awful, though beautiful. I looked with awe at the ground I trod on, to see what the Powers had made there, the form and fashion and material of their work. This was that Earth of which we have heard, made out of Chaos and Old Night. Here was no man's garden, but the unhandselled globe. It was not lawn, nor pasture, nor mead, nor woodland, nor lea, nor arable, nor waste land. It was the fresh and natural surface of the planet Earth, as it was made forever and ever,—to be the dwelling of man, we say,—so Nature made it, and man may use it if he can. Man was not to be associated with it. It was Matter, vast, terrific,—not his Mother Earth that we have heard of, not for him to tread on, or be buried in,—no, it were being too familiar even to let his bones lie there,—the home, this, of Necessity and Fate. There was clearly felt the presence of a force not bound to be kind to man. It was a place for heathenism and superstitious rites,—to be inhabited by men nearer of kin to the rocks and to wild animals than we. We walked over it with a certain awe, stopping, from time to time, to pick the blueberries which grew there, and had a smart and spicy taste. Perchance where *our* wild pines stand, and leaves lie on their forest floor, in Concord, there were once reapers, and husbandmen planted grain; but here not even the surface had been scarred by man, but it was a specimen of what God saw fit to make this world. What is it to be admitted to a museum, to see a myriad of particular things, compared with being shown some star's surface, some hard matter in its home! I stand in awe of my body, this matter to which I am bound has become so strange to me. I fear not spirits, ghosts, of which I am one,—*that* my body might,—but I fear bodies, I tremble to meet them. What is this Titan that has possession of me? Talk of mysteries! Think of our life in nature,—daily to be shown matter, to come in contact with it,— rocks, trees, wind on our cheeks! the *solid* earth! the *actual* world! the *common sense! Contact! Contact! Who* are we? *where* are we?

A LADY'S LIFE IN THE ROCKY MOUNTAINS

Isabella Byrd

As this account of the ascent of Long's Peak could not be written at the time, I am much disinclined to write it, especially as no sort of description within my powers could enable another to realize the glorious sublimity, the majestic solitude, and the unspeakable awfulness and fascination of the scenes in which I spent Monday, Tuesday, and Wednesday.

Long's Peak, 14,700 feet high, blocks up one end of Estes Park, and dwarfs all the surrounding mountains. From it on this side rise, snow-born, the bright St. Vrain, and the Big and Little Thompson. By sunlight or moonlight its splintered grey crest is the one object which, in spite of wapiti and bighorn, skunk and grizzly, unfailingly arrests the eyes. From it come all storms of snow and wind, and the forked lightnings play round its head like a glory. It is one of the noblest of mountains, but in one's imagination it grows to be much more than a mountain. It becomes invested with a personality. In its caverns and abysses one comes to fancy that it generates and chains the strong winds, to let them loose in its fury. The thunder becomes its voice, and the lightnings do it homage. Other summits blush under the morning kiss of the sun, and turn pale the next moment; but it detains the first sunlight and holds it round its head for an hour at least, till it pleases to change from rosy red to deep blue; and the sunset, as if spellbound, lingers latest on its crest. The soft winds which hardly rustle the pine needles down here are raging rudely up there round its motionless summit. The mark of fire is upon it; and though it has passed into a grim repose, it tells of fire and upheaval as truly, though not as eloquently, as the living volcanoes of Hawaii. Here under its shadow one learns how naturally nature worship, and the propitiation of the forces of nature, arose in minds which had no better light.

Longs Peak, "the American Matterhorn," as some call it, was ascended five years ago for the first time. I thought I should like to attempt it, but up to Monday, when Evans left for Denver, cold water was thrown upon the project. It was too late in the season, the winds were likely to be strong, etc.; but just before leaving, Evans said that the weather was looking more settled, and if I did not get farther than the timber line it would be worth going. Soon after he left, "Mountain Jim" came in, and he would go up as guide, and the two youths who rode here with me from Longmount and I caught at the proposal. Mrs. Edwards at once baked bread for three days, steaks were cut from the steer which hangs up conveniently, and tea, sugar, and butter were benevolently added. Our picnic was not to be a luxurious or "well-found" one, for, in order to avoid the expense of a pack mule, we limited our luggage to what our saddle horses could carry. Behind my saddle I carried three pair of camping blankets and a quilt, which reached to my shoulders. My own boots were so much worn that it was painful to walk, even about the park, in them, so Evans had lent me a pair of his hunting boots, which hung to the horn of my saddle. The horses of the two young men were equally loaded, for we had to prepare for many degrees of frost. "Jim" was a shocking figure; he had on an old pair of high boots, with a baggy pair of old trousers made of deer hide, held on by an old scarf tucked into them; a leather shirt, with three or four ragged unbuttoned waistcoats over it; an old smashed wideawake, from under which his tawny, neglected ringlets hung; and with his one eye, his one long spur, his knife in his belt, his revolver in his waistcoat pocket, his saddle covered with an old beaver skin, from which the paws hung down; his camping blankets behind him, his rifle laid across the saddle in front of him, and his axe, canteen, and other gear hanging to the horn, he was as awful-looking a ruffian as one could see. By way of contrast he rode a small Arab mare, of exquisite beauty, skittish, high spirited, gentle, but altogether too light for him, and he fretted her incessantly to make her display herself.

Heavily loaded as all our horses were, "Jim" started over the half-mile of level grass at a hard gallop, and then throwing his mare on her haunches, pulled up alongside of me, and with a grace of manner which soon made me forget his appearance, entered into a conversation which lasted for more than three hours, in spite of the manifold checks of fording streams, single file, abrupt ascents and descents, and other incidents of mountain travel. The ride was one series of glories and surprises, of "park" and glade, of lake and stream, of mountains on mountains, culminating in the rent pinnacles of Longs Peak, which looked yet grander and ghastlier as we crossed an attendant mountain 11,000 feet high. The slanting sun added fresh beauty every hour. There were dark pines against a lemon sky, grey peaks reddening and etherealizing, gorges of deep and infinite blue, floods of golden glory pouring through canyons of enormous depth, an atmosphere of absolute purity, an occasional foreground of cotton-wood and aspen flaunting in red and gold to intensify the blue gloom of the pines, the trickle and murmur of streams fringed with icicles, the strange *sough* of gusts moving among the pine tops—sights and sounds not of the lower earth, but of the solitary, beast-haunted, frozen upper altitudes. From the dry, buff grass of Estes Park we turned off up a trail on the side of a pine-hung gorge, up a steep pine-clothed hill, down to a small valley, rich in fine, sun-cured hay about eighteen inches high, and enclosed by high mountains whose deepest hollow contains a lily-covered lake, fitly named "The Lake of the Lilies." Ah, how magical its beauty was, as it slept in silence, while *there* the dark pines were mirrored motionless in its pale gold, and *here* the great white lily cups and dark green leaves rested on amethyst-colored water!

From this we ascended into the purple gloom of great pine forests which clothe the skirts of the mountains up to a height of about 11,000 feet, and from their chill and solitary depths we had glimpses of golden atmosphere and rose-lit summits, not of "the land very far off," but of the land nearer now in all its grandeur, gaining in sublimity by nearness—glimpses, too, through a broken vista of purple gorges, of the illimitable Plains lying idealized in the late sunlight, their baked, brown expanse transfigured into the likeness of a sunset sea rolling infinitely in waves of misty gold.

We rode upwards through the gloom on a steep trail blazed through the forest, all my intellect concentrated on avoiding being dragged off my horse by impending branches, or having the blankets badly torn, as those of my companions were, by sharp dead limbs, be-

23

tween which there was hardly room to pass—the horses breathless, and requiring to stop every few yards, though their riders, except myself, were afoot. The gloom of the dense, ancient, silent forest is to me awe inspiring. On such an evening it is soundless, except for the branches creaking in the soft wind, the frequent snap of decayed timber, and a murmur in the pine tops as of a not distant waterfall, all tending to produce *eeriness* and a sadness "hardly akin to pain." There no lumberer's axe has ever rung. The trees die when they have attained their prime, and stand there, dead and bare, till the fierce mountain winds lay them prostrate. The pines grew smaller and more sparse as we ascended, and the last stragglers wore a tortured, warring look. The timber line was passed, but yet a little higher a slope of mountain meadow dipped to the south-west towards a bright stream trickling under ice and icicles, and there a grove of the beautiful silver spruce marked our camping ground. The trees were in miniature, but so exquisitely arranged that one might well ask what artist's hand had planted them, scattering them here, clumping them there, and training their slim spires towards heaven. Hereafter, when I call up memories of the glorious, the view from this camping ground will come up. Looking east, gorges opened to the distant Plains, then fading into purple grey. Mountains with pine-clothed skirts rose in ranges, or, solitary, uplifted their grey summits, while close behind, but nearly 3,000 feet above us, towered the bald white crest of Longs Peak, its huge precipices red with the light of a sun long lost to our eyes. Close to us, in the caverned side of the Peak, was snow that, owing to its position, is eternal. Soon the afterglow came on, and before it faded a big half-moon hung out of the heavens, shining through the silver blue foliage of the pines on the frigid background of snow, and turning the whole into fairyland. The "photo" which accompanies this letter is by a courageous Denver artist who attempted the ascent just before I arrived, but, after camping out at the timber line for a week, was foiled by the perpetual storms, and was driven down again, leaving some very valuable apparatus about 3,000 feet from the summit.

Unsaddling and picketing the horses securely, making the beds of pine shoots, and dragging up logs for fuel, warmed us all. "Jim" built up a great fire, and before long we were all sitting around it at supper. It didn't matter much that we had to drink our tea out of the battered meat tins in which it was boiled, and eat strips of beef reeking with pine smoke without plates or forks.

"Treat Jim as a gentleman and you'll find him one," I had been told; and though his manner was certainly bolder and freer than that of gentlemen generally, no imaginary fault could be found. He was very agreeable as a man of culture as well as a child of nature; the desperado was altogether out of sight. He was very courteous and even kind to me, which was fortunate, as the young men had little idea of showing even ordinary civilities. That night I made the acquaintance of his dog "Ring," said to be the best hunting dog in Colorado, with the body and legs of a collie, but a head approaching that of a mastiff, a noble face with a wistful human expression, and the most truthful eyes I ever saw in an animal. His master loves him if he loves anything, but in his savage moods ill-treats him. "Ring's" devotion never swerves, and his truthful eyes are rarely taken off his master's face. He is almost human in his intelligence, and, unless he is told to do so, he never takes notice of any one but "Jim." In a tone as if speaking to a human being, his master, pointing to me, said, "Ring, go to that lady, and don't leave her again to-night." "Ring" at once came to me, looked into my face, laid his head on my shoulder, and then lay down beside me with his head on my lap, but never taking his eyes from "Jim's" face.

The long shadows of the pines lay upon the frosted grass, an aurora leaped fitfully, and the moonlight, though intensely bright, was pale beside the red, leaping flames of our pine logs and their red glow on our gear, ourselves, and "Ring's" truthful face. One of the young men sang a Latin student's song and two Negro melodies; the other "Sweet Spirit, hear my Prayer." "Jim" sang one of Moore's melodies in a singular falsetto, and all together sang, "The Star-spangled Banner" and "The Red, White, and Blue." Then "Jim" recited a very clever poem of his own composition, and told some fearful Indian stories. A group of small silver spruces away from the fire was my sleeping place. The artist who had been up there had so woven and interlaced their lower branches as to form a bower, affording at once shelter from the wind and a most agreeable privacy. It was thickly strewn with young pine shoots, and these, when covered with a blanket, with an inverted saddle for a pillow, made a luxurious bed. The mercury at 9 P.M. was 12° below the freezing point. "Jim," after a last look at the horses, made a huge fire, and stretched himself out beside it, but "Ring" lay at my back to keep me warm. I could not sleep, but the night passed rapidly. I was anxious about the ascent, for gusts of ominous sound swept through the pines at intervals. Then wild animals howled, and

"Ring" was perturbed in spirit about them. Then it was strange to see the notorious desperado, a red-handed man, sleeping as quietly as innocence sleeps. But, above all, it was exciting to lie there, with no better shelter than a bower of pines, on a mountain 11,000 feet high, in the very heart of the Rocky Range, under twelve degrees of frost, hearing sounds of wolves, with shivering stars looking through the fragrant canopy, with arrowy pines for bed-posts, and for a night lamp the red flames of a camp-fire.

Day dawned long before the sun rose, pure and lemon colored. The rest were looking after the horses, when one of the students came running to tell me that I must come farther down the slope, for "Jim" said he had never seen such a sunrise. From the chill, grey Peak above, from the everlasting snows, from the silvered pines, down through mountain ranges with their depths of Tyrian purple, we looked to where the Plains lay cold, in blue-grey, like a morning sea, against a far horizon. Suddenly, as a dazzling streak, at first, but enlarging rapidly into a dazzling sphere, the sun wheeled above the grey line, a light and glory as when it was first created. "Jim" involuntarily and reverently uncovered his head, and exclaimed, "I believe there is a God!" I felt as if, Parsee-like, I must worship. The grey of the Plains changed to purple, the sky was all one rose-red flush, on which vermilion cloud-streaks rested; the ghastly peaks gleamed like rubies, the earth and heavens were new created. Surely "the Most High dwelleth not in temples made with hands!" For a full hour those Plains simulated the ocean, down to whose limitless expanse of purple, cliff, rocks, and promontories swept down.

By seven we had finished breakfast, and passed into the ghastlier solitudes above, I riding as far as what, rightly or wrongly, are called the "Lava Beds," an expanse of large and small boulders, with snow in their crevices. It was very cold; some water which we crossed was frozen hard enough to bear the horse. "Jim" had advised me against taking any wraps, and my thin Hawaiian riding dress, only fit for the tropics, was penetrated by the keen air. The rarefied atmosphere soon began to oppress our breathing, and I found that Evans's boots were so large that I had no foothold. Fortunately, before the real difficulty of the ascent began, we found, under a rock, a pair of small overshoes, probably left by the Hayden exploring expedition, which just lasted for the day. As we were leaping from rock to rock, "Jim" said, "I was thinking in the night about your traveling alone, and wondering where you carried your Derringer, for I could see no signs of it." On my telling him that I traveled unarmed, he could hardly believe it, and adjured me to get a revolver at once.

On arriving at the "Notch" (a literal gate of rock), we found ourselves absolutely on the knifelike ridge or backbone of Longs Peak, only a few feet wide, covered with colossal boulders and fragments, and on the other side shelving in one precipitous, snow-patched sweep of 3,000 feet to a picturesque hollow, containing a lake of pure green water. Other lakes, hidden among dense pine woods, were farther off, while close above us rose the Peak, which, for about 500 feet, is a smooth, gaunt, inaccessible-looking pile of granite. Passing through the "Notch," we looked along the nearly inaccessible side of the peak, composed of boulders and *débris* of all shapes and sizes, through which appeared broad, smooth ribs of reddish-colored granite, looking as if they upheld the towering rock mass above. I usually dislike bird's-eye and panoramic views, but, though from a mountain, this was not one. Serrated ridges, not much lower than that on which we stood, rose, one beyond another, far as that pure atmosphere could carry the vision, broken into awful chasms deep with ice and snow, rising into pinnacles piercing the heavenly blue with their cold, barren grey, on, on for ever, till the most distant range upbore unsullied snow alone. There were fair lakes mirroring the dark pine woods, canyons dark and blue-black with unbroken expanses of pines, snow-slashed pinnacles, wintry heights frowning upon lovely parks, watered and wooded, lying in the lap of summer; North Park floating off into the blue distance, Middle Park closed till another season, the sunny slopes of Estes Park, and winding down among the mountains the snowy ridge of the Divide, whose bright waters seek both the Atlantic and Pacific Oceans. There, far below, links of diamonds showed where the Grand River takes its rise to seek the mysterious Colorado, with its still unsolved enigma, and lose itself in the waters of the Pacific; and nearer the snow-born Thompson bursts forth from the ice to begin its journey to the Gulf of Mexico. Nature, rioting in her grandest mood, exclaimed with voices of grandeur, solitude, sublimity, beauty, and infinity, "Lord, what is man, that Thou art mindful of him? or the son of man, that Thou visitest him?" Never-to-be-forgotten glories they were, burnt in upon my memory by six succeeding hours of terror.

You know I have no head and no ankles, and never ought to dream of mountaineering; and had I known that the ascent was a real mountaineering feat I should not have felt the slightest ambition to perform it. As it is, I am only humiliated by my success, for "Jim" dragged me up, like a bale of goods, by sheer force of muscle. At the "Notch" the real business of the ascent began. Two thousand feet of solid rock towered above us, four thousand feet of broken rock shelved precipitously below; smooth granite ribs, with barely foothold, stood out here and there; melted snow refrozen several times, presented a more serious obstacle; many of the rocks were loose, and tumbled down when touched. To me it was a time of extreme terror. I was roped to "Jim," but it was of no use; my feet were paralyzed and slipped on the bare rock, and he said it was useless to try to go that way, and we retraced our steps. I wanted to return to the "Notch," knowing that my incompetence would detain the party, and one of the young men said almost plainly that a woman was a dangerous encumbrance, but the trapper replied shortly that if it were not to take a lady up he would not go up at all. He went on the explore, and reported that further progress on the correct line of ascent was blocked by ice; and then for two hours we descended, lowering ourselves by our hands from rock to rock along a boulder-strewn sweep of 4,000 feet, patched with ice and snow, and perilous from rolling stones. My fatigue, giddiness, and pain from bruised ankles, and arms half pulled out of their sockets, were so great that I should never have gone half-way had not "Jim," *nolens volens*, dragged me along with a patience and skill, and withal a determination that I should ascend the Peak, which never failed. After descending about 2,000 feet to avoid the ice, we got into a deep ravine with inaccessible sides, partly filled with ice and snow and partly with large and small fragments of rock, which were constantly giving away, rendering the footing very insecure. That part to me was two hours of painful and unwilling submission to the inevitable; of trembling, slipping, straining, of smooth ice appearing when it was least expected, and of weak entreaties to be left behind while the others went on. "Jim" always said that there was no danger, that there was only a short bad bit ahead, and that I should go up even if he carried me!

Slipping, faltering, gasping from the exhausting toil in the rarefied air, with throbbing hearts and panting lungs, we reached the top of the gorge and squeezed ourselves between two gigantic fragments of rock by a passage called the "Dog's Lift," when I climbed on the shoulders of one man and then was hauled up. This introduced

us by an abrupt turn round the south-west angle of the Peak to a narrow shelf of considerable length, rugged, uneven, and so overhung
by the cliff in some places that it is necessary to crouch to pass at all.
Above, the Peak looks nearly vertical for 400 feet; and below, the
most tremendous precipice I have ever seen descends in one unbroken fall. This is usually considered the most dangerous part of the ascent, but it does not seem so to me, for such foothold as there is is secure, and one fancies that it is possible to hold on with the hands.
But there, and on the final, and, to my thinking, the worst part of
the climb, one slip, and a breathing, thinking, human being would
lie 3,000 feet below, a shapeless, bloody heap! "Ring" refused to traverse the Ledge, and remained at the "Lift" howling piteously.

From thence the view is more magnificent even than that from
the "Notch." At the foot of the precipice below us lay a lovely lake,
wood embosomed, from or near which the bright St. Vrain and other
streams take their rise. I thought how their clear cold waters, growing turbid in the affluent flats, would heat under the tropic sun, and
eventually form part of that great ocean river which renders our far-
off islands habitable by impinging on their shores. Snowy ranges,
one behind the other extended to the distant horizon, folding in
their wintry embrace the beauties of Middle Park. Pike's Peak, more
than one hundred miles off, lifted that vast but shapeless summit
which is the landmark of southern Colorado. There were snow
patches, snow slashes, snow abysses, snow forlorn and soiled looking,
snow pure and dazzling, snow glistening above the purple robe of
pine worn by all the mountains; while away to the east, in limitless
breadth, stretched the green-grey of the endless Plains. Giants
everywhere reared their splintered crests. From thence, with a single
sweep, the eye takes in a distance of 300 miles—that distance to the
west, north, and south being made up of mountains ten, eleven,
twelve, and thirteen thousand feet in height, dominated by Longs
Peak, Gray's Peak, and Pike's Peak, all nearly the height of Mont
Blanc! On the Plains we traced the rivers by their fringe of cottonwoods to the distant Platte, and between us and them lay glories of
mountain, canyon, and lake, sleeping in depths of blue and purple
most ravishing to the eye.

As we crept from the ledge round a horn of rock I beheld what
made me perfectly sick and dizzy to look at—the terminal Peak itself—a smooth, cracked face or wall of pink granite, as nearly perpen-

dicular as anything could well be up which it was possible to climb, well deserving the name of the "American Matterhorn."[1]

Scaling, not climbing, is the correct term for this last ascent. It took one hour to accomplish 500 feet, pausing for breath every minute or two. The only foothold was in narrow cracks or on minute projections on the granite. To get a toe in these cracks, or here and there on a scarcely obvious projection, while crawling on hands and knees, all the while tortured with thirst and gasping and struggling for breath, this was the climb; but at last the Peak was won. A grand, well-defined mountain top it is, a nearly level acre of boulders, with precipitous sides all round, the one we came up being the only accessible one.

It was not possible to remain long. One of the young men was seriously alarmed by bleeding from the lungs, and the intense dryness of the day and the rarefication of the air, at a height of nearly 15,000 feet, made respiration very painful. There is always water on the Peak, but it was frozen hard as a rock, and the sucking of ice and snow increases thirst. We all suffered severely from the want of water, and the gasping for breath made our mouths and tongues so dry that articulation was difficult, and the speech of all unnatural.

From the summit were seen in unrivalled combination all the views which had rejoiced our eyes during the ascent. It was something at last to stand upon the storm-rent crown of this lonely sentinel of the Rocky Range, on one of the mightiest of the vertebrae of the backbone of the North American continent, and to see the waters start for both oceans. Uplifted above love and hate and storms of passion, calm amidst the eternal silences, fanned by zephyrs and bathed in living blue, peace rested for that one bright day on the Peak, as if it were some region

> Where falls not rain, or hail, or any snow,
> Or ever wind blows loudly.

We placed our names, with the date of ascent, in a tin within a crevice, and descended to the Ledge, sitting on the smooth granite, getting our feet into cracks and against projections, and letting ourselves down by our hands, "Jim" going before me, so that I might

[1] Let no practical mountaineer be allured by my description into the ascent of Long's Peak. Truly terrible as it was to me, to a member of the Alpine Club it would not be a feat worth performing.

steady my feet against his powerful shoulders. I was no longer giddy, and faced the precipice of 3,500 feet without a shiver. Repassing the Ledge and Lift, we accomplished the descent through 1,500 feet of ice and snow, with many falls and bruises, but no worse mishap, and there separated, the young men taking the steepest but most direct way to the "Notch," with the intention of getting ready for the march home, and "Jim" and I taking what he thought the safer route for me—a descent over boulders for 2,000 feet, and then a tremendous ascent to the "Notch." I had various falls, and once hung by my frock, which caught on a rock, and "Jim" severed it with his hunting knife, upon which I fell into a crevice full of soft snow. We were driven lower down the mountains than he had intended by impassable tracts of ice, and the ascent was tremendous. For the last 200 feet the boulders were of enormous size, and the steepness fearful. Sometimes I drew myself up on hands and knees, sometimes crawled; sometimes "Jim" pulled me up by my arms or a lariat, and sometimes I stood on his shoulders, or he made steps for me of his feet and hands, but at six we stood on the "Notch" in the splendor of the sinking sun, all color deepening, all peaks glorifying, all shadows purpling, all peril past.

"Jim" had parted with his *brusquerie* when we parted from the students, and was gentle and considerate beyond anything, though I knew that he must be grievously disappointed, both in my courage and strength. Water was an object of earnest desire. My tongue rattled in my mouth, and I could hardly articulate. It is good for one's sympathies to have for once a severe experience of thirst. Truly, there was

> Water, water, everywhere,
> But not a drop to drink.

Three times its apparent gleam deceived even the mountaineer's practised eye, but we found only a foot of "glare ice." At last, in a deep hole, he succeeded in breaking the ice, and by putting one's arm far down one could scoop up a little water in one's hand, but it was tormentingly insufficient. With great difficulty and much assistance I recrossed the "Lava Beds," was carried to the horse and lifted upon him, and when we reached the camping ground I was lifted off him, and laid on the ground wrapped up in blankets, a humiliating termination of a great exploit. The horses were saddled, and the young men were all ready to start, but "Jim" quietly said, "Now, gentlemen, I want a good night's rest, and we shan't stir from here to-night." I believe they

were really glad to have it so, as one of them was quite "finished." I retired to my arbor, wrapped myself in a roll of blankets, and was soon
asleep.

When I woke, the moon was high shining through the silvery
branches, whitening the bald Peak above, and glittering on the great
abyss of snow behind, and pine logs were blazing like a bonfire in the
cold still air. My feet were so icy cold that I could not sleep again, and
getting some blankets to sit in, and making a roll of them for my back,
I sat for two hours by the camp-fire. It was weird and gloriously beautiful. The students were asleep not far off in their blankets with their
feet towards the fire. "Ring" lay on one side of me with his fine head
on my arm, and his master sat smoking, with the fire lighting up the
handsome side of his face, and except for the tones of our voices, and
an occasional crackle and splutter as a pine knot blazed up, there was
no sound on the mountain side. The beloved stars of my far-off home
were overhead, the Plough and Pole Star, with their steady light; the
glittering Pleiades, looking larger than I ever saw them, and "Orion's
studded belt" shining gloriously. Once only some wild animals
prowled near the camp, when "Ring," with one bound, disappeared
from my side; and the horses, which were picketed by the stream,
broke their lariats, stampeded, and came rushing wildly towards the
fire, and it was fully half an hour before they were caught and quiet
was restored. "Jim," or Mr. Nugent, as I always scrupulously called
him, told stories of his early youth, and of a great sorrow which had
led him to embark on a lawless and desperate life. His voice trembled,
and tears rolled down his cheek. Was it semi-conscious acting, I wondered, or was his dark soul really stirred to its depths by the silence,
the beauty, and the memories of youth?

We reached Estes Park at noon of the following day.

CROSSING THE CUMBERLAND MOUNTAINS

John Muir

I had climbed but a short distance when I was overtaken by a young man on horseback, who soon showed that he intended to rob me if he should find the job worth while. After he had inquired where I came from, and where I was going, he offered to carry my bag. I told him that it was so light that I did not feel it at all a burden; but he insisted and coaxed until I allowed him to carry it. As soon as he had gained possession I noticed that he gradually increased his speed, evidently trying to get far enough ahead of me to examine the contents without being observed. But I was too good a walker and runner for him to get far. At a turn of the road, after trotting his horse for about half an hour, and when he thought he was out of sight, I caught him rummaging my poor bag. Finding there only a comb, brush, towel, soap, a change of underclothing, a copy of Burns's poems, Milton's Paradise Lost, and a small New Testament, he waited for me, handed back my bag, and returned down the hill, saying that he had forgotten something.

I found splendid growths of shining-leaved *Ericaceæ* [heathworts] for which the Alleghany Mountains are noted. Also ferns of which *Osmunda cinnamomea* [Cinnamon Fern] is the largest and perhaps the most abundant. *Osmunda regalis* [Flowering Fern] is also common here, but not large. In Wood's[1] and Gray's Botany *Osmunda cinnamomea* is said to be a much larger fern than *Osmunda Claytoniana*. This I found to be true in Tennessee and southward, but in Indiana, part of Illinois, and Wisconsin the opposite is true. Found here the beautiful, sensitive *Schrankia*, or sensitive brier. It is a long, prickly, leguminous vine, with dense heads of small, yellow fragrant flowers.

Vines growing on roadsides receive many a tormenting blow, simply because they give evidence of feeling. Sensitive people are served in the same way. But the roadside vine soon becomes less sensitive, like people getting used to teasing—Nature, in this instance, making for the comfort of flower creatures the same benevolent arrangement as for man. Thus I found that the *Schrankia* vines growing along footpaths leading to a backwoods schoolhouse were much less sensitive than those in the adjacent unfrequented woods, having learned to pay but slight attention to the tingling strokes they get from teasing scholars.

It is startling to see the pairs of pinnate leaves rising quickly out of the grass and folding themselves close in regular succession from the root to the end of the prostate stems, ten to twenty feet in length. How little we know as yet of the life of plants—their hopes and fears, pains and enjoyments!

Traveled a few miles with an old Tennessee farmer who was much excited on account of the news he had just heard. "Three kingdoms, England, Ireland, and Russia, have declared war agin the United States. Oh, it's terrible, terrible," said he. "This big war comin' so quick after our own big fight. Well, it can't be helped, and all I have to say is, Amerricay forever, but I'd a heap rather they didn't fight."

"But are you sure the news is true?" I inquired. "Oh, yes, quite sure," he replied, "for me and some of my neighbors were down at the store last night, and Jim Smith can read, and he found out all about it in a newspaper."

Passed the poor, rickety, thrice-dead village of Jamestown, an incredibly dreary place. Toward the top of the Cumberland grade, about two hours before sundown I came to a log house, and as I had been warned that all the broad plateau of the range for forty or fifty miles

---

[1]Alphonso Wood, *Class-book of Botany, with a Flora of the United States and Canada*. The copy of this work, carried by Mr. Muir on his wanderings, is still extant. The edition is that of 1862.

was desolate, I began thus early to seek a lodging for the night. Knocking at the door, a motherly old lady replied to my request for supper and bed and breakfast, that I was welcome to the best she had, provided that I had the necessary change to pay my bill. When I told her that unfortunately I had nothing smaller than a five-dollar greenback, she said, "Well, I'm sorry, but cannot afford to keep you. Not long ago ten soldiers came across from North Carolina, and in the morning they offered a greenback that I couldn't change, and so I got nothing for keeping them, which I was ill able to afford." "Very well," I said, "I'm glad you spoke of this beforehand, for I would rather go hungry than impose on your hospitality."

As I turned to leave, after bidding her good-bye, she, evidently pitying me for my tired looks, called me back and asked me if I would like a drink of milk. This I gladly accepted, thinking that perhaps I might not be successful in getting any other nourishment for a day or two. Then I inquired whether there were any more houses on the road, nearer than North Carolina, forty or fifty miles away. "Yes," she said, "it's only two miles to the next house, but beyond that there are no houses that I know of except empty ones whose owners have been killed or driven away during the war."

Arriving at the last house, my knock at the door was answered by a bright, good-natured, good-looking little woman, who in reply to my request for a night's lodging and food, said, "Oh, I guess so. I think you can stay. Come in and I'll call my husband." "But I must first warn you," I said, "that I have nothing smaller to offer you than a five-dollar bill for my entertainment. I don't want you to think that I am trying to impose on your hospitality."

She then called her husband, a blacksmith, who was at work at his forge. He came out, hammer in hand, bare-breasted, sweaty, begrimed, and covered with shaggy black hair. In reply to his wife's statement, that this young man wished to stop over night, he quickly replied, "That's all right; tell him to go into the house." He was turning to go back to his shop, when his wife added, "But he says he hasn't any change to pay. He has nothing smaller than a five-dollar bill." Hesitating only a moment, he turned on his heel and said, "Tell him to go into the house. A man that comes right out like that beforehand is welcome to eat my bread."

When he came in after his hard day's work and sat down to dinner, he solemnly asked a blessing on the frugal meal, consisting solely of corn bread and bacon. Then, looking across the table at me, he said, "Young man, what are you doing down here?" I replied that I was looking at plants. "Plants? What kind of plants?" I said, "Oh, all kinds; grass, weeds, flowers, trees, mosses, ferns—almost everything that grows is interesting to me."

"Well, young man," he queried, "you mean to say that you are not employed by the Government on some private business?" "No," I said, "I am not employed by any one except just myself. I love all kinds of plants, and I came down here to these Southern States to get acquainted with as many of them as possible."

"You look like a strong-minded man," he replied, "and surely you are able to do something better than wander over the country and look at weeds and blossoms. These are hard times, and real work is required of every man that is able. Picking up blossoms doesn't seem to be a man's work at all in any kind of times."

To this I replied, "You are a believer in the Bible, are you not?" "Oh, yes." "Well, you know Solomon was a strong-minded man, and he is generally believed to have been the very wisest man the world ever saw, and yet he considered it was worth while to study plants; not only to go and pick them up as I am doing, but to study them; and you know we are told that he wrote a book about plants, not only of the great cedars of Lebanon, but of little bits of things growing in the cracks of the walls.[1]

"Therefore, you see that Solomon differed very much more from you than from me in this matter. I'll warrant you he had many a long ramble in the mountains of Judea, and had he been a Yankee he would likely have visited every weed in the land. And again, do you not remember that Christ told his disciples to 'consider the lilies how they grow,' and compared their beauty with Solomon in all his glory? Now, whose advice am I to take, yours or Christ's? Christ says, 'Consider the lilies.' You say, 'Don't consider them. It isn't worth while for any strong-minded man.' "

This evidently satisfied him, and he acknowledged that he had never thought of blossoms in that way before. He repeated again and again that I must be a very strong-minded man, and admitted that no doubt I was fully justified in picking up blossoms. He then told me

---

[1]The previously mentioned copy of Wood's Botany, used by John Muir, quotes on the title page 1 Kings iv, 33: "He spake of trees, from the cedar of Lebanon even unto the hyssop that springeth out of the wall."

that although the war was over, walking across the Cumberland Mountains still was far from safe on account of small bands of guerrillas who were in hiding along the roads, and earnestly entreated me to turn back and not to think of walking so far as the Gulf of Mexico until the country became quiet and orderly once more.

I replied that I had no fear, that I had but very little to lose, and that nobody was likely to think it worth while to rob me; that, anyhow, I always had good luck. In the morning he repeated the warning and entreated me to turn back, which never for a moment interfered with my resolution to pursue my glorious walk.

September 11. Long stretch of level sandstone plateau, lightly furrowed and dimpled with shallow groove-like valleys and hills. The trees are mostly oaks, planted wide apart like those in the Wisconsin woods. A good many pine trees here and there, forty to eighty feet high, and most of the ground is covered with showy flowers. Polygalas [milkworts], solidagoes [goldenrods], and asters were especially abundant. I came to a cool clear brook every half mile or so, the banks planted with *Osmunda regalis, Osmunda cinnamomea*, and handsome sedges. The few larger streams were fringed with laurels and azaleas. Large areas beneath the trees are covered with formidable green briers and brambles, armed with hooked claws, and almost impenetrable. Houses are far apart and uninhabited, orchards and fences in ruins— sad marks of war.

About noon my road became dim and at last vanished among desolate fields. Lost and hungry, I knew my direction but could not keep it on account of the briers. My path was indeed strewn with flowers, but as thorny, also, as mortal ever trod. In trying to force a way through these cat-plants one is not simply clawed and pricked through all one's clothing, but caught and held fast. The toothed arching branches come down over and above you like cruel living arms, and the more you struggle the more desperately you are entangled, and your wounds deepened and multiplied. The South has plant fly-catchers. It also has plant man-catchers.

After a great deal of defensive fighting and struggling I escaped to a road and a house, but failed to find food or shelter. Towards sundown, as I was walking rapidly along a straight stretch in the road, I suddenly came in sight of ten mounted men riding abreast. They undoubtedly had seen me before I discovered them, for they had stopped their horses and were evidently watching me. I saw at once that it was useless to attempt to avoid them, for the ground thereabout was quite open. I knew that there was nothing for it but to face them fearlessly, without showing the slightest suspicion of foul play. Therefore, without halting even for a moment, I advanced rapidly with long strides as though I intended to walk through the midst of them. When I got within a rod or so I looked up in their faces and smilingly bade them "Howdy." Stopping never an instant, I turned to one side and walked around them to get on the road again, and kept on without venturing to look back or to betray the slightest fear of being robbed.

After I had gone about one hundred or one hundred and fifty yards, I ventured a quick glance back, without stopping, and saw in this flash of an eye that all the ten had turned their horses toward me and were evidently talking about me; supposedly, with reference to what my object was, where I was going, and whether it would be worth while to rob me. They all were mounted on rather scrawny horses, and all wore long hair hanging down on their shoulders. Evidently they belonged to the most irreclaimable of the guerrilla bands who, long accustomed to plunder, deplored the coming of peace. I was not followed, however, probably because the plants projecting from my plant press made them believe that I was a poor herb doctor, a common occupation in these mountain regions.

About dark I discovered, a little off the road, another house, inhabited by negroes, where I succeeded in obtaining a much needed meal of string beans, buttermilk, and corn bread. At the table I was seated in a bottomless chair, and as I became sore and heavy, I sank deeper and deeper, pressing my knees against my breast, and my mouth settled to the level of my plate. But wild hunger cares for none of these things, and my curiously compressed position prevented the too free indulgence of boisterous appetite. Of course, I was compelled to sleep with the trees in the one great bedroom of the open night.

September 12. Awoke drenched with mountain mist, which made a grand show, as it moved away before the hot sun. Passed Montgomery, a shabby village at the head of the east slope of the Cumberland Mountains. Obtained breakfast in a clean house and began the descent of the mountains. Obtained fine views of a wide, open country, and distant flanking ridges and spurs. Crossed a wide cool stream [Emory River], a branch of the Clinch River. There is nothing more eloquent in Nature than a mountain stream, and this is the first I ever saw. Its banks are luxuriantly peopled with rare and lovely flowers and overarching trees, making one of Nature's coolest and most hospitable places. Every tree, every flower, every ripple and eddy of this lovely stream seemed solemnly to feel the presence of the great Creator. Lingered in this sanctuary a long time thanking the Lord with all my heart for his goodness in allowing me to enter and enjoy it.

Discovered two ferns, *Dicksonia* and a small matted polypod on trees, common farther South. Also a species of magnolia with very large leaves and scarlet conical fruit. Near this stream I spent some joyous time in a grand rock-dwelling full of mosses, birds, and flowers. Most heavenly place I ever entered. The long narrow valleys of the mountainside, all well watered and nobly adorned with oaks, magnolias, laurels, azaleas, asters, ferns, Hypnum mosses, Madotheca [Scale-mosses], etc. Also towering clumps of beautiful hemlocks. The hemlock, judging from the common species of Canada, I regarded as the least noble of the conifers. But those of the eastern valleys of the Cumberland Mountains are as perfect in form and regal in port as the pines themselves. The latter abundant. Obtained fine glimpses from open places as I descended to the great valley between these mountains and the Unaka Mountains on the state line. Forded the Clinch, a beautiful clear stream, that knows many of the dearest mountain retreats that ever heard the music of running water. Reached Kingston before dark. Sent back my plant collections by express to my brother in Wisconsin.

September 13. Walked all day across small parallel valleys that flute the surface of the one wide valley. These flutings appear to have been formed by lateral pressure, are fertile, and contain some fine forms, though the seal of war is on all things. The roads never seem to proceed with any fixed purpose, but wander as if lost. In seeking the way to Philadelphia [in Loudon County, Tennessee], I was told by a buxom Tennessee "gal" that over the hills was much the nearer way, that she always went that way, and that surely I could travel it.

I started over the flint-ridges, but soon reached a set of enchanted little valleys among which, no matter how or in what direction I traveled, I could not get a foot nearer to Philadelphia. At last, consulting my map and compass, I neglected all directions and finally reached the house of a negro driver, with whom I put up for the night. Received a good deal of knowledge which may be of use should I ever be a negro teamster.

September 14. Philadelphia is a very filthy village in a beautiful situation. More or less of pine. Black oak most abundant. *Polypodium hexagonopterum* and *Aspidium acrostichoides* [Christmas Fern] most abundant of ferns and most generally distributed. *Osmunda claytoniana* rare, not in fruit, small. *Dicksonia* abundant, after leaving the Cumberland Mountains. *Asplenium ebeneum* [Ebony Spleenwort] quite common in Tennessee and many parts of Kentucky. *Cystopteris* [Bladder Fern], and *Asplenium filixfœmina* not common through the same range. *Pteris aquilina* [Common Brake] abundant, but small.

Walked through many a leafy valley, shady grove, and cool brooklet. Reached Madisonville, a brisk village. Came in full view of the Unaka Mountains, a magnificent sight. Stayed over night with a pleasant young farmer.

September 15. Most glorious billowy mountain scenery. Made many a halt at open places to take breath and to admire. The road, in many places cut into the rock, goes winding about among the knobs and gorges. Dense growth of asters, liatris,[1] and grapevines.

Reached a house before night, and asked leave to stop. "Well, you're welcome to stop," said the mountaineer, "if you think you can live till morning on what I have to live on all the time." Found the old gentleman very communicative. Was favored with long "bar" stories, deer hunts, etc., and in the morning was pressed to stay a day or two.

September 16. "I will take you," said he, "to the highest ridge in the country, where you can see both ways. You will have a view of all the world on one side of the mountains and all creation on the other. Besides, you, who are traveling for curiosity and wonder, ought to see our gold mines." I agreed to stay and went to the mines. Gold is found in small quantities throughout the Alleghanies, and many farmers work at mining a few weeks or months every year when their time is not more valuable for other pursuits. In this neighborhood miners are earning from half a dollar to two dollars a day. There are several large quartz mills not far from here. Common labor is worth ten dollars a month.

September 17. Spent a day in botanizing, blacksmithing, and examining a grist mill. Grist mills, in the less settled parts of Tennessee and North Carolina, are remarkably simple affairs. A small stone, that

---

[1]Wood's Botany, edition of 1862, furnishes the following interesting comment on *Liatris odoratissima* (Willd.), popularly known as Vanilla Plant or Deer's Tongue: "The fleshy leaves exhale a rich fragrance even for years after they are dry, and are therefore by the southern planters largely mixed with their cured tobacco, to impart its fragrance to that nauseous weed."

a man might carry under his arm, is fastened to the vertical shaft of a little home-made, boyish-looking, back-action water-wheel, which, with a hopper and a box to receive the meal, is the whole affair. The walls of the mill are of undressed poles cut from seedling trees and there is no floor, as lumber is dear. No dam is built. The water is conveyed along some hillside until sufficient fall is obtained, a thing easily done in the mountains.

On Sundays you may see wild, unshorn, uncombed men coming out of the woods, each with a bag of corn on his back. From a peck to a bushel is a common grist. They go to the mill along verdant footpaths, winding up and down over hill and valley, and crossing many a rhododendron glen. The flowers and shining leaves brush against their shoulders and knees, occasionally knocking off their coon-skin caps. The first arrived throws his corn into the hopper, turns on the water, and goes to the house. After chatting and smoking he returns to see if his grist is done. Should the stones run empty for an hour or two, it does no harm.

This is a fair average in equipment and capacity of a score of mills that I saw in Tennessee. This one was built by John Vohn, who claimed that he could make it grind twenty bushels a day. But since it fell into other hands it can be made to grind only ten per day. All the machines of Kentucky and Tennessee are far behind the age. There is scarce a trace of that restless spirit of speculation and invention so characteristic of the North. But one way of doing things obtains here, as if laws had been passed making attempts at improvement a crime. Spinning and weaving are done in every one of these mountain cabins wherever the least pretensions are made to thrift and economy. The practice of these ancient arts they deem marks of advancement rather than of backwardness. "There's a place back heah," said my worthy entertainer, "whar there's a mill-house, an' a store-house, an' a still-house, an' a spring-house, an' a blacksmith shop—all in the same yard! Cows too, an' heaps of big gals a-milkin' them."

This is the most primitive country I have seen, primitive in everything. The remotest hidden parts of Wisconsin are far in advance of the mountain regions of Tennessee and North Carolina. But my host speaks of the "old-fashioned unenlightened times," like a philosopher in the best light of civilization. "I believe in Providence," said he. "Our fathers came into these valleys, got the richest of them, and skimmed off the cream of the soil. The worn-out ground won't yield no roastin' ears now. But the Lord foresaw this state of affairs, and prepared something else for us. And what is it? Why, He meant us to bust open these copper mines and gold mines, so that we may have money to buy the corn that we cannot raise." A most profound observation.

September 18. Up the mountain on the state line. The scenery is far grander than any I ever before beheld. The view extends from the Cumberland Mountains on the north far into Georgia and North Carolina to the south, an area of about five thousand square miles. Such an ocean of wooded, waving, swelling mountain beauty and grandeur is not to be described. Countless forest-clad hills, side by side in rows and groups, seemed to be enjoying the rich sunshine and remaining motionless only because they were so eagerly absorbing it. All were united by curves and slopes of inimitable softness and beauty. Oh, these forest gardens of our Father! What perfection, what divinity, in their architecture! What simplicity and mysterious complexity of detail! Who shall read the teaching of these sylvan pages, the glad brotherhood of rills that sing in the valleys, and all the happy creatures that dwell in them under the tender keeping of a Father's care?

September 19. Received another solemn warning of dangers on my way through the mountains. Was told by my worthy entertainer of a wondrous gap in the mountains which he advised me to see. "It is called Track Gap," said he, "from the great number of tracks in the rocks—bird tracks, bar tracks, hoss tracks, men tracks, all in the solid rock as if it had been mud." Bidding farewell to my worthy mountaineer and all his comfortable wonders, I pursued my way to the South.

As I was leaving, he repeated the warnings of danger ahead, saying that there were a good many people living like wild beasts on whatever they could steal, and that murders were sometimes committed for four or five dollars, and even less. While stopping with him I noticed that a man came regularly after dark to the house for his supper. He was armed with a gun, a pistol, and a long knife. My host told me that this man was at feud with one of his neighbors, and that they were prepared to shoot one another at sight. That neither of them could do any regular work or sleep in the same place two nights in succession. That they visited houses only for food, and as soon as the one that I saw had got his supper he went out and slept in the woods, without of course making a fire. His enemy did the same.

My entertainer told me that he was trying to make peace between these two men, because they both were good men, and if they would agree to stop their quarrel, they could then both go to work.

Most of the food in this house was coffee without sugar, corn bread, and sometimes bacon. But the coffee was the greatest luxury which these people knew. The only way of obtaining it was by selling skins, or, in particular, "sang," that is ginseng,[1] which found a market in far-off China.

My path all to-day led me along the leafy banks of the Hiwassee,[2] a most impressive mountain river. Its channel is very rough, as it crosses the edges of upturned rock strata, some of them standing at right angles, or glancing off obliquely to right and left. Thus a multitude of short, resounding cataracts are produced, and the river is restrained from the headlong speed due to its volume and the inclination of its bed.

All the larger streams of uncultivated countries are mysteriously charming and beautiful, whether flowing in mountains or through swamps and plains. Their channels are interestingly sculptured, far more so than the grandest architectural works of man. The finest of the forests are usually found along their banks, and in the multitude of falls and rapids the wilderness finds a voice. Such a river is the Hiwassee, with its surface broken to a thousand sparkling gems, and its forest walls vine-draped and flowery as Eden. And how fine the songs it sings!

In Murphy [North Carolina] I was hailed by the sheriff who could not determine by my colors and rigging to what country or craft I belonged. Since the war, every other stranger in these lonely parts is supposed to be a criminal, and all are objects of curiosity or apprehensive concern. After a few minutes' conversation with this chief man of Murphy I was pronounced harmless, and invited to his house, where for the first time since leaving home I found a house decked with flowers and vines, clean within and without, and stamped with the comforts of culture and refinement in all its arrangements. Striking contrast to the uncouth transitionist establishments from the wigwams of savages to the clumsy but clean log castle of the thrifty pioneer.

---

[1]Muir's journal contains the following additional note: "M. County produces $5000 worth a year of ginseng root, valued at seventy cents a pound. Under the law it is not allowed to be gathered until the first of September."

[2]In his journal Muir spells the name "Hiawassee," a form which occurs on many of the older maps. The name probably is derived from the Cherokee Indian "Ayuhwasi," a name applied to several of their former settlements.

September 20. All day among the groves and gorges of Murphy with Mr. Beale. Was shown the site of Camp Butler where General Scott had his headquarters when he removed the Cherokee Indians to a new home in the West. Found a number of rare and strange plants on the rocky banks of the river Hiwassee. In the afternoon, from the summit of a commanding ridge, I obtained a magnificent view of blue, softly curved mountain scenery. Among the trees I saw *Hex* [Holly] for the first time. Mr. Beale informed me that the paleness of most of the women in his neighborhood, and the mountains in general hereabouts, was caused chiefly by smoking and by what is called "dipping." I had never even heard of dipping. The term simply describes the application of snuff to the gum by means of a small swab.

September 21. Most luxuriant forest. Many brooks running across the road. Blairsville [Georgia], which I passed in the forenoon, seems a shapeless and insignificant village, but grandly encircled with banded hills. At night I was cordially received by a farmer whose wife, though smart and neat in her appearance, was an inveterate smoker.

September 22. Hills becoming small, sparsely covered with soil. They are called "knob land" and are cultivated, or scratched, with a kind of one-tooth cultivator. Every rain robs them of their fertility, while the bottoms are of course correspondingly enriched. About noon I reached the last mountain summit on my way to the sea. It is called the Blue Ridge and before it lies a prospect very different from any I had passed, namely, a vast uniform expanse of dark pine woods, extending to the sea; an impressive view at any time and under any circumstances, but particularly so to one emerging from the mountains.

Traveled in the wake of three poor but merry mountaineers—an old woman, a young woman, and a young man—who sat, leaned, and lay in the box of a shackly wagon that seemed to be held together by spiritualism, and was kept in agitation by a very large and a very small mule. In going down hill the looseness of the harness and the joints of the wagon allowed the mules to back nearly out of sight beneath the box, and the three who occupied it were slid against the front boards in a heap over the mules' ears. Before they could unravel their limbs from this unmannerly and impolite disorder, a new ridge in the road frequently tilted them with a swish and a bump against the back boards in a mixing that was still more grotesque.

I expected to see man, women, and mules mingled in piebald ruin at the bottom of some rocky hollow, but they seemed to have full confidence in the back board and front board of the wagonbox. So they continued to slide comfortably up and down, from end to end, in slippery obedience to the law of gravitation, as the gardens demanded. Where the jolting was moderate, they engaged in conversation on love, marriage, and camp-meeting, according to the custom of the country. The old lady, through all the vicissitudes of the transportation, held a bouquet of French marigolds.

The hillsides hereabouts were bearing a fine harvest of asters. Reached Mount Yonah in the evening. Had a long conversation with an old Methodist slaveholder and mine owner. Was hospitably refreshed with a drink of fine cider.

$\mathscr{N}$AVAHO $\mathscr{M}$OUNTAIN

Rob Schultheis

$\mathscr{T}$he first time I went down to the Navaho reservation, driving south from Cortez, Colorado, the country struck me with the force of a foreign land: Mongolia during the reign of the Khans or eighteenth-century Afghanistan, perhaps. The men looked like Central Asian cowboys (later, in Tibetan refugee camps in India, I would see the same faces): flat, cuprous, epicanthic faces, many with long hair topped by incongruous felt Stetsons. Many of the women wore long satin dresses and shining velveteen blouses; they looked like desert princesses (and, in a way, perhaps they are). Off in the sagebrush were the beehive-shaped houses called hogans—built out of timber, planks, solid adobe—that Navahos believe are the only proper dwellings under the sun.

Driving south to Shiprock and then west to Kayenta that first day on the reservation, I found I had entered a whole other cognitive universe; everything was different. Vast deserts of sage swept away to distant surreal mountains. An old Buddha-faced man walked away across the dunes, driving a herd of goats before him. Turquoise pickup trucks rolled down the endless highways. I heard a Navaho talking about the Bible on the car radio. "Jesus was a Navaho," I thought I heard him say. In a café near Teec Nos Pos I ate something called a Navaho taco: ground beef, chili sauce, onions and cheese, on a heavy slab of Indian fry bread. The café was full of big Indians in tall twenty-gallon hats. Two girls came in and ordered coffee. They began to talk in Navaho, a language that manages to sound both slurred and bitten off at the same time. Every once in a while, an English word would pop up in the soft stream of Athabascan*: "basketball game," "Chevy pickup," "cheeseburger." One of the girls went over to the jukebox, put in a quarter and punched three songs: "Okie From Muskogee," "Purple Haze" and "Wasted Days and Wasted Nights," by Freddy Fender. Later that afternoon I picked up a hitch-hiker, a kid on his way home to Kayenta: "My cousins and I started a rock-'n'-roll band," he told me. "We were doing great till Marvin got scared by witches and got sick."

I had traveled down to the Navaho Nation to study something called "acculturation, education and social adjustment"; but it seemed like something much stranger, and more wonderful, was happening. It was as if you sat down to study German irregular verbs, and suddenly a mad message in fire leapt out of the gray grammar, astounding you.

Anglo geographers rate a fifth of the Navaho land base as totally useless for farming or grazing, and another 50 percent as only poor to fair. But what do Anglo geographers know? To the Navahos this is holy land, loaded with divine energy; they have never heard of "real estate." They fought the Utes, the Spanish and then the Anglos to hold on to it. In 1863–64, Kit Carson, who is the Eichmann of Navaho history (old men still spit at his name), came through with the U.S. Army, slaughtered the tribe's flocks, burned their corn fields and peach orchards and marched them into exile at Bosque Redondo on the harsh prairies of eastern New Mexico. Of the 8,000 Navahos sent on the Long Walk, as it was called, a third perished of hunger, exposure, disease and outright murder; many others were sold into slavery.

When the Treaty of 1868 was signed, allowing the surviving remnants of the Dineh to return home, Barboncito, one of the headmen, said, "After we get back to our country, it will brighten up again and the Navahos will be as happy as the land, black clouds will rise and there will be plenty of rain. Corn will grow in abundance and everything will look happy." The Navahos see their country through the eyes of lovers; their songs reiterate its beauty, refract it, enunciate

---

*The Navaho language is part of the Athabascan language family. Other Athabascan peoples include the Apache as well as the Dogribs, Carriers, Na-Denes, Yellowknives and other tribes of the Canadian Arctic and Alaska. The Navahos themselves came down from the north into the Southwestern desert only three or four centuries ago.

it, over and over. Those furrowed, dull hills, like knees and laps draped with rose-colored silk in the light of dusk; that distant mountain, jade in a flint shroud of unfallen rain; green corn against roan cliff: all these are beautiful; beautiful and therefore holy, an equation Anglos have missed. The Navaho word for god is *Yei*, or "beautiful one."

One summer day in Window Rock, the tribal capital, I peered over a floor covered with aerial photographs of the eastern border of the reservation, from Window Rock north to Shiprock. It reminded me of nothing so much as a flight I once took from New Delhi to Teheran over the high, rugged plateau of Central Asia. There were the same naked mountains, the hogback ridges and cuestas; the same tenuous scrub forests surviving in what little rain shadow the mountains provided. Arroyos feathered down into the valleys, joining together to form rivers that were more mud and sand than water.

Life in such a land requires patience, cunning and nerve. Looking at the photographs of the Navaho country, I could see where, in the crook of a wash, an Indian had built a dam out of alluvial stones to hold and trap the occasional water that ran down out of the Chuskai Mountains. There was a fenced rectangle of corn and a tiny peach orchard, the usual crude brush sheep corral, the same kind desert people build all across the earth from Jordan to Tibet to Dinetah. A cluster of hogans, representing several families, cottonwoods and a skein of pickup tire tracks leading off toward the highway and the trading post. Mutton, wool, blankets, turquoise and silver, traded for trucks, gas, coffee, guns and, of course, sugar and salt, the magic white powders of the white man; and the "water that banishes reason," alcohol—cheap red wine, brandy, whiskey that goes down your throat like napalm, burning your spirit away.

It is a delicate way of life; it all leads back, ultimately, to that intermittent thread of water that sometimes, sometimes, doesn't trickle down out of the mountains. If the rains and snows fail, the corn and sage and peach trees and piñon will perish, the sheep and goats and cattle and horses will die; and the people, too, if they do not move. It has happened down here before. Chaco Canyon, Mesa Verde, Betatakin and Keet Seel, the pueblos of the San Juan, all were abandoned because of drought; sinister lacunae, those empty rooms and fields gone to brush and thorn. All history down here is merely a thin skin on the surface of hydrology, a pluvial accident.

One summer up on the northern part of the reservation I drove down from Shonto to the Black Mesa Trading Post to buy groceries and pick up my mail. A very drunk Navaho cowboy came in, bent and bow-legged: a twisty little man doused with dust, Stetson pushed back, boot heels run down. He came up to me, breathing wine like a dragon, and took my arm. "Hey, man," he said, leaning his face close, "I heard old Elvis died. I was sure sorry to hear that." I didn't know what to say; it was as if he thought Elvis and I were clan brothers, friends or something. "Yeah, it was too bad," I said finally. "I guess his heart gave out or something." "Yeah," said the Navaho cowboy as if he hadn't heard me, "Elvis died. Elvis and Hitler, two of your greatest leaders, dead." He shook his head in commiseration and stumbled away down the aisle of saddles and ropes and hats.

One collects incidents like this on the reservation, hoping to put together some kind of mosaic that makes sense—or, rather, *Anglo* sense; but all one ends up with is a bigger, better cryptogram. Was the Navaho cowboy completely ignorant of Anglo ways and boozily mis-connecting two Anglo names he had happened to remember? Or was he (as I suspect) subtly joking me about the quality of Anglo heroes? Navahos have an acute sense of humor, especially when it comes to *belagonas,* as they call us Anglos.

I dated a Navaho girl for a time; her name was Barbara Salt, and she had been brought up off the reservation, in Los Angeles, where her father worked in a defense plant. She was too, too beautiful. When she combed her shining black hair or spent hours piecing together beadwork on a tiny loom (barbaric colors: it looked as if she were weaving a new coat for a Gila monster), she looked so out-of-time, it stole your heart away. Yet her talk was half filled with surfboards and flying saucers and smoking dope in convertibles speeding down Mulholland Drive, and half with remembered childhood stories of life back on the reservation and visits to her relatives, who lived north of Kayenta. Her grandparents still ran sheep up there, though they were both nearly blind and could barely hobble after their flocks on brittle legs. Like many radical young Indians, Barbara refused to admit that her people had come across into the Americas from Asia. "We were always here," she said. "We always lived right where we live now, between the four sacred mountains."

Anthropologists, with their blood-type maps and archeological burrowings and trait lists, have pretty well established that the first Americans came across Beringia tens of thousands of years ago, and that the Navahos drifted down from the Arctic only three or four hundred years ago—these American Bedouin are, remarkably, transplanted tundra-dwellers. But when I tried to tell Barbara that, she would have none of it. "Look, I don't know how we got here—maybe we evolved here, maybe we came out of a spaceship—but I know one thing, I ain't no damn Chinese!" Actually, Navaho origin myth says that the People emerged from an ice cave, a bleak, wintry womb in the side of a mountain in southwestern Colorado. Old-time Navahos still make pilgrimages to this birthing place of their tribe. Perhaps, in one way or another, all of these stories are equally true—all dreams, all songs.

Sometimes I think everything is crazy down there; or, rather, that *we* are so crazy we will never comprehend it: *Dineh* are *Dineh*, *belagona* are *belagona*, and never the twain shall meet.

One spring afternoon I rode north out of Flagstaff with an old Navaho in a brand-new supercharged pickup truck. He wore a purple-satin cowboy shirt with white piping, Tony Lama boots, doubleknit Western slacks, a heavy beaver-felt twenty-gallon hat, a string tie with a silver thunderbird at his throat and a digital timepiece with a fire-coral-studded band. There was an eagle plume hanging from the rear-view mirror. He was a fine-looking man, a person of substance. "I'm goin' as far as Tuba City," he said.

We accelerated out of Flagstaff, faster and faster, settling down to a rock-steady hundred miles an hour up that bumpy road that curved northeast into the Navaho Nation. The tape player blasted out an Indian chant. There was a lot of traffic on the road, but the old man never slowed down.

"I'm gonna drive you home in my '52 pickup truck. Hey ya ya ya, hey ya ya ya," the cassette player chanted: one of those modern Indian songs, called "Forty-niners."

We passed Magic Mountain and then Gray Mountain, that honky-tonk reservation border town with its string of hitch-hiking drunks, and crossed the corroded red desert that descends to the Little Colorado River. The old man pulled a Cobra CB microphone from under the dash and talked away to somebody in the intricate, slurred Navaho tongue—wool and mutton futures? An epidemic of *chinde*, or ghosts, out by Chilchinbito? On we went, at one hundred miles per hour, steady and sure as fate.

Finally, close to Tuba City, we hit a jammed herd of tourist traffic snailing up a long, winding hill behind a Winnebago. There were a lot of cars ahead of us—a dozen, maybe—and a blind curve ahead. The old man pulled out around them without a pause and floored it.

We were about two thirds of the way past the pack when another Indian in a pickup truck, also speeding, rounded the curve above us. He leaned on his horn; the old grandfather leaned on *his*. Neither touched the brake. We headed toward each other like a couple of jousting bighorns.

There was no way we could get by. There was the Winnebago on our right, blocking the right lane, and an arroyo to the left, dropping off steeply, going over which would have been like steering straight into the grave. But the old wizard, deadpan, kept the pedal to the floor, as if there was nobody else on the road. I instinctively cringed and punched my foot down on an imaginary brake pedal.

At the last instant, the old man simply pulled over into the right-hand lane, veering into the Winnebago broadside, driving it off the road, over the shoulder and into the desert. I looked back to see the colossal recreational vehicle, big as five hogans and costing more than the annual income of ten Navaho sheepherding families, bouncing away across the dunes, tearing through a barbed-wire fence.

We were still doing a hundred. When I looked over at the old Navaho, he was grinning at me out of the corner of his face; and then he began to laugh, "Eh 'eh 'eh," and suddenly we were both laughing together at the mad perfection of it all.

Strange things happen down on the Navaho Nation, things that seem to have leaked out of a dream into the real, solid world. Witches, for instance: Navahos believe that some people who lead everyday, normal lives on the surface are in reality *brujos*, black magicians. Navaho witches are a particularly bad lot: they eat human flesh and dig up corpses to make a dust called corpse powder, which they squirt on their sleeping victims to kill them—a kind of infectious death. You never know who might be a witch: you might see a coyote sneaking around your sheep pen at night and take a shot at it with your varmint rifle and the next morning find your brother or mother or cousin lying there dead, with your bullet in them. Suspected witches are still occasionally executed in the back country of the reservation.

Reality is, when you get right down to it, consensual: a tribe or a society makes up its mind what it is going to see and then it sees it; delusion by plurality. What the Navahos see and feel is no truer, no falser than our own sensory world; but it certainly has more magic than ours. And I like that. We have exorcised our world too well: "Before Christianity, all power came from magic," Lawrence Durrell wrote. "After it, from money." All too true.

There is magic going on down in the Nation, but it is illusive. The great rituals of the tribe, the Sings or Ways, are not given at set places and times. They are performed when a family or a clan wants to accomplish something, often a curing or healing: they are usually given far from towns and highways, and whites are not welcome. In fact, Navahos from other clans are not welcome. When Peter Mac-Donald, tribal chairman (known to some young Navahos as "the Navaho Nixon"), showed up at a ceremony near Teec Nos Pos, his bodyguards were beaten and his limousine trashed, and he had to flee in a tribal police car.

Ghost stories are a kind of spiritual pornography, but I have one that is too good not to tell. An anthropologist friend and his wife, who worked on the same anomalous research project that employed me, were driving across the reservation one night on one of the back roads. It was way past midnight, they saw nothing except an occasional goat, a gaunt feral steer, a half-wild horse . . .

Suddenly, out of nowhere, an ancient Navaho woman appeared in their headlights, hobbling along in the same direction they were going, alone. They pulled up next to her and my friend's wife rolled down the window. "Would you like a ride?" she asked, looking into the oldest face in North America, wrinkled and seamed like an ancient tortoise's. But instead of answering, the crone began to screech at them, shaking her fists in the air. They drove away, and when they looked back, the old woman had vanished and a big, pale dog was running down the road after them.

They told a Navaho friend about it later, and he said, "Witch." "What would you have done?" they asked him. "Shoot her or run over her with the truck. Or just get the hell out of there."

I know a couple of other stories just as unbelievable, but I think I'll save them; stories, like certain cheeses, improve with age.

There are tales you hear down on the reservation of stranger, more powerful medicine men: not Singers, the men who give the great rituals, or herb doctors or witches, but *magi*, something like the siddhis of the East. There is one, for instance, who is supposed to be several hundred years old and lives in a cave with two mountain lions up a nameless canyon somewhere. I believe these stories somehow: they remind me irresistibly of tales of such Asian saints as Milarepa, Han

Shan, Lao-Tse and Bodhidharma. And there is no reason why such sumptuous mysteries should reveal themselves to white Americans, spiritual paupers that we are. Native America has always guarded its secrets jealously. Who built Tiahuanaco, that cryptic Andean city on the Altiplano? The Saint Louis Snake Mound? There are no photographs of Crazy Horse; both he and Wovoka, prophet of the ghost dance, are buried in unknown graves, one near Pyramid Lake, the other on the Powder River, somewhere on the lost continent of America.

Nowhere in this continent are people and land so inextricably bound together as in Dinetah. Navaho place-names celebrate the actualities of survival—the Zen of earth, if you will. Cornfields. Many Farms. The Chuskai ("White Fir Trees") Mountains. Dinnehotso, "The Edge of the Meadow." Bad Water, Sweetwater, Mexican Water, Bitter Water; Chilchinbite ("Water in the Sumacs"), Oljeto ("Moonlit Water"), Shato ("Sunshine Water Springs"). Black Rock, Rough Rock, Round Rock, Window Rock, Spider Rock, Red Rock, Owl Rock, Kicking Rock, Baby Rocks; Two Gray Hills, Hummingbird, Burnt Corn, Greasewood . . . Each name is a piece of primitive *musique concrète*; and each name is also the germ of a story, the thread around which a yarn is spun . . .

Kicking Rock, for instance, along the San Juan: They say old Kicking Rock sat by a narrow place in the trail high above the river, and when travelers passed by, he would say, "Um, my knee is feelin' kind of stiff. I'd better stretch it." And then he would kick the travelers into the river below, where his monstrous children fed on their bodies. One day the Hero Twins came along—monster-slayers; they cut Kicking Rock into pieces with their potent obsidian daggers and threw the pieces into the river. Kicking Rock's children devoured their father, exclaiming how delicious the meat was: "Father killed us a *good* traveler this time!" Typical Navaho humor.

Some of the other place-names tell a different kind of story: Laguna Canyon and Marsh Pass, for instance, between Kayenta and Cow Springs, north of Black Mesa. Within living memory (two generations perhaps), these were rich sloughs, oases. There are tales of great migratory flocks of geese and ducks gathering there, and deer, elk, beaver. But about a century ago, as the Navahos became successful herders, their sheep and goats multiplied far beyond the carrying capacity of the land; they literally devoured these microenvironments by "strip grazing"—the pastoral equivalent of strip mining. The range was gnawed to the roots, the soil was sucked away by the wind, the waters ran off through a maze of arroyos. Wasteland with green, ironic names: a Marsh Pass dry as a mummy, a Laguna Canyon with lakes of sand.

But however poor the earth is, down here it is loved. Earth, land, is the ultimate Navaho reality. There is nothing greater. Navaho political power does not grow out of the barrel of a gun: it grows out of the land, like corn, like sagebrush, like the dream flowers of jimson weed. Gods sprout like dry weeds from exhausted soil.

In the remotest northern part of the Navaho Nation, just to the south of the San Juan River, north of No Man's and Skeleton mesas, is the mountain called Navaho. It is as remote as a place can be these days: it is a long, long way from anywhere to this jade-and-cobalt peak that rises like an apparition from the rose-colored desert.

Navaho Mountain—they also call it Pollen, or War, or War God Mountain—is the grandest thing in the landscape. It draws the eye for hundreds of miles, from Page, Arizona, to Cedar Mesa, Utah. In the summer it pulls rain from the dry sky: you see a great hump of nickel cumulus, a gray plume of rain and the black mass of the mountain itself. If you took peyotl, closed your eyes and thought "Mountain," this is the mountain you would see: Navaho. From the first time I sighted it peering at me over the edge of the world as I drove west from Black Mesa Trading Post toward Cow Springs, I wanted to go there. It seemed the essence of everything reticent, unknowable, in the country of the Navaho.

It took me almost a year to get there; and by that time I had picked up a whole bagful of stories about the place. An old anthropologist I met in Gallup who was studying Navaho alcoholism by drinking himself into stupefaction at the Club Mexico and the All-American every night told me of an odd Navaho clan who lived north of the mountain. When the Dineh were deported to Bosque Redondo in 1863, a few of the northernmost Navahos escaped to the furrowed, confused country between the San Juan River and Navaho Mountain. They intermarried with a renegade band of Piutes who lived in the area, and avoided all contact with Anglos for a long, long time. Their descendants still live up there around the mountain, a kind of lost tribe: tall, diffident, backward people. Many of them still shun pickup trucks in favor of horses—and pickup trucks are as Navaho as turquoise or sheep. (What horses were to the nineteenth-century Plains tribes, pickups are to Navahos—objects so perfect that they are endowed with *mana,* bulging beyond their physical boundaries. One tribal government pamphlet, out of Canoncito, New Mexico, begins a short history of the Navaho with the classic line, "A long, long time ago, there weren't any pickup trucks"—as if the first black Model A pickup rattling onto the reservation back in the twenties, full of Ute Peyote Church missionaries from Sleeping Ute Mountain, were some kind of primal alpha. Someone should trace the spread of pickup trucks through the Navaho Nation: it would make a fascinating history.) At Navaho Mountain, the old anthropologist said, truck time had not yet begun.

The old anthropologist reminded me of some old, fuddled Colonel Blimp in India in the heyday of the raj: dry, caustic, foolish, with a colossal red nose and steel-gray hair that looked as if it was cut with a bad knife. Decades ago he had done one of the first Indian drinking studies, in the rough-and-tumble bars of Los Angeles and Reno. He told a hundred tales of endless nights bar-hopping in jalopies with the last Kickapoos, a hundred hilarious disasters. Now he and his thin, sarcastic wife were living in a fine adobe on the highest hill in Gallup; she collected Navaho blankets, while he poured the whiskey down far into the night, in the name of Science.

Other stories about the mountain told of eagles, turquoise, witches on the roads and lions in the trees. The funny thing was, no one I talked to had actually been there: all the stories I heard were well-used, rubbed blurry and vague with age. This lent them, and the mountain itself, an even deeper aura of mystery.

Almost a year after my first summer on the reservation, Barbara Salt and I drove down from Colorado to walk around the western edge of the mountain to Rainbow Bridge. A friend had a friend who had hiked there years ago, and we had a set of directions: "Drive north from Shonto (road bad); at Utah state line, road forks—take left-hand fork (road worse); drive approx. ten miles, to ruins of old Rainbow Lake (stone walls, hard to find); look for north by northwest, possibly marked, possibly not (WATCH TRAIL CAREFULLY—easy to wander off on herding trails and waste half a day); first reliable water is at Eight-Mile Camp, a spring in the cliff on the right-hand side; the trail the rest of the way is easy to follow, if you don't miss the turn to Redbud Pass."

Ironically, Barbara didn't know much more about the geography of the Navaho country than I did. It was her lost homeland, her Palestine; but like anyone drifting home from Diaspora, she had more emotions about her homeland than facts. After all, she spoke only a few phrases of Navaho, while most reservation Navahos, even the young, are unfluent in English; and Barbara was a real city girl, pure Los Angeles, while Navaho reservation life is old-timey, cowboy, like nothing else in America, really.

As we crossed that strip of sleazy borderland around Farmington, she went through something like culture shock. Shops full of junk, mean-faced police, the alky squalor of the Turquoise and Zia bars: it looked like something out of Tijuana or Landi Kotal on the Khyber Pass, the same poverty, vice and bald avarice, the evil electricity generated wherever the First World rubs up too hard against the Third. "What is this place, anyway?" she muttered.

"Ugliness on the way to the magic mountain."

We passed the Four Corners Power Plant, the tall stacks trickling across the sky a subtle pall of Navaho coal burning, the tall, high-tension lines leading toward LA. It was a hot, bright day; the hills glinted like heaps of broken glass. We passed through Shiprock, that classic Navaho town; people were selling melons, corn, tamales and fry bread by the intersection, where one highway ran south ninety-nine miles to Gallup and the other road led west to Biklabito, Rattlesnake, Kayenta, Tuba City. We turned west there for Navaho Mountain.

From Shiprock to Black Mesa Trading Post, where you turn north for Navaho Mountain, is an airy journey; the land is so immense that you feel as if you are levitating, swooping and soaring across the desert fifty, a hundred feet up. That road turns people into hawks. The wind howls across the bronze land, with scattered humps of hogans here and there and the delicate litter of pastoral camps, sheep pens, corals, a tin trailer . . . A herd of pied horses trembles in the uncertain sun.

We camped that night up near the ruined Anasazi city of Betatakin. It took us half of the next day to drive to the base of Navaho Mountain. The road, through Shonto and Inscription House, past a lone ugly mission, was terrible: bedrock, wind-drifted sand, big loose stones. We had worried about a spring blizzard catching us, but the weather, as usual, had doubled back on itself: the sky was cloudless, and desperately hot.

Just past the Utah state line the road forked, right to Navaho Mountain Trading Post, left to nowhere. We turned left across a flat stony desert broken by ravines, studded with brush. A field of dead corn, a collapsed fence of sticks. When this road ran out, we started walking. The upper slopes of Navaho Mountain, still white with snow, loomed over us to the southeast. But down where we were, down in the rocks, it was like a blast furnace.

We crossed Chaiyahi Flats and a series of deep canyons: First Canyon, Horse Canyon, Dome. I had expected to find water, lots of it, in the canyon bottoms, but there was none, not a drop. Lizards watched us from the rocks with cold, uncaring eyes. A buzzard hovered in the sky, motionless, as if hung on a hook. We hiked a trail of broken rocks that cut our feet and blazed as if they had spilled out of a forge.

As the afternoon wore on, the land fell away to the north and west, toward Lake Powell. We looked down into the earth, into enormous basements of bedrock. Here were cruel iron buttes, moon-colored domes, mosques of melting butter, rocks pulled and twisted like putty and shot full of holes, seraglios and languorous blond stone.

We crossed Sunset Pass (Yabuts Pass is the Piute name for it) toward evening; the trail dropped off headlong into Cliff Canyon. We picked our way down the crumbling trail. It was slow going. Dark fell just as we came out onto the narrow canyon floor; we stumbled on down to Eight-Mile Camp by dim flashlight. I found the spring, dribbling corrosive green from a crack in the cliff, and filled our empty canteens; we hadn't seen a drop of water all day till then. Barbara built a fire of cottonwood sticks, dry, frost pale, that burned quickly. We boiled up tea and dried stew. A gritty wind rattled the trees, sobbed in the cliffs. The canyon was narrow there, and across the narrow seam of sky, dark tufts of cloud scudded south.

"Is there a storm coming in?"

"Maybe. This weather is real neurotic. Can't tell what it's going to do."

"Well, I wish it would do something," she said. "I'd just as soon hike through snow; at least you can melt it and drink it. Is it always this dry?"

"We must just be in the wrong canyon. With all that snow up on the mountain, there must be melt water somewhere. It's strange there's none here."

"The mountain is keeping it all for himself."

We wouldn't see Navaho Mountain, the cold, dark mass of it, anymore. But actually we were inside one of the cracks in the great bulge of sandstone over magma that forms the peak; we were down in the hard hide of the mountain itself. We slept uneasily, disturbed by the wind, the squeaky plucked violins of the bats and thoughts that flashed like fire in the blackness. When we touched, the static jumped between our skins.

The next day we left most of our gear at camp and hiked on for Rainbow Bridge. The sky was powder blue and hot as a skillet. We saw only a few sheep tracks, probably strays, and the prints of a lone horse. Farther on, where the trail met a red stone cliff and turned east, was another spring and a row of Anasazi petroglyphs—big-headed gods, squiggling snakes, forked lightning—scratched there on the rock to guard the place. Next to the petroglyphs some Navaho had scrawled his own proprietary sign: INDIAN COUNTRY, it said. Below it was a rough drawing of an archetypal Navaho family, a man in a tall Stetson, a woman in a long dress, a son and daughter, all holding hands in a row. "Here we are," the drawing seemed to say. "Now *we* live here: this land is ours."

"Only an Indian could live down here," Barbara said, sounding proud.

"Yeah. No one else is stubborn or simple enough."

She thought that over, decided it wasn't an insult, said "Yeah" and laughed. Anyhow, it was true. You would have to go to the back country of Central Asia or the Andean Plateau of South America to find people still living in such desiccated, marginal microenvironments, patching subsistence together out of scraps and leavings of runoff and alluvium. In the right hands, poverty can be a fine art: Indians are masters of it.

Later that morning we came to Redbud Pass. Wetherill and his party, the first whites to visit Rainbow Bridge, came through in 1909, led by the Piute guide Nasjah Begay (his name means "son of Mr. Spider"). They had to blast their way through Redbud Pass with dynamite to get their horses up and over. The defile is still narrow and steep; the trail winds its way through boulders and scrub juniper trees. As we descended into Bridge Canyon, we passed a barricade built out of brush and a falling-down gate of sticks and wire—a Navaho stock fence. On a boulder by the trail, someone had written: LOST A HORSE HERE. CLYDE WHISKERS. Whiskers is a not uncommon family name among Navahos. Like Redhouse, Tso ("Skinny"), Begay ("Son of"),

Greyeyes, Yellowhair, Starlight, Salt, Manygoats, Peaches, it was a name with a living, vivid nucleus. I liked "Clyde Whiskers." I wondered who he was, how he lived back here—sheepherding, of course—and whether he ever found his horse. A mile or so down Bridge Canyon, we came to a long pool of water under the overhanging rock; the reflected ripples licked like flames on the sandstone roof. The water was shockingly cold and clear as a lens; the dust boiled off of us like smoke when we bathed.

Just about everyone who knows anything about the American West has read about Rainbow Bridge and seen a photograph of it. It is one of those geological anomalies, like Half Dome or Old Faithful, that Americans seize on and sentimentalize, while they lay waste the rest of the wilderness. I suppose at one time, before Lake Powell was backed up to it, this soaring ribbon of sandstone three-hundred-odd feet above Bridge Creek must have been a compelling place. Powerful. The Navahos once treated it as a shrine: they called it *non-nezoshi*, or "the rainbow of stone." Rainbows are one of the cornerstones of Navaho metaphysics, personified as the Rainbow People, guardians of the universe. (Tibetans have a similar belief.)

But with Lake Powell and its marinas, powerboats and vacationers only two miles down canyon (today the lake reaches all the way to the base of the rainbow), most of the magic was gone. Accessibility, ease, the great vices of America, had squeezed the juice out of the metaphor and turned the power off. The gods had left for wherever gods go.

When Barbara and I got there that afternoon, there was a mob of houseboaters from the lake gathered around the base of the bridge where the trail runs under the arch. They clicked away with their cameras and chattered like daws. A radio was playing, and its tinny music itched in our ears after the profound stillness of the canyons.

We didn't like running into the lake people: after all of our bloody hard traveling, it just didn't seem fair to find them there. And I doubt if they liked seeing us much, either: a dark, sumptuous girl who looked like she *lived* back in those terrible sandstone mazes, and some kind of back-country bohemian mountaineer, both of them with huge packs and cottonwood walking sticks.

"How'd you folks get here?" one pink old man asked us querulously; he wore a billed cap that said: ALL FISHERMEN ARE LIARS, INCLUDING ME. When we told him we had walked in from the far side of Navaho Mountain, two days, the lake people all shook their heads:

"Should've taken the boat. It's easy as pie. In another couple of years the lake will be right here, and you won't have to walk at all then."

"Are you an Indian, honey?" a woman asked Barbara sweetly.

They weren't bad people, of course; you would have had to be a real fundamentalist archdruid not to feel at least a sneaky liking for them: good old middle Americans, stolid, salty, with a dour brand of humor. But we really didn't want to see them or their lake *down there* in that country whose body is petrified sand, whose spirit is denial. Some places should be left alone; this was one of them.

After a few minutes Barbara and I went off a ways by ourselves, found a spot of shade below a rock, drank our water and shared a Mandarin orange. A half hour later we headed back toward Eight-Mile Camp and the silence and solitude of the canyons.

The rest of the trip was much more interesting. We found we had forgotten to pack one of the stuff sacks of food, and we ran completely out of provisions. Dinner that night was a lump of cheese and a chip of chocolate apiece, and that was it. The next day we had to hike out hungry. It was another cloudless, baleful day; the land seemed rinsed in fire. We left early, but the sun caught us on the climb up to Yabuts Pass. It was a 1,500-vertical-foot slog; perhaps 95 degrees and zero humidity. We drank our canteens dry halfway up, and then we were out of water.

The hike to the car was the worst walk I have ever done, six and a half miles that seemed endless. The quiet of the canyons was suddenly not peaceful at all, but oppressive, vaguely menacing. The cold white summit of Navaho Mountain looked disdainfully down on us, toiling through the chaos of stone. I poured out a spoonful of blood from my boots when we reached the car.

We didn't make it to the highway till after dark, and it was another hour east to Kayenta, where there was a café open. We bought Navaho tacos there and mutton stew and coffee. The food tasted better than any mystery. I didn't care if I never saw Navaho Mountain again; that short-order greasy spoon was shrine enough for me.

That night we drove back up to Colorado, staying awake on Methedrine tablets from the medical kit, bitter as gall; listening to Wolf Man Jack on the radio. A few weeks later Barbara drove north for Alaska, to work on a salmon boat for the summer. I never heard a word from her again.

In time, of course, the miseries and disappointments of the trip went away, and what I remembered probably never happened, except in the imagination. I dreamed about that crazy journey many times—it stuck deep in my psyche, down in the vague part of the mind where memory recombines, fantastical, to form dreams. Again and again, I walked those hard trails, following Barbara around the edge of a shadow mountain, a mountain of unknowing . . . It had become a kind of a fairy tale.

Three years later I came back, again in the spring, to walk all the way around the mountain. This year the desert was wet with rain, the road up from Shonto ran red with earth, the skies were cool and cloudy. The rain had wet the range till it glowed. The top of Navaho Mountain was hidden in mists.

It was strange, and a shade melancholy, walking the trail to Eight-Mile Camp alone. I thought of Barbara and wondered where she was, whether she had ever come back here and walked these lonely trails again. I even imagined, foolishly, coming to Eight-Mile Camp in the evening and finding her there, under the cottonwood trees, combing her long brooding hair . . . But of course there was no one there; Eight-Mile Camp was deserted.

The next day I hiked down to Rainbow Bridge and camped a couple of miles up canyon from the bridge. And the day after that I crossed the while north side of the mountain.

This was the country I had dreamed was there, a tangled web of cliffs, towers, mesas, ravines. It drizzled on and off that morning. I crossed a stony mesa, a herd of sheep in the distance, but no people. Oak Canyon was a cleft of green, green cottonwoods, like jade set in bone. Beyond was a maze of canyons; looking at my USGS map only gave names to the confusion. Nasjah (Navaho for spider) Canyon. Moepitz Canyon, a Piute name whose meaning I did not know. Lehi Canyon, a name dug up out of the Bible, probably Mormon in origin. Trail, Desha, Anasazi canyons. Cha Canyon: *cha* is Navaho for either beaver or excrement. (I favored the latter, as there was a huge rock of suggestive shape where the trail dipped into what should have been Cha Canyon.)

I kept thinking I would run into somebody. I passed more herds of sheep and goats, and messages written on the rock by the omnipresent Clyde Whiskers: "CLYDE WHISKERS & MARY MANYGOATS." "CLYDE WHISKERS '70." "CLYDE WHISKERS WAS HERE." Perhaps, I thought, Clyde Whiskers was a Navaho Everyman, a Native American Kilroy; perhaps, like them, he was always there, but he had never been there at all: like Coyotl, or Avalokitesvara.

It was a day of omens and portents. About midday I found an abandoned hogan in a draw full of cottonwoods. There was still a metal cot inside and a little iron stove with a frying pan and a coffeepot on top; but the cobwebs in the door hung in thick shrouds, and one of the dried-mud walls was falling in. No one had been there for a long, long time. The canyon was full of a loud, buzzing silence. Death, I thought. Among the traditional Navahos, when somebody dies in a hogan, everybody moves away, for death is unclean, *wrong*, a kind of contagious darkness. That must have happened here; and now the place belonged only to the *chinde,* those who have left the bright world of the living behind and who have no love for the living.

I thought for a moment of taking the coffeepot, tying it on my pack—it was a good old enameled one, blue, with white flecks like snow—but then I thought, No, I don't want to drink coffee with the dead, and so I left it and walked on.

It was one of those days in which everything is supernaturally charged with a meaning almost readable, but cryptic; the world strains with revelation. To the south the whole northern face of Navaho Mountain—cliffs, gorges, steep forests—took up the horizon; to the north the country grew more and more intricate, tessellations of ruby, rust and chalk under haze; above, a skyful of clouds pulled east in the wind. I walked east with it, crossing mesa after mesa, canyon after canyon. I saw more herds of sheep and goats in the distance, grazing on the stony brush; a clump of beehive-shaped hogans with smoke spiraling up, and a dog barking; a log sheep pen against a far canyon wall; but no people, no one at all . . . Only sitting beneath a Douglas fir in midafternoon, something moved out of the corner of my eye, and I looked up to see a mountain lion, like a long, golden shadow, flow up over the rimrock and vanish. Like a shooting star, it all happened in an instant. A beautiful disturbance rippled slowly across my eye and mind.

Toward the end of the day, a horseman rode out of the southeast. He came riding up to me, a rawboned old man on a big gaunt horse, riding slow, with a sack slung over his saddlehorn. He was long and narrow, with a long, curious face. He grinned and raised a huge hand in greeting as he reined in his horse. "*Yaatahey,*" he said.

"*Yaatahey.* How far is it to the trading post?"

He cocked his head and laughed. "*St'o'*," he said, pointing south over the edge of the mountain. He pointed to the sack: "*Co'n.*" Then he gestured at me with his great hand: "*Ca'fon'ya'?*"

"California?" He nodded. "No, Colorado."

"*Co'lo'a'do*. Ah." He pointed to himself: "*Oo'tah*."

He sat up there on his horse, that giant, ancient man—he almost creaked in the wind—smiling down at me, studying me, a *belagona* walking around he sacred mountain alone with a crazy orange thing strapped to his back like a hump. It would make a good story to tell his friends later: "I met this crazy *belagona* crossing Desha Canyon . . . mebbe he was a lost missionary . . . mebbe he was looking for gold . . ."

He raised his hand again, as if in benediction, spurred his horse gently into motion and headed on down the trail. I looked back once; he was turned in the saddle, watching me. I waved; he turned away. I started on my way again, heading for the wrong side of the mountain, while the old man rode home into the time of stone.

I crossed No Man's Mesa just as dusk fell; the trail became a rough road, and there were more hogans off toward Navaho Begay, "Son of Navaho," the small peak on the eastern shoulder of the big mountain. The desert was radiant. To the northeast the goblin country of the San Juan submerged in a slumberous glow. I was dog-tired. Twenty-two miles today, according to the map.

As darkness fell, a pickup truck came speeding out of No Man's Mesa: a young Navaho man, two sleek young women and two children. The women wore heavy silver, velvet in slurred colors of maroon and green. "Going to the trading post?" one asked in soft, broken English. "You can have a ride."

I rode in the back; the stars came out; it got cold. We came to the trading post about eight o'clock, and I slept that night out back in the tall grass under the dark, hunched shoulder of the mountain.

I read somewhere that one of the highest peaks in North America once stood in the center of what is now Lake Superior. The story sounds too good to be true, but I pass it on to you for what it's worth. The mountain, the story goes, vanished millenniums ago, ground down by ice, wind, time. There is nothing left to show where it stood—only the invisible whorls in the magnetic skin of the earth, deep in the bedrock beneath the deep black waters of the lake. But the migrating geese that cross the lake still turn, they say, to avoid the vanished mountain. It still exists in their piano rolls of memory, rolled tight in those airy skulls.

Navaho Mountain is like that. There is the mountain of stone and soil, covered with timber; and there is the thick electric sediment

of memories and dreams, arched in a mountain more perfect than anything on earth.

I went to Navaho Mountain one last time, determined to climb to the
summit. There, I thought, I would find some kind of transcendent
sign, some kind of answer (though I wasn't even sure what the question was). If the sides of the mountain were so powerful, would not the
summit be a capstone of pure mystery? So ran my thoughts, full of
half-digested Jodorowsky and René Daumal.

I drove north from Tucson, where I had been staying with
friends, up the long road through Phoenix, Flagstaff, Tuba City.
Northeast of Tuba City there was snow on the ground; the sky was
black and windy. It was November and the mountain would be cold,
but I kept going.

The dirt roads north of Shonto were deep in red muck and
molten snow, hard going. I bought candy bars, canned beef stew and
cheese at Navaho Mountain Trading Post, and asked the trader about
the route to the top. "No problem," he said. "Blind man couldn't miss
it. Construction crew's been workin' on the road up there for weeks. If
you had a four-wheel drive, you could drive all the way to the top."

This wasn't at all what I had expected, but it was too late to turn
back now. I followed his directions, and as the sun set I was crawling
my way up the rutted mud and stone of the mesa. Finally I came to a
collection of heavy equipment, pickup trucks, Cats and Thiokol trac-
tors, parked in a circle of gouged earth. The road went up steeply from
there. It was already getting cold and there was nobody around, so I
decided to camp. I unfolded the back seat of the station wagon, spread
out my sleeping bag, ate the beef stew cold out of the can and fell
asleep.

Sometime later I awoke to the sound of a diesel grumbling
around about fifty feet from my car. I looked out and there were four
or five men in hard hats trying to load a small diesel tractor up onto a
trailer in the dark. "Just a cunt hair to the left, Joe!" one of them
shouted. "Well, *you* try it then, smartass!" "Shut up and back it in
again." "*Haw haw haw!* If ya can't aim any better'n that, I don't see
how ya ever get a piece a ass." Night on the sacred mountain. I felt
like the king of fools.

The next morning there was no one around, and I put on my
pack and began to trudge up the mountain. The road ran between
steep forests and sandstone cliffs, following a power line. The snow

got deeper the higher I climbed, and it was hard going. Off to the south, a storm was brewing: darkness over Black Mesa, the horizon gone in red-tinged clouds, like glowing heaps of slag. The treetops shook in the wind.

The road gave out, or I lost it. I began to slog straight up the mountainside, breaking through snow up to my waist. I was near the top now, and suddenly it seemed worthwhile: the whole long drive up the length of Arizona and the hike up through the frozen mud and the wet snow.

I looked up, and a face was looking down at me, silhouetted against the sky. Round, brown and smiling, it wore a plastic hard hat with the words NAVAHO POWER AUTHORITY printed across it. "Hey what you doin' up here?" the Navaho asked.

I didn't know what to say. "Oh, just looking around. How about you?"

A couple of other Navahos appeared. "We're working on the power line up here. The line got blown down in a windstorm, and we're puttin' it back up again. Navaho Power Authority and Arizona Public Service."

"I heard there were mountain lions up here," I said, grasping at a last wild straw.

They looked at each other: "Nope, never heard of any. No mountain lion up here. I live here fifty years, I never heard of one. But," he added brightly, obviously trying to help this deranged *belagona*, "two weeks ago, I seen the biggest jackrabbit you ever saw, not two miles west of here. He must a been two feet long!"

The wind roared, cold and blue, over the summit of Pollen Mountain. They offered me a ride back down the mountain in their Thiokol, and I accepted. I figured that they were *kind of* medicine men—they were the only ones up there, anyway—and that was good enough for me. On the way down they told me a joke about a Hopi who went to a whorehouse, but I forget it.

INFERNAL PARADISE

Barbara Kingsolver

In the darkness before dawn I stood on the precipice of a wilderness. Inches in front of my toes, a lava cliff dropped away into the mammoth bowl of Haleakala, the world's largest dormant volcano. Behind me lay a long green slope where clouds rolled up from the sea, great tumbleweeds of vapor, passing through the pastures and eucalyptus forests of upland Maui to the volcano's crest, then spilling over its edge into the abyss.

Above the rimrock and roiling vapor, the sun was about to break. Far from the world where "Aloha Oe" whines through hotel lobbies, I stood in a remote place at an impossibly silent hour.

But pandemonium had an appointment. Grunting, hissing, a dozen buses pulled up behind me and threw open their doors. Tourists swarmed like ants over the tiny visitors' center at the crater's edge. Loading cameras, dancing from foot to foot in the cold, they positioned for the spectacle. "Darn," a man griped through his viewfinder, "I can't get it all in."

"Take two shots, then," his wife advised.

In the throng I lost and then relocated Steven, my fellow traveler. In his hiking boots, sturdy fedora, and backpack, he apparently struck such a picturesque silhouette against the dawn he'd been cornered by a pro and enlisted as foreground. "Perfect for a wilderness catalog," the photographer testified, while his camera whirred meaningfully.

Sunrise over Haleakala is a packaged Maui tradition: tourists in the beachfront hotels can catch a bus at 3 A.M., ride the winding road to the summit, witness the daybreak moment, and return in time for a late breakfast. As religious experiences go, this one is succinct. In fifteen minutes the crowd was gone.

I wandered a hundred yards back to the parking lot, where a second troop was assembling. For about $120, intrepid sightseers can get a one-way bus ride to the summit for a different thrill: outfitted with helmets, Day-Glo safety vests, and rental bikes, they speed back down to the coast in a huge mob, apparently risking life and limb for a thirty-eight-mile exercise in handbraking. The group leaders, who presumably knew the score, were padded from head to toe like hockey goalies. As they lined up their herds of cyclers, they delivered flat monologues about hand signals and road conditions. "Ready to go play in traffic?" demanded a guide, straddling his mount. "Okay, let's go play in traffic." With the hiss of a hundred thin tires on a ribbon of asphalt, this crowd vanished too.

I blinked in the quiet light, feeling passed over by a raucous visitation. Now the crater lay deserted in the howling wind, by all but one pair of picturesque stragglers. The toes of our boots turned toward the rim and found purchase on a rough cinder trail called Sliding Sands, which would lead us down into the belly of Haleakala. The price: a $6.95 waterproof trail map, and whatever else it might take to haul ourselves down and back again.

Entering the crater at dawn seemed unearthly, though Haleakala is entirely of the earth, and nothing of human artifice. The cliffs absorbed and enclosed us in a mounting horizon of bleak obsidian crags. A lake of cloud slid over the rim, wave by wave, and fell into the crater's separate atmosphere, dispersing in vapor trails. The sharp perimeter of cliffs contains a volcanic bowl three thousand feet deep and eight miles across as the crow flies (or twice that far as the hiker hikes). The depression would hold Manhattan, though fortunately it doesn't.

We walked and slid down miles of gravelly slope toward the crater floor, where the earth had repeatedly disgorged its contents. Black sworls of bubbling lava had once flowed around red cinder cones, then cooled to a tortured standstill. I stood still myself, allowing my eye a minute to take in the lunatic landscape. In the absence of any human construction or familiar vegetation like, say, trees, it was impossible to judge distances. An irregular dot on the trail ahead might be a person or a house-sized boulder. Down below, sections of the trail were sketched across the valley, crossing dark lava flows and green fields, disappearing into a velvet fog that hid the crater's eastern half.

The strange topography of Haleakala Crater makes its own weather. Some areas are parched as the Sahara, while others harbor fern forests under a permanent veil of cloud. Any part of the high-altitude crater can scorch in searing sun, or be lashed by freezing rain, or both, on just about any day of the year. Altogether it is one of the most difficult landscapes ever to host natural life. It is also one of the few places in Hawaii that looks as it did two hundred years ago—or for that matter, two thousand. Haleakala is a tiny, threatened ark.

To learn about the natural history of Hawaii is to understand a story of unceasing invasion. These islands, when they first lifted their heads out of the waves a million years ago, were naked, defiant rock—the most isolated archipelago in the world. Life, when it landed here, arrived only through powerful stamina or spectacular accident: a fern's spore drifting on the trade wind, a seed in the craw of a bird, the bird itself. If it survived, that was an accident all the more spectacular. Natural selection led these survivors to become new species unique in the world: the silversword, for example, a plant that lives in lava beds and dies in a giant flowery starburst; or the nēnē, a crater-dwelling goose that has lost the need for webbed feet because it shuns the sea, foraging instead in foggy meadows, grown languid and tame in the absence of predators. Over the course of a million years, hundreds of creatures like these evolved from the few stray immigrants. Now they are endemic species, living nowhere on earth but here. For many quiet eons they thrived in their sequestered home.

Then humans arrived, also through stamina and spectacular accident. The Polynesians came first, bringing along some thirty plants and animals they considered indispensable, including bananas, taro, sugar cane, pigs, dogs, chickens. And also a few stowaways: rats, snails, and lizards. All of these went forth and multiplied throughout the islands. Each subsequent wave of human immigration brought fresh invasions. Sugar cane and pineapples filled the valleys, crowding out native herbs. Logging operations decimated the endemic rain forests. Pigs, goats, and cattle uprooted and ate whatever was left. Without a native carnivore to stop them, rats flourished like the Pied Piper's dream. Mongooses were imported in a harebrained plan to control them, but the mongoose forages by day and the rat by night, so these creatures rarely encounter one another. Both, though, are happy to feast on the eggs of native birds.

More species have now become extinct in Hawaii than in all of North America. At least two hundred of the islands' endemic plant species are gone from the earth for good, and eight hundred more are endangered. Of the original cornucopia of native birds, many were never classified, including fifty species that were all flightless like the dodo—and now, like the dodo, all gone. A total of only thirty endemic bird species still survive.

It's quite possible now to visit the Hawaiian Islands without ever laying eyes on a single animal or plant that is actually Hawaiian—from the Plumeria lei at the airport (this beloved flower is a Southeast Asian import) to the farewell bouquet of ginger (also Asian), African flame trees, Brazilian jacarandas, mangos and banyans from India, coffee from Africa, macadamia nuts from Australia—these are beautiful impostors all, but to enjoy them is to dance on a graveyard. Exotics are costing native Hawaii its life.

Haleakala Crater is fortified against invasion, because of its protected status as a national park, and because its landscape is hostile ground for pineapples and orchids. The endemics had millennia to adapt to their difficult niche, but the balance of such a fine-tuned ecosystem is precarious, easily thrown into chaos: the plants fall prey to feral pigs and rats, and are rendered infertile by insect invaders like Argentine ants and yellow jacket wasps, which destroy the native pollinators.

Humans have sated their strange appetites in Haleakala too, and while a pig can hardly be blamed for filling its belly, people, it would seem, might know better. The dazzling silverswords, which grow nowhere else on earth, have been collected for souvenirs, leis, scientific study, Oriental medicine, and—of all things—parade floats. These magical plants once covered the ground so thickly a visitor in 1873 wrote that Haleakala's slopes glowed silvery white "like winter in moonlight." But in 1911 a frustrated collector named Dr. Aiken complained that "wild cattle had eaten most of the plants in places of easy access." However, after much hard work he "obtained gunny sacks full." By 1930, it was possible to count the surviving members of this species.

The nēnē suffered an even more dire decline, nearly following the dodo. Since it had evolved in the absence of predators, nothing in this gentle little goose's ground-dwelling habits prepared it for egg-eating rodents, or a creature that walked upright and killed whenever it found an easy mark. By 1951, there were thirty-three nēnē geese left living in the world, half of them in zoos.

Midway through the century, Hawaiians began to protect their islands' biodiversity. Today, a tourist caught with a gunnysack of silverswords would find them pricey souvenirs—there's a $10,000 fine. The Park Service and The Nature Conservancy, which owns adjacent land, are trying to exclude wild pigs from the crater and native forests by means of a fence, though in such rugged ground it's a task akin to dividing needles from haystacks. Under this fierce protection, the silverswords are making a gradual comeback. Nēnē geese have been bred in captivity and reintroduced to the crater as well, but their population, numbered at two hundred and declining, is not yet considered saved. Meanwhile, the invasion creeps forward: even within the protected boundaries of a national park, 47 percent of the plant species growing in Haleakala are aliens. The whole ecosystem is endangered. If the silverswords, nēnē geese, and other colorful endemics of Hawaii survive this century, it will be by the skin of their teeth. It will only happen because we decided to notice, and hold on tight.

Like a child anticipating sleighbells at Christmas, I saw illusory silverswords everywhere. I fixed my binoculars on every shining dot in the distance, and located a lot of roundish rocks in the noonday sun. Finally I saw the real thing. I was not prepared for how they would appear to glow from within, against the dark ground. They are actually silver. For all the world, they look like huge, spherical bouquets of curved silver swords. Cautiously I leaned out and touched one that grew near the path. The knives were soft as bunnies' ears. Unlike the spiny inhabitants of other deserts, the arid-adapted silverswords evolved without the danger of being eaten. Defenseless, they became a delicacy for wild pigs. Such bad luck. This landscape was so unready for what has come to pass.

I never saw "winter in moonlight," but as we trudged deep into the crater we saw silverswords by twos and threes, then clumps of a dozen. Finally, we saw them in bloom. Just once, before dying, the knee-high plant throws up a six-foot flower spike—a monstrous, phallic bouquet of purple asters. If a florist delivered this, you would hide it in a closet. Like a torrid sunset or a rousing thunderstorm, it's the kind of excess that only nature can pull off to rave reviews.

The sun blazed ferociously. My pack was stuffed with a wool sweater, sleeping bag, and rain gear—ludicrous baggage I'd brought at the insistence of Park Service brochures. The gallon of water, on the other hand, was a brilliant idea. The trail leveled out on the valley floor and dusty cinders gave way to fields of delicate-looking ferns, which felt to the touch like plastic. Under a white-hot sky, blue-black cinder cones rose above the fern fields. From the cliffs came the gossipy chatter of petrels, rare endemic gull-like birds that hunt at sea and nest in Haleakala. I envied them their shady holes.

When we topped a small rise, a tin-roofed cabin and water tank greeted us like a mirage. The Park Service maintains a primitive cabin in each of three remote areas of the crater, where hikers, with advance permission, can avail themselves of bunks, a woodstove, and water. (There are no other water sources within Haleakala.) We had a permit for a cabin, but not this one—we would spend the night at Paliku, six miles on down the trail. The next day we would backtrack across the crater by a different path, and exit Haleakala via a formidable set of switchbacks known as the Halemau'u Trail. Even on the level the trail was hard, skulking over knife-edged rocks, requiring exhaustive attention; I could hardly imagine doing this up the side of a cliff. I decided I'd think about that tomorrow.

Meanwhile, we flopped on a grassy knoll at the Kapaloa cabin, devouring our lunchtime rations and most of our water. Steven, my ornithologist companion, observed that we were sitting on a litter of excrement whose source could only be the nēnē. He was very excited about this. I lay down on endangered goose pop and fell asleep.

I woke up groggy, weary of the sun and grateful to be more than halfway to Paliku. We marched through a transition zone of low scrub that softened the lava fields. Ahead of us hung the perpetual mystery of fog that had obscured the crater's eastern end all day, hiding our destination.

Suddenly we walked through that curtain into another world: cool gray air, a grassy meadow where mist dappled our faces and dripped from bright berries that hung in tall briar thickets. We had passed from the mouth of hell to the gates of heaven—presuming heaven looks like the Smoky Mountains or Ireland. Awestruck, and possessed of aching feet, we sat down on the ground. Immediately we heard a quiet honking call. A little zebra-striped goose materialized out of mist and flew very low, circling over our heads. It landed a stone's throw away, cocked its head, and watched us. "Perfect for a wilderness catalog," it might have been thinking. In the past I have scoffed at anthropomorphic descriptions of Hawaii's state bird, which people like to call "friendly" and "curious." Now you can scoff at mine.

Soaked to the bone and suddenly shivering, we walked through miles of deep mist, surrounded by the honking of invisible nēnēs. The world grew quiet, white, punctuated with vermilion berries. The trail ended in Paliku meadow. Beyond the field, a wall of cliffs rose straight up like a Japanese carving of a mountainside in jade. The vertical rock faces were crisscrossed with switchback crevices where gnarled trees and giant ferns sprang out in a sidesaddle forest. On these impossible ledges dwell the last traces of native rain forest. They survive there for only one reason: pigs can't fly.

Paliku cabin, nestled among giant ferns, was a sight for sore muscles. Its iron stove was an antique giant, slow to warm up but ultimately unstoppable. Rain roared on the tin roof of our haven. In the thickening dark we lit candles and boiled water for coffee. I hugged the sleeping bag and heavy wool sweater which, at lunchtime, I'd secretly longed to bury under a rock. It was impossible now to recall the intensity of the morning's heat. And tomorrow I would have trouble believing I'd stood tonight fogging the window-pane with my breath, looking out on the wet tangle of a Hawaiian rain forest. Where does it go when it leaves us, the memory of beautiful, strange things?

At dawn the sun broke over the cliffs and parted the pink mantle of clouds, reaching down like a torch to light the tops of red cinder cones in the crater, one at a time. For half a minute, sunlight twinkled star-like against what must have been the glass front of the visitors' center, all those miles away. I pictured the rowdy scene that must have been playing there. I found I couldn't really believe in any other world but the perfect calm of where I stood.

The mist cleared. Fern trees dripped. Nēnēs flew across the cliff face by twos and threes, in heartbreaking imitation of a Japanese pen-and-ink drawing. Birds called from the trees, leading us on a goose chase through soggy vegetation. We spotted the red 'apapane, the yellow Maui creeper, and the 'i'nvi, an odd crimson creature with a downcurved bill—all three gravely threatened species.

I would happily have turned over rocks in search of endangered worms—anything to postpone packing up and striking out. But we had eleven miles to go, all uphill, and the sun was gaining ground. I groaned as I shouldered my pack. "We can still do everything we could when we were twenty," Steven pointed out companionably, "except now it hurts."

We backtracked through the meadows on a trail that grew steadily less muddy. We rested under a crooked acacia, the last tree in an increasingly arid landscape, before taking a new, more northerly trail that would lead us back up and out. Like an old-fashioned hologram, the crater offered two views of itself that were impossible to integrate: all day yesterday we'd walked toward white mist and green cliffs at the crater's wet eastern side; today we did the opposite, facing the drought-stricken western slopes. Planting one boot carefully in front of the other, we crossed acres of black lava flow, where the ground seemed to hula-dance in the heat. We skirted tall cinder cones whose sides were striped yellow and orange like paint pots. Several times I stopped and took note of the fact that there was not, in my whole field of vision, anything living. It might well have been the moon.

The trail graduated from rugged to punishing, and in the afternoon the mists returned. The landscape flowed from lava field to meadow and back again, until we were tossed up at last on the Halemau'u switchbacks. We spent the next two hours scaling the cliff face. With each turn the panorama broadened. We ascended through layers of cloud and emerged on top—nearly two miles above sea level. I invented new names for the Halemau'u trail, which I will keep to myself.

Back home again, still nursing a few aches, I found myself deflecting odd looks from friends who seemed to think a trek through scorched desert and freezing rain in Hawaii was evidence of poor vacation skills.

I would do it all again, in a heartbeat. There are few enough places in the world that belong entirely to themselves. The human passion to carry all things everywhere, so that every place is home, is well on its way to homogenizing our planet. The casualties are the species trampled and lost, extinguished forever, at the rate of tens of thousands per year.

It's a painful, exhausting thing to try to argue logically for the preservation of all the world's species—like trying to debate spirituality with your accountant. Causing extinctions, especially at such a staggering rate, feels dangerous and wrong, but proving scientifically that it's wrong is ultimately very much like proving the existence of God. Commonly environmentalists fall back upon the "pharmacopeia" argument, and it's true enough—any one of these small fallen soldiers might have held some magic bullet to save humanity, like the antirejection drug cyclosporine, derived from a peat-bog fungus, that has made organ transplants a matter of course, or the powerful new anticancer agents extracted from a yew tree. But this seems a pale, selfish reason to care about preserving biodiversity, and near sacrilege in the face of a power so howling and brilliant as life on earth. To love life, really, must mean caring not only for the garden plot but also the wilderness beyond the fence, beauty and mystery for their own sake, because of how meager a world would be without them.

We're familiar enough, across all cultures, with ancestor worship. Why have we never put a second, parallel candle on that altar for "progeny worship"? How can we proceed with such pure disregard for the ones who will come after—not just our own heirs, but all of life? How do we fail to realize we are a point in a grand procession, with equal responsibilities to past and future? "Maybe we need new stories," Linda Hogan writes in the anthology *Heart of the Land*, "new terms and conditions that are relevant to the love of land. . . . We need to reach a hand back through time and a hand forward, stand at the zero point of creation to be certain that we do not create the absence of life, of any species, no matter how inconsequential it might appear to be."

The first tragedy I remember having really understood in my life was the extinction of the dodo. I was four years old. I'd found its picture in the dictionary and asked my mother if we could see a bird like that. I was dismayed by her answer. Not "Yes, at the zoo," or "When you grow up, if you travel to a faraway country." Just: No. The idea that such a fabulous creature had existed, and then simply stopped being—this is the kind of bad news that children refuse to accept. I hauled the dictionary off to bed with me and prayed for the restoration of the dodo to this earth. I vowed that if I could only see such a creature in my lifetime, I would throw myself in front of its demise.

Haleakala Crater is such a creature in our lifetime. In its great cupped hand it holds a bygone Hawaii, a vision of curled fern leaves, a held-back breath of bird song, things that mostly lie buried now under fields of brighter flowers. The memory of beautiful, strange things slips so far beyond reach, when it goes. If I hadn't seen it, I couldn't care half well enough.

Mountaineering in the Sierra Nevada

Clarence King

We had now an easy slope to the summit, and hurried up over rocks and ice, reaching the crest at exactly twelve o'clock. I rang my hammer upon the topmost rock; we grasped hands and I reverently named the grand peak Mount Tyndall.

To our surprise, upon sweeping the horizon with my level, there appeared two peaks equal in height with us, and two rising even higher. That which looked highest of all was a cleanly cut helmet of granite upon the same ridge with Mount Tyndall, lying about six miles south, and fronting the desert with a bold, square bluff which rises to the crest of the peak, where a white fold of snow trims it gracefully. Mount Whitney, as we afterward called it, in honor of our chief, is probably the highest land within the United States. Its summit looked glorious, but inaccessible.

The general topography overlooked by us may be thus simply outlined. Two parallel chains, enclosing an intermediate trough, face each other. Across this deep, enclosed gulf, from wall to wall, juts the thin but lofty and craggy ridge, or "divide," before described, which forms an important watershed, sending those streams which enter the chasm north of it into King's River, those south forming the most important sources of the Kern, whose straight, rapidly deepening valley

Clarence King

stretches south, carved profoundly in granite, while the King's, after flowing longitudinally in the opposite course for eight or ten miles, turns abruptly west round the base of Mount Brewer, cuts across the western ridge, opening a gate of its own, and carves a rock channel transversely down the Sierra to the California plain.

Fronting us stood the west chain, a great mural ridge watched over by two dominant heights, Kaweah Peak and Mount Brewer, its wonderful profile defining against the western sky a multitude of peaks and spires. Bold buttresses jut out through fields of ice, and reach down stone arms among snow and *débris*. North and south of us the higher, or eastern, summit stretched on in miles and miles of snow peaks, the farthest horizon still crowded with their white points. East the whole range fell in sharp, hurrying abruptness to the desert, where, ten thousand feet below, lay a vast expanse of arid plain intersected by low, parallel ranges, traced from north to south. Upon the one side, a thousand sculptures of stone, hard, sharp, shattered by cold into infiniteness of fractures and rift, springing up, mutely severe, into the dark, austere blue of heaven; scarred and marked, except where snow or ice, spiked down by ragged granite bolts, shields with its pale armor these rough mountain shoulders; storm-tinted at summit, and dark where, swooping down from ragged cliff, the rocks plunge over cañon-walls into blue, silent gulfs.

Upon the other hand, reaching out to horizons faint and remote, lay plains clouded with the ashen hues of death; stark, wind-swept floors of white, and hill-ranges, rigidly formal, monotonously low, and lying under an unfeeling brilliance of light, which, for all its strange, unclouded clearness, has yet a vague half-darkness, a suggestion of black and shade more truly pathetic than fading twilight. No greenness soothes, no shadow cools the glare. Owen's Lake, an oval of acrid water, lies dense blue upon the brown sage-plain, looking like a plate of hot metal. Traced in ancient beach-lines, here and there upon hill and plain, relics of ancient lakeshore outline the memory of a cooler past—a period of life and verdure when the stony chains were green islands among basins of wide, watery expanse.

The two halves of this view, both in sight at once, express the highest, the most acute, aspects of desolation—inanimate forms out of which something living has gone forever. From the desert have been dried up and blown away its seas. Their shores and white, salt-strewn bottoms lie there in the eloquence of death. Sharp, white light glances from all the mountain-walls, where in marks and polishings

78

has been written the epitaph of glaciers now melted and vanished into air. Vacant cañons lie open to the sun, bare, treeless, half shrouded with snow, cumbered with loads of broken *débris*, still as graves, except when flights of rocks rush down some chasm's throat, startling the mountains with harsh, dry rattle, their fainter echoes from below followed too quickly by dense silence.

The serene sky is grave with nocturnal darkness. The earth blinds you with its light. That fair contrast we love in lower lands, between bright heavens and dark, cool earth, here reverses itself with terrible energy. You look up into an infinite vault, unveiled by clouds, empty and dark, from which no brightness seems to ray, an expanse with no graded perspective, no tremble, no vapory mobility, only the vast yawning of hollow space.

With an aspect of endless remoteness burns the small, white sun, yet its light seems to pass invisibly through the sky, blazing out with intensity upon mountain and plain, flooding rock details with painfully bright reflections, and lighting up the burnt sand and stone of the desert with a strange, blinding glare. There is no sentiment of beauty in the whole scene; no suggestion, however far remote, of sheltered landscape; not even the air of virgin hospitality that greets us explorers in so many uninhabited spots which by their fertility and loveliness of grove or meadow seem to offer man a home, or us nomads a pleasant camp-ground. Silence and desolation are the themes which nature has wrought out under this eternally serious sky.

A faint suggestion of life clings about the middle altitudes of the eastern slope, where black companies of pine, stunted from breathing the hot desert air, group themselves just beneath the bottom of perpetual snow, or grow in patches of cloudy darkness over the moraines, those piles of wreck crowded from their pathway by glaciers long dead. Something there is pathetic in the very emptiness of these old glacier valleys, these imperishable tracks of unseen engines. One's eye ranges up their broad, open channel to the shrunken white fields surrounding hollow amphitheatres which were once crowded with deep burdens of snow,—the birthplace of rivers of ice now wholly melted; the dry, clear heavens overhead blank of any promise of ever rebuilding them. I have never seen Nature when she seemed so little "Mother Nature" as in this place of rocks and snow, echoes and emptiness. It impresses me as the ruins of some bygone geological period, and no part of the present order, like a specimen of chaos which has defied the finishing hand of Time.

Of course I see its bearings upon climate, and could read a lesson quite glibly as to its usefulness as a condenser, and tell you gravely how much California has for which she may thank these heights, and how little Nevada; but looking from this summit with all desire to see everything, the one overmastering feeling is desolation, desolation!

Next to this, and more pleasing to notice, is the interest and richness of the granite forms; for the whole region, from plain to plain, is built of this dense, solid rock, and is sculptured under chisel of cold in shapes of great variety, yet all having a common spirit, which is purely Gothic.

In the much discussed origin of this order of building I never remember to have seen, though it can hardly have escaped mention, any suggestion of the possibility of the Gothic having been inspired by granite forms. Yet, as I sat on Mount Tyndall, the whole mountains shaped themselves like the ruins of cathedrals,—sharp roof-ridges, pinnacled and statued; buttresses more spired and ornamented than Milan's; receding doorways with pointed arches carved into black façades of granite, doors never to be opened, innumerable jutting points, with here and there a single cruciform peak, its frozen roof and granite spires so strikingly Gothic I cannot doubt that the Alps furnished the models for early cathedrals of that order.

I thoroughly enjoyed the silence, which, gratefully contrasting with the surrounding tumult of form, conveyed to me a new sentiment. I have lain and listened through the heavy calm of a tropical voyage, hour after hour, longing for a sound; and in desert nights the dead stillness has many a time wakened me from sleep. For moments, too, in my forest life, the groves made absolutely no breath of movement; but there is around these summits the soundlessness of a vacuum. The sea stillness is that of sleep; the desert, of death—this silence is like the waveless calm of space.

All the while I made my instrumental observations the fascination of the view so held me that I felt no surprise at seeing water boiling over our little faggot blaze at a temperature of one hundred and ninety-two degrees F., nor in observing the barometrical column stand at 17.99 inches; and it was not till a week or so after that I realized we had felt none of the conventional sensations of nausea, headache, and I don't know what all, that people are supposed to suffer at extreme altitudes; but these things go with guides and porters, I believe, and with coming down to one's hotel at evening there to scold one's picturesque *aubergiste* in a French which strikes upon his ear as a foreign tongue; possibly all that will come to us with advancing time, and what is known as "doing America." They are already shooting our buffaloes; it cannot be long before they will cause themselves to be honorably dragged up and down our Sierras, with perennial yellow gaiter, and ostentation of bath-tub.

Having completed our observations, we packed up the instruments, glanced once again round the whole field of view, and descended to the top of our icicle ladder. Upon looking over, I saw to my consternation that during the day the upper half had broken off. Scars traced down upon the snow-field below it indicated the manner of its fall, and far below, upon the shattered *débris*, were strewn its white relics. I saw that nothing but the sudden gift of wings could possibly take us down to the snow-ridge. We held council, and concluded to climb quite round the peak in search of the best mode of descent.

As we crept about the east face, we could look straight down upon Owen's Valley, and into the vast glacier gorges, and over piles of moraines and fluted rocks, and the frozen lakes of the eastern slope. When we reached the southwest front of the mountain we found that its general form was that of an immense horseshoe, the great eastern ridge forming one side, and the spur which descended to our camp the other, we having climbed up the outer part of the toe. Within the curve of the horseshoe was a gorge, cut almost perpendicularly down two thousand feet, its side rough-hewn walls of rocks and snow, its narrow bottom almost a continuous chain of deep blue lakes with loads of ice and *débris* piles. The steam which flowed through them joined the waters from our home grove, a couple of miles below the camp. If we could reach the level of the lakes, I believed we might easily climb round them and out of the upper end of the horseshoe, and walk upon the Kern plateau round to our bivouac.

It required a couple of hours of very painstaking, deliberate climbing to get down the first descent, which we did, however, without hurting our barometer, and fortunately without the fatiguing use of the lasso; reaching finally the uppermost lake, a granite bowlful of cobalt-blue water, transparent and unrippled. So high and enclosing were the tall walls about us, so narrow and shut in the cañon, so flattened seemed the cover of sky, we felt oppressed after the expanse and freedom of our hours on the summit.

The snow-field we followed, descending farther, was irregularly honeycombed in deep pits, circular or irregular in form, and melted to a greater or less depth, holding each a large stone embedded in the bottom. It seems they must have fallen from the overhanging heights with sufficient force to plunge into the snow.

Brilliant light and strong color met our eyes at every glance—the rocks of a deep purple-red tint, the pure alpine lakes of a cheerful sapphire blue, the snow glitteringly white. The walls on either side for half their height were planed and polished by glaciers, and from the smoothly glazed sides the sun was reflected as from a mirror.

Mile after mile we walked cautiously over the snow and climbed round the margins of lakes, and over piles of *débris* which marked the ancient terminal moraines. At length we reached the end of the horseshoe, where the walls contracted to a gateway, rising on either side in immense, vertical pillars a thousand feet high. Through this gateway we could look down the valley of the Kern, and beyond to the gentler ridges where a smooth growth of forest darkened the rolling plateau. Passing the last snow, we walked through this gateway and turned westward round the spur toward our camp. The three miles which closed our walk were alternately through groves of *Pinus flexilis* and upon plains of granite.

The glacier sculpture and planing are here very beautiful, the large crystals of orthoclase with which the granite is studded being cut down to the common level, their rosy tint making with the white base a beautiful, burnished porphyry.

The sun was still an hour high when we reached camp, and with a feeling of relaxation and repose we threw ourselves down to rest by the log, which still continued blazing. We had accomplished our purpose.

During the last hour or two of our tramp Cotter had complained of his shoes, which were rapidly going to pieces. Upon examination we found to our dismay that there was not over half a day's wear left in them, a calamity which gave to our difficult homeward climb a new element of danger. The last nail had been worn from my own shoes, and the soles were scratched to the quick, but I believed them stout enough to hold together till we should reach the main camp.

We planned a pair of moccasins for Cotter, and then spent a pleasant evening by the camp-fire, rehearsing our climb to the detail, sleep finally overtaking us and holding us fast bound until broad daylight next morning, when we woke with a sense of having slept for a week, quite bright and perfectly refreshed for our homeward journey.

After a frugal breakfast, in which we limited ourselves to a few cubic inches of venison, and a couple of stingy slices of bread, with a single meagre cup of diluted tea, we shouldered our knapsacks, which now sat lightly upon toughened shoulders, and marched out upon the granite plateau.

We had concluded that it was impossible to retrace our former way, knowing well that the precipitous divide could not be climbed from this side; then, too, we had gained such confidence in our climbing powers, from constant victory, that we concluded to attempt the passage of the great King's Cañon, mainly because this was the only mode of reaching camp, and since the geological section of the granite it exposed would afford us an exceedingly instructive study.

The broad granite plateau which forms the upper region of the Kern Valley slopes in general inclination up to the great divide. This remarkably pinnacled ridge, where it approaches the Mount Tyndall wall, breaks down into a broad depression where the Kern Valley sweeps northward, until it suddenly breaks off in precipices three thousand feet down into the King's Cañon.

The morning was wholly consumed in walking up this gently inclined plane of granite, our way leading over the glacier-polished foldings and along graded undulations among labyrinths of alpine garden and wildernesses of erratic boulders, little lake-basins, and scattered clusters of dwarfed and sombre pine.

About noon we came suddenly upon the brink of a precipice which sank sharply from our feet into the gulf of the King's Cañon. Directly opposite us rose Mount Brewer, and up out of the depths of those vast sheets of frozen snow swept spiry buttress-ridges, dividing the upper heights into those amphitheatres over which we had struggled on our outward journey. Straight across from our point of view was the chamber of rock and ice where we had camped on the first night. The wall at our feet fell sharp and rugged, its lower two thirds hidden from our view by the projections of a thousand feet of crags. Here and there, as we looked down, small patches of ice, held in rough hollows, rested upon the steep surface, but it was too abrupt for any great fields of snow. I dislodged a boulder upon the edge and watched it bound down the rocky precipice, dash over caves a thousand feet below us, and disappear, the crash of its fall coming up to us from the unseen depths fainter and fainter, until the air only trembled with confused echoes.

A long look at the pass to the south of Mount Brewer, where we had parted from our friends, animated us with courage to begin the descent, which we did with utmost care, for the rocks, becoming more and more glacier-smoothed, afforded us hardly any firm footholds. When down about eight hundred feet we again rolled rocks ahead of us, and saw them disappear over the eaves, and only heard the sound of their stroke after many seconds, which convinced us that directly below lay a great precipice.

At this juncture the soles came entirely off Cotter's shoes, and we stopped upon a little cliff of granite to make him moccasins of our provision bags and slips of blanket, tying them on as firmly as we could with the extra straps and buckskin thongs. Climbing with these proved so insecure that I made Cotter go behind me, knowing that under ordinary circumstances I could stop him if he fell.

Here and there in the clefts of the rocks grew stunted pine bushes, their roots twisted so firmly into the crevices that we laid hold of them with the utmost confidence whenever they came within our reach. In this way we descended to within fifty feet of the brink, having as yet no knowledge of the cliffs below, except our general memory of their aspect from the Mount Brewer wall.

The rock was so steep that we descended in a sitting posture, clinging with our hands and heels. I heard Cotter say, "I think I must take off these moccasins and try it barefooted, for I don't believe I can make it." These words were instantly followed by a startled cry, and I looked round to see him slide quickly toward me, struggling and clutching at the smooth granite. As he slid by I made a grab for him with my right hand, catching him by the shirt, and, throwing myself as far in the other direction as I could, seized with my left hand a little pine tuft, which held us. I asked Cotter to edge along a little to the left, where he could get a brace with his feet and relieve me of his weight, which he cautiously did. I then threw a couple of turns with the lasso round the roots of the pine bush, and we were safe, though hardly more than twenty feet from the brink. The pressure of curiosity to get a look over that edge was so strong within me that I lengthened out sufficient lasso to reach the end, and slid slowly to the edge, where, leaning over, I looked down, getting a full view of the wall for miles. Directly beneath, a sheer cliff of three or four hundred feet stretched down to a pile of *débris* which rose to unequal heights along its face, reaching the very crest not more than a hundred feet south of us. From that point to the bottom of the cañon, broken rocks, ridges rising through vast sweeps of *débris*, tufts of pine and frozen bodies of ice covered the further slope.

I returned to Cotter, and, having loosened ourselves from the pine bush, inch by inch we crept along the granite until we supposed ourselves to be just over the top of the *débris* pile, where I found a firm brace for my feet, and lowered Cotter to the edge. He sang out, "All right!" and climbed over on the uppermost *débris*, his head only remaining in sight of me; when I lay down upon my back, making knapsack and body do friction duty, and, letting myself move, followed Cotter and reached his side.

From that point the descent required two hours of severe, constant labor, which was monotonous of itself, and would have proved excessively tiresome but for the constant interest of glacial geology beneath us. When at last we reached the bottom and found ourselves upon a velvety green meadow, beneath the shadow of wide-armed pines, we realized the amount of muscular force we had used up, and threw ourselves down for a rest of half an hour, when we rose, not quite renewed, but fresh enough to finish the day's climb.

In a few minutes we stood upon the rocks just above King's River,—a broad, white torrent fretting its way along the bottom of an impassable gorge. Looking down the stream, we saw that our right bank was a continued precipice, affording, so far as we could see, no possible descent to the river's margin, and indeed, had we gotten down, the torrent rushed with such fury that we could not possibly have crossed it. To the south of us, a little way up stream, the river flowed out from a broad, oval lake, three quarters of a mile in length, which occupied the bottom of the granite basin. Unable to cross the torrent, we must either swim the lake or climb round its head. Upon our side the walls of the basin curved to the head of the lake in sharp, smooth precipices, or broken slopes of *débris*, while on the opposite side its margin was a beautiful shore of emerald meadow, edged with a continuous grove of coniferous trees. Once upon this other side, we should have completed the severe part of our journey, crossed the gulf, and have left all danger behind us; for the long slope of granite and ice which rose upon the west side of the cañon and the Mount Brewer wall opposed to us no trials save those of simple fatigue.

Around the head of the lake were crags and precipices in singularly forbidding arrangement. As we turned thither we saw no possible way of overcoming them. At its head the lake lay in an angle of the vertical wall, sharp and straight like the corner of a room; about three hundred feet in height, and for two hundred and fifty feet of this a pyramidal pile of blue ice rose from the lake, rested against the corner, and reached within forty feet of the top. Looking into the deep blue water of the lake, I concluded that in our exhausted state it was madness to attempt to swim it. The only alternative was to scale that slender pyramid of ice and find some way to climb the forty feet of smooth wall above it; a plan we chose perforce, and started at once to put into execution, determined that if we were unsuccessful we would fire a dead log which lay near, warm ourselves thoroughly, and attempt the swim. At its base the ice mass overhung the lake like a roof, under which the water had melted its way for a distance of not less than a hundred feet, a thin cave overhanging the water. To the very edge of this I cautiously went, and, looking down into the lake, saw through its beryl depths the white granite blocks strewn upon the bottom at least one hundred feet below me. It was exceedingly transparent, and, under ordinary circumstances, would have been a most tempting place for a dive; but at the end of our long fatigue, and with the still unknown tasks ahead, I shrank from a swim in such a chilly temperature.

We found the ice-angle difficultly steep, but made our way successfully along its edge, clambering up the crevices melted between its body and the smooth granite to a point not far from the top, where the ice had considerably narrowed, and rocks overhanging it encroached so closely that we were obliged to change our course and make our way with cut steps out upon its front. Streams of water, dropping from the overhanging rock-eaves at many points, had worn circular shafts into the ice, three feet in diameter and twenty feet in depth. Their edges offered us our only foothold, and we climbed from one to another, equally careful of slipping upon the slope itself, or falling into the wells. Upon the top of the ice we found a narrow, level platform, upon which we stood together, resting our backs in the granite corner, and looked down the awful pathway of King's Cañon, until the rest nerved us up enough to turn our eyes upward at the forty feet of smooth granite which lay between us and safety. Here and there were small projections from its surface, little protruding knobs of feldspar, and crevices riven into its face for a few inches.

As we tied ourselves together, I told Cotter to hold himself in readiness to jump down into one of these in case I fell, and started to climb up the wall, succeeding quite well for about twenty feet. About two feet above my hands was a crack, which, if my arms had been long enough to reach, would probably have led me to the very top; but I judged it beyond my powers, and, with great care, descended to the side of Cotter, who believed that his superior length of arm would enable him to make the reach.

I planted myself against the rock, and he started cautiously up the wall. Looking down the glare front of ice, it was not pleasant to consider at what velocity a slip would send me to the bottom, or at what angle, and to what probable depth, I should be projected into the ice-water. Indeed, the idea of such a sudden bath was so annoying that I lifted my eyes toward my companion. He reached my farthest point without great difficulty, and made a bold spring for the crack, reaching it without an inch to spare, and holding on wholly by his fingers. He thus worked himself slowly along the crack toward the top, at last getting his arms over the brink, and gradually drawing his body up and out of sight. It was the most splendid piece of slow gymnastics I ever witnessed. For a moment he said nothing; but when I asked if he was all right, cheerfully repeated, "All right."

It was only a moment's work to send up the two knapsacks and barometer, and receive again my end of the lasso. As I tied it round my breast, Cotter said to me, in an easy, confident tone, "Don't be afraid to bear your weight." I made up my mind, however, to make that climb without his aid, and husbanded my strength as I climbed from crack to crack. I got up without difficulty to my former point, rested there a moment, hanging solely by my hands, gathered every pound of strength and atom of will for the reach, then jerked myself upward with a swing, just getting the tips of my fingers into the crack. In an instant I had grasped it with my right hand also. I felt the sinews of my fingers relax a little, but the picture of the slope of ice and the blue lake affected me so strongly that I redoubled my grip, and climbed slowly along the crack until I reached the angle and got one arm over the edge, as Cotter had done. As I rested my body upon the edge and looked up at Cotter, I saw that, instead of a level top, he was sitting upon a smooth, roof-like slope, where the least pull would have dragged him over the brink. He had no brace for his feet, nor hold for his hands, but had seated himself calmly, with the rope tied around his breast, knowing that my only safety lay in being able to make the climb entirely unaided; certain that the least waver in his tone would have disheartened me, and perhaps made it impossible. The shock I received on seeing this affected me for a moment, but not enough to throw me off my guard, and I climbed quickly over the edge. When we had walked back out of danger we sat down upon the granite for a rest.

In all my experience of mountaineering I have never known an act of such real, profound courage as this of Cotter's. It is one thing, in a moment of excitement, to make a gallant leap, or hold one's nerves in the iron grasp of will, but to coolly seat one's self in the door of death, and silently listen for the fatal summons, and this all for a friend,—for he might easily have cast loose the lasso and saved himself,—requires as sublime a type of courage as I know.

But a few steps back we found a thicket of pine overlooking our lake, by which there flowed a clear rill of snow-water. Here, in the bottom of the great gulf, we made our bivouac; for we were already in the deep evening shadows, although the mountaintops to the east of us still burned in the reflected light. It was the luxury of repose which kept me awake half an hour or so, in spite of my vain attempts at sleep. To listen for the pulsating sound of waterfalls and arrowy rushing of the brook by our beds was too deep a pleasure to quickly yield up.

Under the later moonlight I rose and went out upon the open rocks, allowing myself to be deeply impressed by the weird Dantesque surroundings—darkness, out of which to the sky towered stern, shaggy bodies of rock; snow, uncertainly moonlit with cold pallor; and at my feet the basin of the lake, still, black, and gemmed with reflected stars, like the void into which Dante looked through the bottomless gulf of Dis. A little way off there appeared upon the brink of a projecting granite cornice two dimly seen forms; pines I knew them to be, yet their motionless figures seemed bent forward, gazing down the cañon; and I allowed myself to name them Mantuan and Florentine, thinking at the same time how grand and spacious the scenery, how powerful their attitude, and how infinitely more profound the mystery of light and shade, than any of those hard, theatrical conceptions with which Doré has sought to shut in our imagination. That artist, as I believe, has reached a conspicuous failure from an overbalancing love of solid, impenetrable darkness. There is in all his Inferno landscape a certain sharp boundary between the real and unreal, and never the infinite suggestiveness of great regions of half-light, in which everything may be seen, nothing recognized. Without waking Cotter, I crept back to my blankets, and to sleep.

The morning of our fifth and last day's tramp must have dawned cheerfully; at least, so I suppose from its aspect when we first came back to consciousness, surprised to find the sun risen from the eastern mountain-wall, and the whole gorge flooded with its direct light. Rising as good as new from our mattress of pine twigs, we hastened to take breakfast, and started up the long, broken slope of the Mount Brewer wall. To reach the pass where we had parted from our friends required seven hours of slow, laborious climbing, in which we took advantage of every outcropping spine of granite and every level expanse of ice to hasten at the top of our speed. Cotter's feet were severely cut; his tracks upon the snow were marked by stains of blood, yet he kept on with undiminished spirit, never once complaining. The perfect success of our journey so inspired us with happiness that we forgot danger and fatigue, and chatted in liveliest strain.

It was about two o'clock when we reached the summit, and rested a moment to look back over our new Alps, which were hard and distinct under direct, unpoetic light; yet with all their dense gray and white reality, their long, sculptured ranks, and cold, still summits, we gave them a lingering, farewell look, which was not without its deep fulness of emotion, then turned our backs and hurried down the *débris* slope into the rocky amphitheatre at the foot of Mount Brewer, and by five o'clock had reached our old camp-ground. We found here a note pinned to a tree, informing us that the party had gone down into the lower cañon, five miles below, that they might camp in better pasturage.

The wind had scattered the ashes of our old campfire, and banished from it the last sentiment of home. We hurried on, climbing among the rocks which reached down to the crest of the great lateral moraine, and then on in rapid stride along its smooth crest, riveting our eyes upon the valley below, where we knew the party must be camped.

At last, faintly curling above the sea of green treetops, a few faint clouds of smoke wafted upward into the air. We saw them with a burst of strong emotion, and ran down the steep flank of the moraine at the top of our speed. Our shouts were instantly answered by the three voices of our friends, who welcomed us to their camp-fire with tremendous hugs.

After we had outlined for them the experience of our days, and as we lay outstretched at our ease, warm in the blaze of the glorious camp-fire, Brewer said to me: "King, you have relieved me of a dreadful task. For the last three days I have been composing a letter to your family, but somehow I did not get beyond, 'It becomes my painful duty to inform you.' "

A Mystery Solved

Debbie Miller

A few winters after our trip across the Brooks Range, I'm poring through a stack of topographic maps inside a 12-by-15-foot log cabin southwest of Arctic Village. With so little daylight and 40-below-zero temperatures, it's a perfect time to dream of summer backpacking trips. Ever since crossing the Brooks Range via the Okpilak, Hulahula, and Chandalar drainages, I've longed to hike a route through the refuge that would follow different northern rivers to their headwaters. This coming summer Dennis will be working as a commercial pilot, so I hope to make the trek with one or two women friends.

Studying the maps, my eyes jog along the Continental Divide, and I find scores of delicate-flowing streams and rivers that are born in mountain provinces such as the Philip Smith, Romanzof, and Davidson mountains. My heart is set on finding an east–west route that would traverse several drainages near the crest of the Brooks Range and cross the divide in at least two places. There are an unlimited number of routes, all with spectacular scenery and great wildlife diversity, so the decision is not an easy one.

After pondering the maps by candlelight, and consulting with Dennis on various choices, I decide on a month-long trip that will have two legs. The first leg will begin at the confluence of Cane Creek and the East Fork of the Chandalar River, follow Cane Creek to its headwaters, then head west across the divide into the upper reaches of the exquisite Marsh Fork of the Canning River.

The second leg of the trip will be more strenuous. The trip will begin along the braided Ivishak River, which lies a couple of drainages west of the Canning River. This route will follow the Ivishak to its headwaters, cross the divide through a 5,700-foot saddle nestled between 7,000- to 8,000-foot rugged mountains, then follow the Wind River drainage south. I have chosen this particular route because the Ivishak–Wind River pass is one of the highest passes along the Continental Divide, and our course will cut through the heart of the remote Philip Smith Mountains. There is always the chance that no one has ever walked this particular route.

Several months later, it is summer, and Dennis is circling over the Ivishak River, trying to locate a gravel bar on which to land the Super Cub. The surfaces of most of the Ivishak's bars resemble a rough washboard, and can be better referred to as boulder bars. Dennis has a difficult time finding a place smooth enough, without plane-eating rocks, to land safely. He finally discovers an acceptable spot, and soon we are rattling across the rocks. After dropping me off, he heads back to the Marsh Fork of the Canning to pick up Sidney Stephens, a teacher-friend with whom I have just completed the first two-week segment of our trip.

Alone in the broad Ivishak River valley, I listen to the peaceful-flowing braided river, and reflect upon the first 75-mile portion of our trip. Sidney and I, with another friend, Mary Clare Andrews, had just hiked up Cane Creek's gentle valley, following the exquisite stream to its headwaters. We passed many upthrusted mountains with unusual pastel, brick red, and coal black layers. Some cone-shaped mountains were folded, twisted, or tilted on their sides, while others had concentric sedimentary layers that spiraled toward the sky. Each bend in the river and foot of elevation gained brought us new mountains with different geologic chapters written on their faces.

For days we walked through undisturbed valleys and along nameless tributaries; we saw no other human footprints. We viewed scores of Dall sheep grazing in the high country or picking their way across talus slopes. One blond grizzly paid us a brief but heart-pounding visit near a campsite surrounded by thickets of soapberry bushes. The bear was scarfing down a breakfast of the bitter red berries when we spotted it. The grizzly evidently caught our scent at about the same time we saw it. Startled, the bear took off through the bushes as though in a steeplechase. Within a minute the galloping bear vanished beyond the sloping crest of tundra. All of us were relieved that the grizzly had left our camp, but at the same time we regretted that it didn't stay longer within binocular range.

The route along Cane Creek and the Marsh Fork also offered a diversity of habitats for a number of birds: arctic warblers and redpolls in the willow bushes; semipalmated plovers and sandpipers on the gravel bars; upland plovers and jaegers on the tussocks; and golden eagles and rough-legged hawks soaring above us. Sidney had been thrilled when she spotted a flock of northern wheatears darting among the rocks just below the divide. She had always wanted to see this mountain-loving bird that breeds in northern Alaska then marathons back to Africa to spend the winter.

I'm brought back to the present when the puttering Super Cub breaks the sound of the Ivishak. Today the river sounds like a steady wind blowing through a pine forest. Soon the broad-winged Cub glides down to the bar like a frigate bird, then bounces off the bar a couple of times before rolling out.

Dennis is anxious to try his luck at fishing for arctic char. He unearths his pole from the back of the Cub and heads over to what look like a couple of deep blue holes at the base of some limestone cliffs. Each summer thousands of the sea-running arctic char migrate up many northern rivers within the refuge to spawn and overwinter. Rivers such as the Ivishak, Hulahula, and Kongakut contain many freshwater springs that provide ideal overwintering habitat for char. The abundant arctic char are a major subsistence resource for local Kaktovik residents, who catch the fish in both summer and winter.

Instead of pulling out our poles, Sidney and I are more interested in eating some of the fresh supplies Dennis had brought. We decide on some avocado, onion, and cheese sandwiches for starters.

"Char!" Dennis shouts as I put the sandwich together. Sure enough, he has caught a good-size char on his first cast.

"Another one!" he yells to us a few minutes later.

With that, I grab my fishing pole and lures and head over to join him. Within a half-hour we have caught seven beautiful silvery pink arctic char. Dennis still has several flights to make from Arctic Village, so Sidney and I send him off with all seven fish, figuring there are more to come. Arctic char are always a welcome surprise for Arctic Village residents, since this particular seafaring cousin of the Dolly Varden is not available in the Arctic Village area. Dennis plans to share the catch.

Soon Dennis takes off and tips the Cub's wings a few times, waving goodbye to the only two human specks of life along this far-reaching northern river. We, indeed, feel isolated. The nearest settlement is Arctic Village, some seventy miles to the southeast. The closest city is Fairbanks, almost three hundred miles due south. If we were to hop into a boat and float about fifty miles down the Ivishak to its confluence with the Sagavanirktok River, we would reach our first sign of civilization: the trans-Alaska pipeline. Following the Sagavanirktok and the silver tube north for another fifty miles, we would eventually reach the Prudhoe Bay oil fields.

Sidney and I decide to walk upriver a couple of miles to find a good campsite and another fishing spot. After a mile of walking on gravel bars, we find another fairly deep, crystal-clear fishing hole with not one visible char. I cast a few times, and there are no nibbles. What if Dennis took off with our only chance of fresh fish, and we end up with another freeze-dried dinner?

Fortunately, that's not the case. Within another mile we discover a deep blue, bottomless hole that looks promising. The pool is bordered by a series of prominent cliffs that apparently have fought the river's erosional force. Springwater gushes out of the upper portion of one cliff, showering the rocks with a fine mist; several birds flit through the water's spray. One lower band of rock is thickly covered with green moss, and for a moment I'm reminded of some of those unusual green-covered pinnacles on the island of Kauai.

After a couple of casts, I catch a three- to four-pounder that will provide plenty for dinner and sandwiches. Now that it is mid-August, most of the insects have vanished, and the char seem to be gobbling my lures. Sidney has packed a fly rod, but she decides to wait until tomorrow to try her hand at the art of fly casting.

That evening we eat a delicious meal of pink char and bannock beside a driftwood fire by the river. For a time the northern sky is painted with sunset colors nearly the same hue as our pink dinner.

The next morning we decide it's too beautiful to leave camp. It's warm, probably in the upper 60s, and the char hole looks inviting for a swim. Sidney spends much of the morning experimenting with the new fly rod, her line sweeping back and forth in great arcs from the gravel bar to the pool. Sometimes she snags a scrubby willow bush or the back of her sweater, and I hear an "Ahhhhh!" of frustration. Most of the time she looks like a wayward music conductor following the tempo of some unconventional piece, arms and hands waving all over the place. Although she doesn't get a nibble, she says she loves going through the motions and doesn't care about the catch.

Later in the afternoon, after swimming in killing-cold water, washing our rank clothes, and catching another whopper for dinner, we head upriver a few miles. As soon as we pack up the tent, black clouds start to consume the sky to the south. Within a mile of char-hole camp, the wind starts gusting into our faces, and soon the rain is soaking us. The squall quickly blows by us, and we're in sunshine once again, although the slate sky hanging over the more distant mountains looks threatening.

We reach a large, mile-wide, nameless tributary that merges with the Ivishak from the west. The tributary has an immense alluvial fan of gravel and boulders that yawns into the Ivishak, yet only a couple of small creeks snake through the clutter of rocks. The broad Ivishak valley is impressively open here, particularly with such a broad-flowing tributary cutting through the 4,000- to 6,000-foot gray mountains that flank the river. Across the floor of the two-mile-wide Ivishak valley, I count at least ten channels weaving through an enormous floodplain of rocks.

On the other side of the tributary, we set up camp, since the weather is looking more ominous to the south and slowly moving our way. We erect the tent and cover our packs while thunder rumbles in the distance and a dark wave of clouds moves down the valley like an incoming tide. Each valley to the south gradually becomes sheathed by veils of rain, shadowed by iron gray clouds, and rapped with thunder. Closer and closer the storm moves toward us, with the constant rumbling of thunder and intermittent jagged bolts of lightning, yet bright sunshine still bathes us as we are a part of that momentary calm before the storm.

Watching thunderstorms move down a valley such as this is an awesome experience. You can actually study and enjoy the movements of the storm for a time without being caught up in it. Instead of struggling to keep dry, or hiding within the shelter of a tent, you can just observe one of nature's wonders in motion. You can soak in the power of the storm and watch the surrounding mountains and valleys get drenched, without getting wet yourself.

Then the wind picks up, and the first raindrops from the periphery of the storm blow into our faces. Sidney and I throw our few needed belongings into the tent and continue to watch the swirling dark clouds and lightning streak toward the mountaintops on the opposite side of the river. The thunder now shakes us. We can hear, as well as see, thick curtains of rain closing in upon us.

"It sounds as if it's ripping the sky apart," Sidney says of the thunderous din.

Then we notice a bull caribou trotting proudly down a gravel bar in the middle of the river. Concentrating on the storm's show, we had almost missed him. The bull is running north, away from the blow. As he passes our campsite, an unusually loud belt of thunder stops the caribou in his tracks.

Startled, the bull first looks behind him at the oncoming storm, then gives our bright orange tent a puzzled look, as though the thunder and tent are somehow connected. The loner, with his new set of ornate antlers, continues to trot north.

Within seconds the rain reaches us, and we crawl into the tent. Soon hailstones are bombarding the flapping tent fly, and we appear to be in the thick of the storm. I look south out the tent's exit hole and see a band of sunlight behind the fast-moving thunderstorm. This storm is grasping the earth in its fury of swirling clouds, wind, and thunder; then it releases its grip, suddenly and deliberately, after showering and pelting the ground with rain and hail. We watch the storm continue to move north, gripping and pounding the valley, until the thunder is muffled in the distant mountains.

Soon we are in sunshine again, and the sky is flecked with beautiful poststorm cumulus clouds. Our day ends with another delicious char dinner with curried rice, and a spectacular sunset of apricot- and pink-washed clouds.

A few days later we have moved several miles upstream, just west of Porcupine Lake, which lies between the Marsh Fork of the Canning River and the Ivishak drainage. We hope to scale a mountain that will give us a good view of the mile-long lake, named by USGS geologists who discovered many porcupines in the area in 1948.

The closer we get to the backbone of the Philip Smith Mountains, the narrower the Ivishak becomes. Along one section of the river a band of cliffs rises some 30 to 40 feet above the main channel. One rock formation has what appears to be a striking band of quartz, curving like a sidewinder through several layers of sedimentary rock. Many of the sedimentary layers are twisted and folded, thrusted and squeezed, in almost every direction by some unimaginable geologic force.

We are camped near a large patch of willows and are surrounded by dense thickets of soapberries and an occasional blueberry bush on which there are ripe berries. Bears and berries go hand in hand this time of year, so, sure enough, we find fresh grizzly signs all over. The bears in this region seem to be most fond of the soapberries, we surmise, since we discover dung containing piles of berries all around our camp. The bears seem to be inhaling the berries whole rather than chewing them.

I begin to worry about the smell of char juice on our clothing and on the pot bags. Even though North Slope grizzlies are generally not considered fish eaters, the smell could certainly attract them. I carry our heavy 30.06 rifle for emergency protection, but pray I will never have to use it. As a precaution, I nervously play my harmonica when we walk through the willows and other areas of poor visibility, figuring that my novice tunes will scare off just about anything.

Male grizzlies on the north side of the Brooks Range weigh an average of 350 to 400 pounds, about one-third the size of their giant cousin, the Kodiak brown bear. Although much smaller, these northern grizzlies are not to be treated with any less respect. Most of the bears we've encountered within the refuge have run away at the first hint of our scent. But there are bears with unpredictable personalities, and they may be more curious or aggressive. One thing is certain. I did not want to take any grizzly by surprise.

One sultry afternoon we decide to climb up a lookout mountain on the east side of the river that we hope will offer a good view of the Porcupine Lake region and the upper Ivishak we have yet to explore. It's a relatively easy hike up the gentle ridgeline. When we reach the top, there is just room enough for the two of us to sit and gaze at the impressive panoramic view. We first discover that others have used this summit for a lookout. The craggy mountaintop is peppered with sheep pellets, and we also find a few owl pellets, some tiny vole teeth, and scattered white feathers. An old bleached caribou antler lies several yards below us on the other side of the mountain.

Although many of the highest peaks along the divide are obscured, there is much scenery to view at the lower elevations. Looking north, we see the silver-gray Ivishak bending west toward our old thunderstorm campsite. To the south, we face a wall of some of the most remote mountains in North America, mountains that we would soon cross over. In the somber light, most of the mountains are the same uniform dusty gray, although they are highlighted by magnificent erosional patterns. Some mountains are streaked with chutes and gullies that curve around barren-looking pinnacles and jagged out-croppings that erupt from the steep slopes.

The tundra slopes still have a hint of green, although we can see the beginning of autumn golds and reds that will soon completely paint this northern landscape. On the west bank of the Ivishak we spot a large group of Dall rams grazing on a tundra bench a few hundred feet above the river. To the east, we can barely see the edge of Porcupine Lake because of a low-lying ridge that blocks our view. Beyond the hidden lake we can see the undulating slopes of tundra falling gently toward the Marsh Fork of the Canning River, some 15 to 20 miles away. All of this, and not a sign of human activity. Since Dennis left us, we have not seen or heard an airplane overhead.

Perhaps at this very moment, somewhere in the halls of Congress, Representative Morris Udall and his many supporters are fighting to pass landmark legislation known as H.R. 39, or the so-called d-2 bill. D-2 refers to Section 17(d)(2) of the 1971 Alaska Native Claims Settlement Act (ANCSA). In addition to distributing a cash settlement and millions of acres to Alaska Natives, ANCSA directed the Secretary of Interior to withdraw up to 80 million acres of Alaska's unreserved public lands deemed suitable for national parks, forests, wildlife refuges, and wild and scenic rivers.

With the passage of ANCSA, subsequent d-2 legislation, passed in 1980, would ultimately establish the most extensive park and refuge system ever enacted by Congress. The Alaska National Interest Lands Conservation Act (ANILCA), in addition to setting aside 97 million new acres of national park and wildlife refuge lands, would designate 56.4 million acres as wilderness and add 26 exquisite Alaskan rivers to the National Wild and Scenic River system. Portions of the Ivishak, Wind, and Shiinjik rivers, in the refuge, would be on that list.

Sidney and I are walking through country that is outside the original Arctic National Wildlife Range. New boundaries are being fought over in Washington, boundaries that will determine whether this land beneath our feet remains under the control of the Bureau of Land Management, or whether it will be managed as a refuge under USFWS. Thanks to those dedicated to protecting wild areas for future generations, to those who beat on doors in Washington, and to the many conservationists and grassroots organizations who lobbied representatives from their home states, ANILCA did become a reality.

The soon-to-be-established Arctic National Wildlife Refuge would encompass all that our eyes can see from this summit. A vast portion of the Ivishak drainage, along with other free-flowing river systems stretching westward toward the pipeline corridor and south to the Yukon Flats, would all be part of the new addition. The 19-million-acre Arctic Refuge would be the second largest unit within the National Wildlife Refuge system, with the Yukon Delta National Wildlife Refuge ranking slightly larger.

A day later we are exploring the narrower portion of the upper Ivishak, which reveals a new series of geologic formations. For a few miles it is as though we are walking through whiskey bottles lying end to end on a table. In several places the Ivishak narrows for several hundred yards, forming small gorges through a buckskin-colored rock formation. As we enter these winding narrow cuts, we expect that the Ivishak gorge will continue, perhaps forming a deeper canyon as we approach the divide.

To the contrary, it's like walking through the skinny neck of a bottle and entering its more spacious bottom. Each time we walk through a narrow gorge, we reach an opening that funnels us into a gentle open valley. The river once again becomes braided, and there is a prevailing feeling of open space, although we are still shouldered by the Ivishak's mountainous valley walls.

Each narrow passageway brings us new surprises as we enter the more open valley. There are new rock formations, unusual upthrusted mountains, with convoluted sedimentary bands, and always the intricate web of tundra plant life along the river.

In one of these valley rooms, the Ivishak's riverbed is covered with parts of an unusual rock band that I have never seen elsewhere in the eastern Brooks Range. Each hunk, piece, or fragment possesses the same characteristics. The rock is composed largely of an iron red base and topped with a thin coal-black layer. The black layer is extensively fractured into small polygonal shapes, and quartz, the color of white icing, has filled all the cracks. I would later find out that the reddish portion of the rock is iron oxide and that the Inupiat word for iron oxide is Ivishak. At one time Eskimos in this region reportedly used iron oxide from this river drainage to make red paint.

We later camp on an ideal bluff that overlooks the valley and is shouldered by impressive 6,000- to 7,000-foot serrated ridges and partially obscured peaks. Along the divide there is one striking, dome-shaped, chocolate-colored mountain with a remnant glacier flowing like marshmallow sauce over its crest and down its brow. We call it sundae mountain.

The following day dawns partly cloudy, with an autumn nip in the air and a fairly stiff breeze. Our tent is beaded with the raindrops that pattered on us most of the night. In the last couple of days there has been a dramatic change in color on the tundra. The willows have turned to yellow and deep gold, the blueberry leaves to a subdued violet, and the bearberry leaves to a brilliant crimson.

"It feels like winter is coming," I say to Sidney as the coffee's steam momentarily warms my face.

We're both anxious to get under way just to warm up. With any luck we might cross the divide today. The first few miles beyond camp offer great walking along tundra-covered river terraces. A couple of stretches of tundra are as smooth as a golf course, and that gives us the opportunity to look around at the precipitous mountains and the remnant north-facing glaciers that form the backbone of the Philip Smith Mountains.

After three to four miles, the valley grows more restrictive, tundra slopes fall steeply to the river, and numerous rivulets and cascades tumble down from the high country. Soon we are walking through a narrow canyon and are forced to make numerous river crossings. Although not deep, the water numbs our feet. The tortuous creek continues through the confining slit for a couple of miles, and our pace slows to the speed of a waddling porcupine as the stream gradient increases. Finally we reach a waterfall and a deep pool, and luckily discover a route that takes us above the canyon so that we don't have to backtrack. While I climb up from the river, a small flock of rosy-crowned finches lands next to me and seems to be studying my progress. They chirp away with such ease, while I huff and puff. Yes, it would be nice to have wings right now.

As we near the Ivishak's headwaters, the terrain grows ever more rugged. No longer would we find stretches of tundra for easy hiking. From now on we pick our way across steep talus slopes and occasionally use both our hands and feet for balance. Although we are only two miles from the hidden pass, we decide to make camp because the weather looks foreboding. Thick, dark clouds are sweeping over the divide, and a mean wind is blowing down the valley. A storm is coming our way.

At 4,200 feet we erect our tent on what may be the only level patch of rocky ground in the immediate area. Within an hour of setting up camp, the storm begins to pound us with sleet and hail, and we quickly realize that this is not a brief thundershower. All evening and through the night we are stuck in our tent, listening to the flapping tent and pounding sleet. At one point I go out in the gusting storm to tighten the guy lines and almost need a flashlight; now that it is the third week of August we are experiencing several hours of darkness.

All through the next day the storm continues, and we occasionally peer out the tent door to watch snow falling about 800 feet above us. I worry about crossing the divide. If the snow continues, it may be a treacherous 1,500-foot ascent to the pass over slippery, rock-cluttered terrain. At this point we have no idea whether our chosen route is feasible. Neither of us has seen the pass from the air, and there could be sheer drop-offs on either side of the divide that wouldn't necessarily show up on our 1:250,000-scale topographic maps.

But this was all part of the adventure of exploring this wild country. I was glad we had not seen our route from an airplane. Wilderness explorer and advocate Bob Marshall once wrote: ". . . one of the greatest values of exploration is in pitting oneself without the aid of machinery against unknown Nature. When you use machinery to get the jump on Nature by making her reveal some of her secrets in advance, it seems to me a little bit like peeping at the end of the book to see how the plot will come out."

If we can cross the divide, we are still 25 miles from where Dennis plans to pick us up in three days. If we can't reach the Wind River drainage, we will have to backtrack about 40 miles down the Ivishak to the closest known landing area. Although it is wearisome to think that our route may not be feasible, there is a tremendous sense of adventure in not knowing what lies ahead. Perhaps one of the greatest value in experiencing this primeval wilderness is the element of discovery.

On the morning of August 23, after we've been trapped in our tent for 36 hours, the skies are blue and clear. Our tent is sheathed in ice and is crisp to the touch. The condensation on our bags is frosted. I did not sleep well through the damp, cold night. The temperature is in the low 30s as we awkwardly crawl out of the tent, stiff as a couple of two-by-fours. The rugged mountains along the divide are beautifully dusted with fresh snow, and although they are only 7,000 to 8,000 feet high, the relief is as impressive as some of the glaciated ranges we've seen at much higher elevations, such as the Alaska Range.

Within the hour the temperature warms a few degrees, and we can see that the snow will melt quickly in the pass area. We break camp and head toward the divide at a fast pace to avoid potential high runoff. Soon the rocky valley slopes narrow into a canyon, and we again make numerous river crossings through knee-deep icy water.

Rounding a sharp bend in the river, we discover an accessible ridge above the canyon that will give us a chance to exit the freezing riverbed and gain a view of what lies ahead. As we near the top of the ridge, we see for the first time the 5,700-foot saddle nestled in the 7,500-foot jagged crestline. With our 50-pound packs, the walk across the steep, loose talus will be difficult, but we're relieved that the route over the divide looks like a go.

Scanning the pass area, we both notice an unusual bright patch of orange about 200 feet below the pass. I assume that it is lichens contrasted against the slate gray ridge. But why are they growing in that one particular spot? We pull out binoculars, and to our amazement we discover that the orange is not lichens. It is the remains of an airplane wreck.

Cautiously we traverse the unstable talus, trying to avoid starting a rock slide. We sometimes hear water trickling well beneath our feet, and occasionally the faint rumbling of rocks shifting beneath us. How long had this plane wreckage been lying in the mountains? Were there any survivors? Why did it crash in this isolated, rugged area?

As we approach the wreckage, I pick up an old duffel bag that has rolled down the mountainside. Written in ink on the canvas is a legible address, and the aluminum zipper still works, so I assume that the plane wreck can't be too old. Inside the bag I find six army sleeping bags.

When we get closer to the wreckage, we realize the plane accident must have happened years ago. Vintage 7-Up and Coke cans lie unopened near the crash site. Rusted debris and crumpled cowling are scattered around what remains of the fuselage. Most of the international-orange, amphibious plane had burned. One engine and wing—with the plane's identification numbers, N720—lie intact on the 40-degree slope.

Sidney spots a metal flight case that was evidently thrown from the plane on impact. Strangely, it rests on a large rock as though someone had placed it there. Enclosed in the case, protected from the elements, are old flight logs. Luckily only the lower right-hand corner of the logs burned, and the entries are perfectly legible.

The logs reveal that the plane belonged to the USFWS and had been piloted by a man named Rhode. The entries indicate that on August 21, 1958, almost 21 years ago to the day, Rhode took off from Porcupine Lake, approximately 25 miles northeast. He departed at 10:10 A.M. and returned to Porcupine Lake at 11:35 A.M. He stayed at the lake for almost two hours and then took off again at 1:26 P.M. That was Rhode's last entry. He gave no destination.

An eerie sensation sweeps through us as wind funnels down from the pass, rattling pieces of metal against the rocks. Who was this man named Rhode, and what was the final destination of this plane? It is obvious that no one could have survived the violent crash. Is it possible that we are the first people to locate these remains? Given that 21 years have passed, we guess that someone has likely spotted the wreckage from the air. Nevertheless, we decide to carry the flight case with us and report the plane as soon as we reach Arctic Village.

Walking up to the pass, I keep wondering who had given up their lives to these enduring mountains. Soon we reach the saddle and can't help but linger on the spine of this rugged range, where each drop of water is given its destination. The Wind and Ivishak rivers are only gently flowing trickles here. Narrow veins of water form a miniature delta within the saddle, the birthplace of these two wild, clear-flowing rivers. The Ivishak will eventually merge with the Sagavanirktok River and continue beyond the oil fields into the Beaufort Sea. The south-flowing Wind will meander some 75 miles through and beyond the Brooks Range, into spruce forests, and merge with the East Fork of the Chandalar. Its waters eventually flow into the Yukon River and on to the Bering Sea, more than a 1,000 miles to the southwest.

Looking down the Wind River valley, we don't expect any great difficulty on our descent. The first portion goes easily as we walk down the scree-covered slope. Then we hear the faint rumbling of water below us. I picture Yosemite Falls around the bend, with us stranded on the brink. As the rumbling grows louder, I notice a void in the distance. Soon we reach a 30-foot drop-off, with the falls spilling below us.

"This vertical plunge doesn't show up on the topo map," I say to Sidney.

Much to our relief, we spot an alternative route skirting the falls. The unstable ground is saturated with water, and we pick our way through many loose rocks. Several times we lose our balance, but neither of us tumbles into the streambed. It takes several hours to cover the two-mile descent to the main river as we continue to encounter more rough terrain and a series of waterfalls.

With only two days remaining, we have to hurry to reach the planned pickup spot. Both of us regret that we don't have more time to enjoy the spectacular scenery along the upper Wind River. We've now spent a full month exploring the refuge, yet, as always, I find that the longer the time I spend in this country, the greater my peace within, and the harder it is to leave. A month is just not long enough. It usually takes a couple of weeks to unwind from the pulse of civilization, to revive the dusty senses, and to become acutely aware of nature's northernmost web of life, with all the subtle sounds and signs that are inherent in this great wilderness.

By the third and fourth weeks, that busy human world has grown more distant and my mind is sharply in tune with its natural surroundings. There is a tremendous sense that I am beginning to feel a part of the country. Or perhaps it's that this wildness has become a part of me, in a moment-to-moment, uninterrupted way. The longer I breathe in the pure air, drink the mountain water, and absorb nature's gifts into my mind, heart, body, and soul, the richer my perspective of life; be it the hardy lichens that have grown for centuries, the gentle eyes of rosy-crowned finches, or the multi-million-year-old rocks that make me feel as insignificant as a speck of dust.

Dennis meets us on schedule on the planned pickup day, and one hour later we arrive in Arctic Village. Dennis uses the community telephone to call the Flight Service Station in Fairbanks to report the plane wreckage and its location. He reaches a longtime employee who is amazed by our discovery. The employee immediately recognizes the N720 identification numbers and tells Dennis that we have solved the 21-year-old mystery of the disappearance of Clarence Rhode; his 22-year-old son, Jack; and USFWS agent Stanley Fredericksen in their twin-engine Grumman Goose. The man informs Dennis that in 1958, Clarence Rhode was Alaska's USFWS regional director.

Within two hours of that telephone conversation, news of the discovery is broadcast on Fairbanks radio stations, and eventually throughout Alaska. The following day, banner headlines on page one of the *Anchorage Times* read: Hikers Find Rhode Plane. Sidney and I are amazed to learn that following Rhode's disappearance, hundreds of air force, government agency, and private aircraft conducted the most extensive rescue search in the history of the Alaska Territory to find

Rhode's plane. Day and night, pilots systematically searched for the plane, scanning more than 280,000 square miles—an area larger than California and Oregon combined.

After a month of intensive searching, and following a few false leads, the air force estimated that the cost of the search had grown to a million dollars. During the search the weather had deteriorated, with days of snow, icing conditions, and fog. Flying conditions continued to worsen as winter in the Brooks Range set in. Although the air force and others discontinued their searching efforts at the onset of winter, the USFWS refused to give up. Until early December USFWS planes continued to check out every possibility: lakes that Rhode might have crash-landed upon, trappers who might have seen the party, remote cabins that might have been used for shelter. There was even speculation that perhaps Rhode's plane had been shot down, or escorted by the Russians into Siberia. The State Department contacted Russian officials to see if they had any contact with a plane meeting the description of the Goose.

With sub-zero temperatures and only a few hours of daylight remaining in December, the search was called off for the remainder of the winter. The 44-year-old Rhode was an accomplished outdoorsman and pilot, and the Goose had been well-equipped with survival gear. Rhode had also taken many trips to the Arctic, a place he dearly loved and knew well. Friends and family refused to give up hope through the winter of 1958–59, having great faith that the party could survive the winter. After a full year had passed, there were still no clues. The missing men were declared dead.

On August 20, 1958, Rhode had left Fairbanks with his son and Fredericksen, en route to the then-proposed Arctic National Wildlife Range. They intended to survey Dall sheep in the Porcupine Lake area and to check out hunting parties in the vicinity. They took 200 gallons of extra gasoline, which was stored in 5-gallon cans in the large nose of the Goose. Rhode planned to make fuel caches in a few locations for future use.

Rhode made his last radio contact from Porcupine Lake on the afternoon of August 20. Later that day the party flew to Peters and Schrader lakes, some 50 miles to the northeast. There they visited with an International Geophysical Year scientific party based at Peters Lake. Those scientists were the last people to see Rhode and his party before they disappeared. The flight logs indicate that after Rhode left Peters Lake, he returned to Porcupine Lake.

Dave Spencer, who was then Alaska's refuge supervisor in charge of 15 other earlier-established refuges, recalls that Rhode planned to return to Fairbanks by August 23, to meet Ira Gabrielson and Clinton "Pink" Gutermuth, then president and vice-president of the Wildlife Management Institute in Washington, D.C. Gabrielson and Gutermuth had hoped to join Rhode and receive a tour of the proposed Arctic National Wildlife Range. Spencer remembers the influential Rhode as being "politically active on a national level" in pushing for the proposed Arctic National Wildlife Range. Rhode was considered the strongest advocate within the Department of Interior to press for the arctic range.

At the time of his death, Rhode was a prominent figure in the field of wildlife conservation. Since the mid-1930s, Rhode had worked extensively as a game warden in Alaska, traveling by horseback in the early days and by plane after he learned how to fly in 1939. He was appointed regional director of the USFWS in 1947, and soon built up the service's fleet of airplanes, which were equipped with the most advanced post–World War II aircraft radio system available. The aircraft radio system helped USFWS effectively manage fish and wildlife resources and nab violators. Dedicated to work in his field, Rhode also helped to establish a department of wildlife management, and a cooperative wildlife research unit at the University of Alaska in Fairbanks.

By no means was Rhode a typical administrative bureaucrat. Instead of being a desk man, Rhode liked to work in the field. During the 1950s, he flew many parties into the proposed arctic range. Rhode's surviving son, Jim, recalls that his father believed that the best way to convince people that the arctic range should be established was by taking individuals to see the area. Rhode was often frustrated with his effort to push for the range because many felt there was no sense of urgency to protect the arctic region; its very vastness and wildness, people seemed to believe, protected it from development. "His philosophy was that if people see it, they will be moved by it and understand the importance of preserving the area," Jim later told me.

Jim remembered that his father had a deep passion for the Arctic because it was the most untouched region in Alaska, and that he believed the proposed arctic range was necessary because one day the pressures of population and economic development would encroach upon that precious region the way they have on so many other areas in the continental United States. The pressure of oil development within Alaska was just beginning on the already-established Kenai Moose Range, south of Anchorage. Rhode feared that such development in southern Alaska also might threaten another important proposed range in the Yukon-Kuskoquim region of southwestern Alaska. At the time of his death, there was no immediate threat of development within the proposed arctic range.

In a letter dated November 8, 1957, Rhode wrote Olaus Murie, president of The Wilderness Society and leading spokesman for the conservation drive to establish the arctic range. In his letter Rhode reported to Murie that progress was being made on setting up the arctic range and that the USFWS had received many endorsements from various places, largely thanks to Murie's influential work. Rhode went on, however, to express his fears concerning oil development within the Kenai Moose Range and the proposed Kuskoquim range (later renamed the Clarence Rhode National Wildlife Range, and still later the Yukon-Delta National Wildlife Refuge). He suggested that Murie might bring some of these issues to the attention of Secretary of Interior Fred Seaton. Part of Rhode's letter to Murie reads:

> This all-important nesting area [the Kuskoquim range] has been "in the mill" for so many years we are getting discouraged. It means so much, as you know, to the wildfowl picture generally and particularly the entire west coast. If oil explorations start out there without safeguards and a film is spilled into those connecting rivers and sloughs, we shudder to think of the consequences. . . .
>
> There is much pressure in Anchorage, backed by the Chamber of Commerce and oil interests, to convince everyone oil exploration and development will not harm moose habitat in any way and might even enhance it on the Kenai Moose Range. Some of the proposals call for a road network in a grid fashion every quarter mile. I cannot agree that would be helpful in maintenance of the type of moose habitat which appeals to me but it is difficult to convince these hungry promoters. It even appeals to some moose hunters who feel they would have no difficulty, with such a network, of killing moose where they could back up the car to load them. They will twist statements referring to adequate cropping for range protection, and roads for fire protection, into statements that make such proposals beneficial for moose and man.
>
> We hope to be able to hold at least half the range intact and limit road building in the remainder.

Tragically, Rhode did not live to see that the Kuskoquim and arctic ranges would become established, nor did he see that more than half of the Kenai Moose Range would be left intact, and that oil development and road building would be limited. Also, Rhode died long before the Prudhoe Bay oil discovery and the subsequent development on the North Slope. As he had feared, the hungry developers would indeed inch their way toward the Arctic and encroach upon America's northernmost wilderness. If Rhode were living today, how disheartened he would be to see his former employer, the Department of Interior, recommend to Congress that oil development occur within the nation's last great stretch of arctic wilderness, within the proposed wildlife range he so deeply cherished.

The following week I'm asked to direct an investigative team to Rhode's crash site. It is late August, and the fall weather is wretched for flying through the Brooks Range. Jon Osgood, from the National Transportation Safety Board; Dick Hemmen, a state fish and wildlife officer representing the coroner's office; Jim Rhode; and I fly by helicopter from Arctic Village to reach the site.

The pilot makes several attempts to reach the Ivishak drainage, following different valleys, searching for clear low-lying passes where we can cross the divide, but the snowstorm makes it impossible to press on. Jim pensively sits in the helicopter, flooded with emotion. For so many years he, his sister Sally, his deceased mother, and other relatives and friends had pondered and grieved over the trio's mysterious disappearance. Now that his father and brother's cause of death had become known, Jim was mourning the loss and painfully reliving the tragedy of 21 years ago.

On the second day the cloud layer lifts, and we reach the snow-covered Ivishak valley. With four inches of fresh snow, I can barely make out the crash site. Because of the elevation of the wreckage, the remote nature of this winding, narrow portion of the upper Ivishak, and the fact that the pass area is covered with snow for as much as ten months of the year, it is easy to understand why the search efforts had failed.

The helicopter has flown us in groups of two up to the pass where Sidney and I had stood only a week ago. With temperatures in the 30s, we carefully climb down across slippery, loose rocks to the crash site and spend more than four hours investigating the wreckage. We fan out across the talus, each of us digging through snow to uncover fragments of the Goose that would give Osgood clues as to how and why the plane had crashed.

A few articles, like Rhode's weathered flight bag, had been thrown from the plane upon impact, escaping fire damage. Inside the flight bag we find many USGS topographical maps, World Aeronautical Charts, and old USFWS forms. The freezing temperatures have prevented deterioration; the maps are damp, but readable. The 1950s vintage topo maps are rudimentary, showing little detail. Instead of the 200-foot contour lines we have today, these old maps were scaled in 1,000-foot contours. Ave Thayer, one of the pilots who searched for the Goose, later told me that pilots in Rhode's day "relied on maps for direction and general topography only." With the lack of navigational aids, detailed maps, and modern radio communication equipment, flying in the 1950s presented challenges unknown today.

Continuing to brush away snow, we find many five-gallon gas cans that had been flattened like pancakes upon impact. When the nose hit the mountainside, the stored gas cans exploded and most of the fuselage burned beyond recognition. Death would have been instantaneous. There are very few human remains because fire and time have eliminated them. But there are enough mechanical clues for Osgood to draw some preliminary conclusions as to the fate of the Goose.

Osgood says there is overwhelming evidence, because of the contour of the twisted and curled propellers, that the engines were under power at the time of the impact. The throttles were in a forward position. Osgood is convinced that, for unknown reasons, the Goose made a left-hand turn as it neared the pass. As the plane ran out of turning space, the left engine and nose hit the mountainside.

Because of the nature of the winding Ivishak, Rhode could not have seen the pass area until he rounded the final bend of the canyon-like valley, about one mile from the pass. That meant he had only a minute or less to make a decision: to either go over the pass or turn around.

Because of the conflicting weather reports at the time, there will always be unknowns as to the possibility of poor visibility, icing conditions, or strong down drafts. A patchwork of varied weather systems can be distributed throughout the Brooks Range on any given day. Was Rhode heading home to Fairbanks? Did he mistakenly fly up the wrong valley? Much remains a mystery.

Flying back to Arctic Village through the rugged eastern Brooks Range, I regret that I would never have the chance to know this far-sighted man named Clarence Rhode. He died on the divide of his beloved mountains on the eve of what would become the national environmental movement of the 1960s. His life ended at the very time the battle began to establish this northeastern corner of Alaska as a wildlife range. Many other individuals and groups would successfully carry on that fight. Those who knew of Rhode would remember his lifelong efforts in the field of wildlife conservation, his love for the Arctic, and his influential role in helping to set aside the Arctic National Wildlife Range.

HISTORY OF THE
DIVIDING LINE

William Byrd

[*Oct. 25, 1728*]   The air clearing up this morning, we were again agreeably surprised with a full prospect of the mountains. They discovered themselves both to the north and south of us on either side, not distant above ten miles, according to our best computation. We could now see those to the north rise in four distinct ledges one above another, but those to the south formed only a single ledge and that broken and interrupted in many places, or rather they were only single mountains detached from each other. One of the southern mountains was so vastly high it seemed to hide its head in the clouds, and the west end of it terminated in a horrible precipice that we called the Despairing Lover's Leap. The next to it, toward the east, was lower except at one end, where it heaved itself up in the form of a vast stack of chimneys. The course of the northern mountains seemed to tend west-southwest and those to the southward very near west. We could descry other mountains ahead of us, exactly in the course of the line though at a much greater distance. In this point of view, the ledges on the right and left both seemed to close and form a natural amphitheater. Thus 'twas our fortune to be wedged in betwixt these two ranges of mountains, insomuch that if our line had run ten miles on either side it had butted before this day either upon one or the other, both of them now stretching away plainly to the eastward of us.

It had rained a little in the night, which dispersed the smoke and opened this romantic scene to us all at once, though it was again hid from our eyes as we moved forward by the rough woods we had the misfortune to be engaged with. The bushes were so thick for near four miles together that they tore the deerskins to pieces that guarded the bread bags. Though, as rough as the woods were, the soil was extremely good all the way, being washed down from the neighboring hills into the plain country. Notwithstanding all these difficulties, the surveyors drove on the line 4 miles and 205 poles.

In the meantime we were so unlucky as to meet with no sort of game the whole day, so that the men were obliged to make a frugal distribution of what little they [had] left in the morning. We encamped upon a small rill, where the horses came off as temperately as their masters. They were by this time grown so thin by hard travel and spare feeding that hence forth, in pure compassion, we chose to perform the greater part of the journey on foot. And as our baggage was by this time grown much lighter, we divided it after the best manner so that every horse's load might be proportioned to the strength he had left. Though after all the prudent measures we could take, we perceived the hills began to rise upon us so fast in our front that it would be impossible for us to proceed much farther.

We saw very few squirrels in the upper parts, because the wildcats devour them unmercifully. Of these there are four kinds: the fox squirrel, the gray, the flying, and the ground squirrel. These last resemble a rat in everything but the tail and the black and russet streaks that run down the length of their little bodies.

[Oct. 26] We found our way grow still more mountainous, after extending the line three hundred poles farther. We came then to a rivulet that ran with a swift current toward the south. This we fancied to be another branch of the Irvin, though some of these men, who had been Indian traders, judged it rather to be the head of Deep River, that discharges its stream into that of Pee Dee, but this seemed a wild conjecture. The hills beyond that river were exceedingly lofty and not to be attempted by our jaded palfreys, which could now hardly drag their legs after them upon level ground. Besides, the bread began to grow scanty and the winter season to advance apace upon us. We had likewise reason to apprehend the consequences of being intercepted by deep snows and the swelling of the many waters between us and home. The first of these misfortunes would starve all our horses and the other ourselves, by cutting off our retreat and obliging us to winter in those desolate woods. These considerations determined us to stop short here and push our adventures no farther. The last tree we marked was a red oak growing on the bank of the river; and to make the place more remarkable, we blazed all the trees around it.

We found the whole distance from Currituck Inlet to the rivulet where we left off to be, in a straight line, 240 miles and 230 poles. And from the place where the Carolina commissioners deserted us, 72 miles and 302 poles. This last part of the journey was generally very hilly, or else grown up with troublesome thickets and underwoods, all which our Carolina friends had the discretion to avoid. We encamped in a dirty valley near the rivulet above-mentioned for the advantage of the canes, and so sacrificed our own convenience to that of our horses. There was a small mountain half a mile to the northward of us, which we had the curiosity to climb up in the afternoon in order to enlarge our prospect. From thence we were able to discover where the two ledges of mountains closed, as near as we could guess about thirty miles to the west of us, and lamented that our present circumstances would not permit us to advance the line to that place, which the hand of Nature had made so very remarkable.

Not far from our quarters one of the men picked up a pair of elk's horns, not very large, and discovered the track of the elk that had shed them. It was rare to find any tokens of those animals so far to the south, because they keep commonly to the northward of thirty-seven degrees, as the buffaloes, for the most part, confine themselves to the southward of that latitude. The elk is full as big as a horse and of the deer kind. The stags only have horns and those exceedingly large and spreading. Their color is something lighter than that of the red deer and their flesh tougher. Their swiftest speed is a large trot, and in that motion they turn their horns back upon their necks and cock their noses aloft in the air. Nature has taught them this attitude to save their antlers from being entangled in the thickets, which they always retire to. They are very shy and have the sense of smelling so exquisite that they wind a man at a great distance. For this reason they are seldom seen but when the air is moist, in which case their smell is not so nice. They commonly herd together, and the Indians say if one of the drove happen by some wound to be disabled from making his escape, the rest will forsake their fears to defend their friend, which they will do with great obstinacy till they are killed upon the spot. Though, otherwise, they are to alarmed at the sight of a man that to avoid him they will sometimes throw themselves down very high precipices into the river.

A misadventure happened here which gave us no small perplexity. One of the commissioners was so unlucky as to bruise his foot against a stump, which brought on a formal fit of the gout. It must be owned there could not be a more unseasonable time, nor a more improper situation for anyone to be attacked by that cruel distemper. The joint was so inflamed that he could neither draw shoe or boot upon it, and to ride without either would have exposed him to so many rude knocks and bruises in those rough woods as to be intolerable even to a stoic. It was happy indeed that we were to rest here the next day, being Sunday, that there might be leisure for trying some speedy remedy. Accordingly, he was persuaded to bathe his foot in cold water in order to repel the humor and assuage the inflammation. This made it less painful and gave us hopes, too, of reducing the swelling in a short time.

Our men had the fortune to kill a brace of bears, a fat buck, and a wild turkey, all which paid them with interest for yesterday's abstinence. This constant and seasonable supply of our daily wants made us reflect thankfully on the bounty of Providence. And that we might not be unmindful of being all along fed by Heaven in this great and solitary wilderness, we agreed to wear in our hats the maosti, which is in Indian the beard of a wild turkey cock, and on our breasts the figure of that fowl with its wings extended and holding in its claws a scroll with this motto, *Vice coturnicum*, meaning that we had been supported by them in the wilderness in the room of quails.

[Oct. 27] This being Sunday, we were not wanting in our thanks to Heaven for the constant support and protection we had been favored with. Nor did our chaplain fail to put us in mind of our duty by a sermon proper for the occasion. We ordered a strict inquiry to be made into the quantity of bread we had left and found no more than would subsist us a fortnight at short allowance. We made a fair distribution of our whole stock and at the same time recommended to the men to manage this, their last stake, to the best advantage, not knowing how long they would be obliged to live upon it. We likewise directed them to keep a watchful eye upon their horses, that none of them might be missing the next morning to hinder our return.

There fell some rain before noon, which made our camp more a bog than it was before. This moist situation began to infect some of the men with fevers and some with fluxes, which however we soon removed with Peruvian bark and ipecacuanha.

In the afternoon we marched up again to the top of the hill to entertain our eyes a second time with the view of the mountains, but a perverse fog arose that hid them from our sight. In the evening we deliberated which way it might be most proper to return. We had at first intended to cross over at the foot of the mountains to the head of James River, that we might be able to describe that natural boundary so far. But, on second thoughts, we found many good reasons against that laudable design, such as the weakness of our horses, the scantiness of our bread, and the near approach of winter. We had cause to believe the way might be full of hills, and the farther we went toward the north, the more danger there would be of snow. Such considerations as these determined us at last to make the best of our way back upon the line, which was the straightest and consequently the shortest way to the inhabitants. We knew the worst of that course and were sure of a beaten path all the way, while we were totally ignorant what difficulties and dangers the other course might be attended with. So prudence got the better for once of curiosity, and the itch for new discoveries gave place to self-preservation.

Our inclination was the stronger to cross over according to the course of the mountains, that we might find out whether James River and Appomattox River head there or run quite through them. 'Tis certain that Potomac passes in a large stream through the main ledge and then divides itself into two considerable rivers. That which stretches away to the northward is called Cohungaroota and that which flows to the southwest hath the name of Sharantow. The course of this last stream is near parallel to the Blue Ridge of mountains, at the distance only of about three or four miles. Though how far it may continue that course has not yet been sufficiently discovered, but some woodsmen pretend to say it runs as far as the source of Roanoke; nay, they are so very particular as to tell us that Roanoke, Sharantow, and another wide branch of Mississippi all head in one and the same mountain. What dependence there may be upon this conjectural geography I won't pretend to say, though 'tis certain that Sharantow keeps close to the mountains, as far as we are acquainted with its tendency. We are likewise assured that the south branch of James River, within less than twenty miles east of the main ledge, makes an elbow and runs due southwest, which is parallel with the mountains on this side. But how far it stretches that way before it returns is not yet certainly known, no more than where it takes its rise.

In the meantime, it is strange that our woodsmen have not had curiosity enough to inform themselves more exactly of these particulars, and it is stranger still that the government has never thought it worth the expense of making an accurate survey of the mountains, that we might be masters of that natural fortification before the French, who in some places have settlements not very distant from it. It therefore concerns His Majesty's service very nearly and the safety of his subjects in this part of the world to take possession of so important a barrier in time, lest our good friends, the French, and the Indians through their means, prove a perpetual annoyance to these colonies. Another reason to invite us to secure this great ledge of mountains is the probability that very valuable mines may be discovered there. Nor would it be at all extravagant to hope for silver mines among the rest, because part of these mountains lie exactly in the same parallel, as well as upon the same continent, with New Mexico and the mines of St. Barb.[1]

[Oct. 28] We had given orders for the horses to be brought up early, but the likelihood of more rain prevented our being overhasty in decamping. Nor were we out in our conjectures, for about ten o'clock it began to fall very plentifully. Our commissioner's pain began now to abate as the swelling increased. He made an excellent figure for a mountaineer, with one boot of leather and the other of flannel. Thus accoutered he intended to mount, if the rain had not happened opportunely to prevent him. Though, in truth, it was hardly possible for him to ride with so slender a defense without exposing his foot to be bruised and tormented by the saplings that stood thick on either side of the path. It was therefore a most seasonable rain for him, as it gave more time for his distemper to abate.

Though it may be very difficult to find a certain cure for the gout, yet it is not improbable but some things may ease the pain and shorten the fits of it. And those medicines are most likely to do this that supple the parts and clear the passage through the narrow vessels that are the seat of this cruel disease. Nothing will do this more suddenly than rattlesnake's oil, which will even penetrate the pores of glass when warmed in the sun. It was unfortunate, therefore, that we

---

[1]Santa Barbara, Chihuahua, Mexico.

had not taken out the fat of those snakes we had killed some time before, for the benefit of so useful an experiment as well as for the relief of our fellow traveler. But lately the Seneca rattlesnake root has been discovered in this country, which, being infused in wine and drank morning and evening, has in several instances had a very happy effect upon the gout, and enabled cripples to throw away their crutches and walk several miles, and, what is stranger still, it takes away the pain in half an hour.

Nor was the gout the only disease amongst us that was hard to cure. We had a man in our company who had too voracious a stomach for a woodsman. He ate as much as any other two, but all he swallowed stuck by him till it was carried off by a strong purge. Without this assistance, often repeated, his belly and bowels would swell to so enormous a bulk that he could hardly breathe, especially when he lay down, just as if he had had an asthma; though, notwithstanding this oddness of constitution, he was a very strong, lively fellow and used abundance of violent exercise, by which 'twas wonderful the peristaltic motion was not more vigorously promoted. We gave this poor man several purges, which only eased him for the present, and the next day he would grow as burly as ever. At last we gave him a moderate dose of ipecacuanha in broth made very salt, which turned all its operation downwards. This had so happy an effect that from that day forward to the end of our journey all his complaints ceased and the passages continued unobstructed.

The rain continued most of the day and some part of the night, which incommoded us much in our dirty camp and made the men think of nothing but eating, even at a time when nobody could stir out to make provision for it.

[Oct. 29] Though we were flattered in the morning with the usual tokens of a fair day, yet they all blew over, and it rained hard before we could make ready for our departure. This was still in favor of our podagrous friend, whose lameness was now grown better and the inflammation fallen. Nor did it seem to need above one day more to reduce it to its natural proportion and make it fit for the boot; and effectually the rain procured this benefit for him and gave him particular reason to believe his stars propitious.

Notwithstanding the falling weather, our hunters sallied out in the afternoon and drove the woods in a ring, which was thus performed: from the circumference of a large circle they all marched inward and drove the game toward the center. By this means they shot a brace of fat bears, which came very seasonably, because we had made clean work in the morning and were in danger of dining with St. Anthony, or His Grace Duke Humphrey.[2] But in this expedition the unhappy man who had lost himself once before straggled again so far in pursuit of a deer that he was hurried a second time quite out of his knowledge; and, night coming on before he could recover the camp, he was obliged to lie down without any of the comforts of fire, food, or covering; nor would his fears suffer him to sleep very sound, because, to his great disturbance, the wolves howled all that night and panthers screamed most frightfully.

In the evening a brisk northwester swept all the clouds from the sky and exposed the mountains as well as the stars to our prospect. That which was the most lofty to the southward and which we called the Lover's Leap, some of our Indian traders fondly fancied was the Kiawan Mountain, which they had formerly seen from the country of the Cherokees. They were the more positive by reason of the prodigious precipice that remarkably distinguished the west end of it. We seemed however not to be far enough south for that, though 'tis not improbable but a few miles farther the course of our line might carry us to the most northerly towns of the Cherokees. What makes this the more credible is the northwest course that our traders take from the Catawbas for some hundred miles together, when they carry goods that roundabout way to the Cherokees.

It was a great pity that the want of bread and the weakness of our horses hindered us from making the discovery. Though the great service such an excursion might have been to the country would certainly have made the attempt not only pardonable but much to be commended. Our traders are now at the vast charge and fatigue of traveling above five hundred miles for the benefit of that traffic which hardly quits cost. Would it not then be worth the Assembly's while to be at some charge to find a shorter cut to carry on so profitable a trade, with more advantage and less hazard and trouble than they do at present? For I am persuaded it will not then be half the distance that our traders make it now nor half so far as Georgia lies from the northern

---

[2]Humphrey, Duke of Gloucester. A statue in old St. Paul's Cathedral, erroneously identified as that of the Duke, was a meeting place for needy gallants and rogues. A penniless gallant with nowhere to go for dinner was said to "dine with Duke Humphrey," meaning to go dinnerless.

clans of that nation. Such a discovery would certainly prove an unspeakable advantage to this colony by facilitating a trade with so considerable a nation of Indians, which have sixty-two towns and more than four thousand fighting men. Our traders at that rate would be able to undersell those sent from the other colonies so much that the Indians must have reason to deal with them preferably to all others. Of late the new colony of Georgia has made an act obliging us to go four hundred miles to take out a license to traffic with these Cherokees, though many of their towns lie out of their bounds and we had carried on this trade eighty years before that colony was thought of.

[*Oct. 30*] In the morning early the man who had gone astray the day before found his way to the camp by the sound of the bells that were upon the horses' necks.

At nine o'clock we began our march back toward the rising sun, for though we had finished the line yet we had not yet near finished our fatigue. We had, after all, two hundred good miles at least to our several habitations, and the horses were brought so low that we were obliged to travel on foot great part of the way, and that in our boots, too, to save our legs from being torn to pieces by the bushes and briers. Had we not done this, we must have left all our horses behind, which could now hardly drag their legs after them; and with all the favor we could show the poor animals we were forced to set seven of them free not far from the foot of the mountains.

Four men were dispatched early to clear the road, that our lame commissioner's leg might be in less danger of being bruised and that the baggage horses might travel with less difficulty and more expedition. As we passed along, by favor of a serene sky we had still from every eminence a perfect view of the mountains, as well to the north as to the south. We could not forbear now and then facing about to survey them, as if unwilling to part with a prospect which at the same time, like some rakes, was very wild and very agreeable. We encouraged the horses to exert the little strength they had and, being light, they made a shift to jog on about eleven miles. . . .

We encamped on Crooked Creek near a thicket of canes. In the front of our camp rose a very beautiful hill that bounded our view at about a mile's distance, and all the intermediate space was covered with green canes. Though to our sorrow, firewood was scarce, which was now the harder upon us because a northwester blew very cold from the mountains.

The Indian killed a stately, fat buck, and we picked his bones as clean as a score of turkey buzzards could have done. By the advantage of a clear night, we made trial once more of the variation and found it much the same as formerly. This being His Majesty's birthday, we drank all the loyal healths in excellent water, not for the sake of the drink (like many of our fellow subjects), but purely for the sake of the toast. And because all public mirth should be a little noisy, we fired several volleys of canes, instead of guns, which gave a loud report. We threw them into the fire, where the air enclosed betwixt the joints of the canes, being expanded by the violent heat, burst its narrow bounds with a considerable explosion.

In the evening one of the men knocked down an opossum, which is a harmless little beast that will seldom go out of your way, and if you take hold of it will only grin and hardly ever bite. The flesh was well tasted and tender, approaching nearest to pig, which it also resembled in bigness. The color of its fur was a goose gray, with a swine's snout and a tail like a rat, but at least a foot long. By twisting this tail about the arm of a tree, it will hang with all its weight and swing to anything it wants to take hold of. It has five claws on the forefeet of equal length, but the hinder feet have only four claws and a sort of thumb standing off at a proper distance. Their feet, being thus formed, qualify them for climbing up trees to catch little birds, which they are very fond of. But the greatest particularity of this creature, and which distinguishes it from most others that we are acquainted with, is the false belly of the female, into which her young retreat in time of danger. She can draw the slit, which is the inlet into this pouch, so close that you must look narrowly to find it, especially if she happen to be a virgin. Within the false belly may be seen seven or eight teats, on which the young ones grow from their first formation till they are big enough to fall off like ripe fruit from a tree. This is so odd a method of generation that I should not have believed it without the testimony of mine own eyes. Besides, a knowing and credible person has assured me he has more than once observed the embryo opossums growing to the teat before they were completely shaped, and afterwards watched their daily growth till they were big enough for birth.[3] And all this he could the more easily pry into because the dam

---

[3]Byrd seems to think that the embryos were formed in the pouch, whereas in fact the mother places the immature embryos there after natural birth.

was so perfectly gentle and harmless that he could handle her just as he pleased.

I could hardly persuade myself to publish a thing so contrary to the course that nature takes in the production of other animals unless it were a matter commonly believed in all countries where that creature is produced and has been often observed by persons of undoubted credit and understanding. They say that the leather-winged bats produce their young in the same uncommon manner; and that young sharks at sea and young vipers ashore run down the throats of their dams when they are closely pursued.

[Oct. 31] The frequent crossing of Crooked Creek and mounting the steep banks of it gave the finishing stroke to the foundering of our horses, and no less than two of them made a full stop here and would not advance a foot farther, either by fair means or foul. We had a dreamer of dreams amongst us who warned me in the morning to take care of myself or I should infallibly fall into the creek; I thanked him kindly and used what caution I could but was not able, it seems, to avoid my destiny, for my horse made a false step and laid me down at my full length in the water. This was enough to bring dreaming into credit, and I think it much for the honor of our expedition that it was graced not only with a priest but also with a prophet. We were so perplexed with this serpentine creek, as well as in passing the branches of the Irvin, which were swelled since we saw them before, that we could reach but five miles this whole day.

In the evening we pitched our tent near Miry Creek, though an uncomfortable place to lodge in, purely for the advantage of the canes. Our hunters killed a large doe and two bears, which made all other misfortunes easy. Certainly no Tartar ever loved horseflesh or Hottentot guts and garbage better than woodsmen do bear. The truth of it is, it may be proper food perhaps for such as work or ride it off, but, with our chaplain's leave, who loved it much, I think it not a very proper diet for saints, because 'tis apt to make them a little too rampant. And, now, for the good of mankind and for the better peopling an infant colony, which has no want but that of inhabitants, I will venture to publish a secret of importance which our Indian disclosed to me. I asked him the reason why few or none of his countrywomen were barren. To which curious question he answered, with a broad grin upon his face, they had an infallible secret for that. Upon my being importunate to know what the secret might be, he informed me that if any Indian woman did not prove with child at a decent time after marriage, the husband, to save his reputation with the women, forthwith entered into a bear diet for six weeks, which in that time makes him so vigorous that he grows exceedingly impertinent to his poor wife, and 'tis great odds but he makes her a mother in nine months. And thus much I am able to say besides for the reputation of the bear diet, that all the married men of our company were joyful fathers within forty weeks after they got home, and most of the single men had children sworn to them within the same time, our chaplain always excepted, who, with much ado, made a shift to cast out that importunate kind of devil by dint of fasting and prayer.

Mount Mazama: The Realm of Becoming

Carol Ann Bassett

For all its heaviness the world seems made of breath.
—Scott Russell Sanders

It begins with a clear sharp line, a crack in the earth and liquid rock pulsing upward—the grind and the rumble, the ooze and the squeeze—the birth of a mountain. Valleys form. Fossils emerge from the convoluted rocks. The earth smells ancient, as though new life simmers just beneath the surface. It happens subtly over the eons: a change in particles holding the world together. I stand on a ridge in the Cascade Range trying to envision the mercurial nature of volcanoes—the impossible measure of time. Far below me, Crater Lake shimmers like a polished sapphire. The water is so blue that no word describes it: azure, cobalt, empyrean, lapis, indigo, cerulean. Gazing down at the startling hues, I know the landscape was not always so, and I try to imagine when Mount Mazama stood in place of the lake. The terrain is stark and bewildering, as though it has turned itself inside out. To the north, Mount Thielsen rises like an icy dagger. Mount Shasta floats above a sea of pale pink ash.

I have come here to learn about change: why a volcano becomes a lake, how rocks breathe, whether Mazama still stirs beneath the water. I have also come to mourn the death of my father only last week. Walking across a jagged flow of basalt high above the water, I feel alone and vulnerable. Who really dies? How do we grieve? What prevails of the human spirit? The answers do not come easily, and as I enter a forest of windswept pines, I search the past for meaning.

I grew up in the snowy mountains of northern Honshu where the Sea of Japan, the Tsugaru Strait and the Pacific Ocean meet. The first time I ever saw Mount Fuji I could not fathom why smoke curled from a mountain made of snow. Fuji means "never dying" or "eternal life," and something about the volcano seemed unknowable like a koan. My father flew jets with the 531st Tactical Fighter Squadron at Misawa Air Force Base. A photograph from 1959 shows a Japanese tori with the slogan: "Through these gates pass the best damn fighter pilots in the world." His name was William Brainard Bassett, a top gun who had earned the Distinguished Flying Cross in the Korean War. One day, hoping to teach his children something about aerodynamics, he brought home a mammoth box kite. It was made of brown paper and stood nearly as high as my brother, sister and I. Off we ran, Billy in the lead, feet wheeling through fields of clover, faces skyward. The kite soared so high it seemed to touch the clouds. Then with a dip, and a jerk, and a snap, it sailed away over the chain-link fence into what we called "the Japanese land." For military kids, the area was strictly off limits.

We scrambled over anyway, dropping into golden fields of mustard. In a small clearing a group of Japanese farmers sat cross-legged, eating rice cakes and fish wrapped in dark strands of seaweed. Women clad in kimonos carried babies on their chests. Seeing us, the workers rose. Then bowing from the waist, they pointed across the field. The mustard was tall and gilt and thick with pollen, licking our cheeks as we ran. In that moment there was a sense of freedom I will never forget—crossing into the unknown. Back home with our new kite still intact we never said a word to my father, but somehow I think he always knew. When the days of summer had passed, he and my mother would drive the family south to Lake Towada in Aomori Prefecture. The pine trees, the dark wet earth always stirred memories of school days—the smell of chalk, or crayons, or the leather of brand new shoes.

Lake Towada could have been a cousin of Crater Lake, but the Oregon landmark is far more striking. It is the deepest lake in the United States and one of the purest of its kind in the world. The Klamath Indians called the lake *gi-was*. Contrary to Anglo beliefs that no Indian would dare gaze at the sacred water, Crater Lake was a place of reverence, a spirit quest site. Prehistoric rock piles still stand near the rim of the lake like offerings where the Klamath would tempt fate by running down the precipitous western rim all the way to the lake. It was believed that those who did not fall had been guided by powerful spirits. Even more courage was needed to swim in the lake. Ethnographer Leslie Spier once quoted the father of one of his sources: "Having lost a child, he went swimming in Crater Lake; before evening he had become a shaman."

The lake was indeed a powerful place. Throughout the centuries it was the battlefield of the gods, a place of chaos and chicanery. Skell was the spirit of the Upper World, who ruled over the marshlands to the south. Llao was the spirit of the Lower World, who lived in the lake. The two were constantly at war, sending explosions throughout the valley and setting the forests on fire. Sometimes the wrath of the gods sent rivers of lava down the mountainside, burying Indian villages. Skell was killed near the base of Mount Mazama but was later restored to life. Llao was slain during the last great battle, his body torn into pieces and tossed in the lake. But the loyal water spirits preserved Llao's head, a dark protrusion in the lake known today as Wizard's Island. In the end, the turmoil that had toppled the gods changed Klamath cosmology forever.

In January 1999, just after my parents celebrated their fiftieth wedding anniversary, both were diagnosed with cancer within the same week—my father with lung cancer and my mother with breast cancer. A successful mastectomy removed all of my mother's disease, and aggressive radiation therapy destroyed most of my father's illness. But in June, when I visited my dad in Phoenix, the cancer we thought was in remission had returned. In the hospital, a stout bespectacled doctor delivered the news that tumors had spread throughout his spine, liver and brain. "Mr. Bassett," he said stoically, "our tests show that you have a terminal illness." Mom and I stared at the doctor, then at Dad, who listened quietly with troubled eyes.

Mom was in shock. She leaned over and hugged him, then blinked back tears, hiding how she really felt—like falling apart. I sat in a metal chair across from his bed weeping.

The next day in the hospital Dad and I watched the History Channel. Footage from the Cuban Missile Crisis in 1962 flickered across the screen. Back then we lived at Homestead Air Force Base in southern Florida, the first base that would have been annihilated in a Soviet attack from the island. The film showed American housewives frantically pushing shopping carts, stockpiling for the apocalypse. "I remember that," I said. The missile crisis was, in fact, my first political memory: our house filled with canned goods, candles, canisters of butane, the bathtub filled with water, mattresses stacked in the hallways, windows taped in giant Xs against the nuclear blast.

"You remember all *that?*" he asked in astonishment.

"Sure," I said. "We thought it was the end of the world."

The end was also near for the Klamath Indians who witnessed Mount Mazama's eruptions and who kept the events alive in their legends. Geologic evidence and radio-carbon dating tend to parallel the stories. When Mazama exploded for the final time about 7,700 years ago, ash and dust blocked out the sunlight for weeks like a nuclear winter. According to legend, the people fled in canoes through a system of marshes, finding refuge in a cave at Fort Rock about 45 miles away. Archeologists have excavated the cave since 1938, when they discovered 9,000-year-old woven sandals. At the bottom of the marsh they found evidence of human occupation dating back more than 13,000 years.

In geologic time, the Cascade Range is relatively young. It was formed about 750,000 years ago after the earth's crust folded, then inched upward. Molten rocks welled up through enormous cracks, building a string of volcanoes from Mount Garibaldi in Canada to Lassen Peak in northern California. Mount Mazama was one of the major volcanoes in the High Cascades, and the largest between Mount Shasta and the Three Sisters volcanoes. It rose to a height of about 12,000 feet and was covered with glaciers. Its final eruption was the greatest known anywhere in the Cascades—42 times greater than that at Mount St. Helens in 1980. The explosion spewed ash across eight states and three Canadian provinces, creating pumice fields several hundred feet deep.

Once the magma chamber beneath the volcano collapsed, a giant caldera formed about six miles wide and 4,000 feet deep. Rain and melting snow collected in the bowl-shaped depression, creating a fragile lake with no inlet or outlet. The lake has maintained a steady temperature of 38 degrees. It is 1,932 feet deep and varies only from 1 to 3 feet per year.

In mythic time, *gi-was* probably always existed. But in written history the first "discovery" of the lake was made by John Wesley Hillman, who climbed to the caldera's rim with a party of gold prospectors on June 12, 1853. Crater Lake became a national park in 1902, after 17 years of lobbying by William Gladstone Steel. As a Kansas schoolboy, Steel first learned of Crater Lake while reading a newspaper used to wrap his lunch. It became his lifelong obsession.

I stand on the northern rim of the caldera gazing across the mythical lake. Though it is July, deep snowfields still sprawl across the northern part of the park. From here I can see most of the southern rim, including Wizard Island and Sun Notch—the U-shaped valley carved by the slow movement of glaciers some 10,000 years ago. Parallel grooves in some rocks were scratched into the hard rock by ice embedded with stone, a kind of glacial signature.

How so beautiful a lake could have such a dull name remains puzzling. Crater Lake is in fact a misnomer. Technically speaking, a crater is a depression surrounded by a wall of lava and ash blasted from a volcano's vent. A caldera is created when the center of a volcano caves in on itself. In either case, quiet volcanoes are not always dead, and in 1989, scientists discovered that Mount Mazama still breathes beneath the frigid lake. Traveling in a small submarine, they discovered warm springs at the bottom of the lake in temperatures of 66 degrees. They also found tiny worms and bright yellow mats of bacteria. Then in 1997, experts declared Crater Lake the purest of its kind in the world when they learned that the water's clarity extended down 142 feet.

Not surprisingly, new vents are still being created within the old volcano. Wizard Island grew inside the mountain after it collapsed. Three vents now lie beneath the lake. Above the water, more pyroclastic testaments remain. Devils Backbone is an andesite dike extending from rim to lake like a petrified dragon's tail. Phantom Ship, which *Harper's Weekly* described in 1896 as "a fantastic object of unspeakable dread to the Klamath Indians," is a volcanic island in the middle of the lake. Sometimes when the light changes the island disappears.

Time and space are also dissolving for my father in Phoenix. One morning my mother tries to help him shave. He shakes the can, smears the foam across the mirror, and scrapes at his own reflection. Which face is more real? In *The Snow Leopard*, Peter Matthiessen writes that form is emptiness and emptiness form. Emptiness is not a void but something without boundaries, "like a mirror across which all things pass." As all the familiar boundaries fall away for my father, my mom and sister take him home from the hospice to die. When I call him from my home in Eugene, his thoughts are erratic, his voice uncertain. Cancer is eating away at his memories, his identity, his sense of purpose. He has been asking for me every single day, and soon I'm on a plane to Phoenix. It's 110 degrees when I arrive at my parents' home on July 2nd.

"Honey, brace yourself," Mom warns me in the kitchen. In a hospital bed in the middle of the living room lies my father. His skin is taut and pallid, his eyes deeply sunken. He has lost almost all of his curly black hair, and he runs his hand unconsciously over his balding head. Without thinking, I join my hands in *gassho*, for he resembles a monk who has spent the last decade in some far-off hermitage. His once muscular frame is so thin it seems he might float away. "Dad?" I say, putting my arm around him. He sits up, rests his head on my shoulder and begins to cry. Surely, he would have rather gone down in a fiery cockpit somewhere over the desert. That evening he eats his last real supper: a small bite of chicken, a piece of potato, some apple-sauce. Then all night long he sits upright in his hospital bed, clutching the metal handrails and staring into space. It seems he is examining his soul—the dark and beautiful truths of his life.

The Dalai Lama says there is an endless cycle in which the universe evolves, disintegrates then comes back into being. What endures after death is consciousness or mind, "the ultimate creative principle" that provides a link between lifetimes. In *The Tibetan Book of Living and Dying*, Sogyal Rinpoche writes that our entire existence is divided into *bardos*, or transitions. We experience four: the "natural" bardo of this lifetime; the "painful" bardo of dying; the "luminous" bardo of the mind's true nature, and the "karmic" bardo of becoming. In the bardo of dying, Dad is becoming a child again. He can no longer speak. His pain medication is given rectally because he can no longer swallow. My sister Bonnie and I change his diapers.

Throughout the house everything we do is more conscious, even our walking. I sit with Dad for long periods in silence practicing *tong-len*, a Buddhist exercise in compassion to help the dying. Breathing in, I absorb his pain and fear like sooty black smoke. Breathing out, I imagine the clear light of healing. Soon his own breathing becomes more natural, and for the first time in days he sleeps peacefully for hours.

On the fourth night of my visit I stand next to his bed, holding his hand. It's late and the room is illuminated only by my mother's plastic Virgin Mary night-light. "This is just another big adventure," I tell him softly. He squeezes my hand in response. "All your work on this earth is finished now, Dad. It's okay to go." He opens his eyes and mouths the words *I love you*. A few hours later he takes his final breath. At sunrise the first summer rains fall on the parched desert terrain, and soon a giant rainbow appears in the western sky. "Now, mountains, rivers, earth, the sun, moon, and stars are mind," wrote the 13th-century Buddhist monk Dogen. "At just this moment, what is it that appears directly in front of you?"

On the day my father's body is cremated in Arizona, I hike down to Crater Lake on Fleetwood Cove Trail. Shasta red fir grows beneath the ridge, and smooth-barked manzanita bushes line the path. I stand at the lake's edge for a long time watching pine pollen swirl across the water like golden snakes. At eye level the water is no longer cobalt, it is a glassy mirror in which I can see my reflection. There is an overwhelming presence here, an innate wisdom in chaos and serenity, joy and grief, life and death. Who knows whether our last breath will be in this life or the next?

I imagine my father's ashes floating away in sunlight. As I try to let go, a deep sadness overcomes me, yet I know the only certainty is change. Reaching into the clear blue water I watch prisms flicker across my fingers like luminous fish. "Your whole body is radiant light. Your whole body is mind in its totality. . . . Your whole body knows no hindrance," wrote Dogen. "Everywhere is round, round, turning over and over."

I climb the steep switchbacks to the top of the rim and walk across a giant snowfield. It is late morning and a white-tailed deer emerges from the forest. She sniffs the air, then saunters off through the blinding white. Her tracks will soon vanish in the afternoon sun.

$\mathscr{B}$ABOQUIVARI!

Dave Petersen

BABOQUIVARI! The very name is like a dream; a hard place to get to—jeeps might do it but will be unwelcome; best come on horseback or like Christ astride a donkey—way past the end of the pavement, beyond the farthest smallest sleepiest town, beyond the barbed wire (invented, some say, by a Carmelite nun), beyond the Papagoan hogans, beyond the last of the windmills, hoving always in the direction of the beautiful mountain.
—from the journals of Edward Abbey, November 1954

$\mathscr{O}$nce upon a time I was granted the bittersweet honor of editing my late friend Edward Abbey's twenty-one volumes of personal journals for publication (*Confessions of a Barbarian*, 1994). Sadly, I had to leave out more than I could fit in. One of the unpublished episodes has haunted me ever since. It's a detailed, exuberantly romantic fantasy of freedom, dignity and place.

A desert place, naturally, anchored by a little island mountain range floating in the prickly midst of the Sonoran Desert southwest of Tucson. Its name is Baboquivari. Westward spreads the sparsely inhabited 2.3-million-acre Tohono O'odham (Papago) Indian Reservation. Immediately east sprawls the Altar Valley and the 120,000-acre Buenos Aires National Wildlife Refuge. To the south lie Old Mexico and the azure Sea of Cortez.

At the time of his Baboquivari journal scratchings, Abbey was a lonesome intellectual of twenty-four years, living in a dank loft in Edinburgh, studying philosophy and literature as a Fulbright Fellow, writing his first novel . . . and building desert sand castles in the air.

Baboquivari—there, somewhere, in that vast desert wasteland, I shall build my festung, retreat, hideout . . . dark womb of the soul—a long low dark sprawling sunbaked stormlashed hacienda of adobe . . . a fat library of esoteric books, an arsenal of music . . . all in one long open room crawling with centipedes, arachnids, vinegaroons.

Years later, Ed would settle on (and for) the west edge of Tucson, almost within sight of Baboquivari Peak, which he visited often and climbed repeatedly. Rising nearly 4500 feet (to 7730 feet ASL) above the desert basins that surround it, Babo's bulbous granite dome offers the only class-six climb in Arizona.

Now Ed is gone, leaving me haunted by that hulking visage. Each March, to hasten the arrival of spring and honor the memory of a friend, Caroline and I flee our snowbound Colorado cabin and point ourselves southwest. This time, our destination is Baboquivari.

BABOQUIVARI! How this name strikes on the romantic heart.

Quite so. Yet it's a name without a language, the final twisted link in a chain of awkward translations from Indian to Spanish to English. The source word, from the tongue of the indigenous Tohono O'odham—the aptly self-named "Desert People"—is *Waw* (say "vav") *Kiwulik*, or "rock drawn in at the middle."

To the O'odham, Baboquivari is holy ground. As detailed by Arizona ethnobiologist Gary Nabhan in his splendid Sonoran study *The Desert Smells Like Rain*, the Baboquivaris shelter a cave that "is *I'itoi Ki*: the home of the Coyote-like character responsible for the Papago emergence into this world. . . . Because Baboquivari Peak towering over the cave can be seen from nearly every village on the reservation, this place is literally and figuratively at the heart of the Papago universe."

Today, but half of the north-south-trending Baboquivaris lie within the O'odham preserve. The boundary traces the ridgeline, with the western slope belonging to the Indians and the eastern slope a checkerboard of private and public parcels. And any way you come at it, access to Baboquivari is a challenge.

You can, if you must, purchase a permit to enter tribal lands and climb Baboquivari from the west, as Abbey did on his initial attempt a quarter of a century ago (as documented in *Cactus Country*). But the O'odham are a private people and less than eager to have swarms of outsiders buzzing over their land and sacred shrines, and I don't blame them.

Fortunately, there exists a little-known route to the flanks of Baboquivari from the east, which Caroline and I snooped out and even now are exploring.

Oh my beloved Baboquivari . . . here the bullbat will resound at night, the greathorned owl hunch on its haunches in the dusk, the coyote yodel wanly on the hill, the mockingbird cry and the thrush hush all; and all about, the cactus.

Cactus? Not so much, as it turns out. Westward, you bet. But here in the Altar Valley to the east of the Babos the elevation is just high enough to exclude the spectacular Sonoran cactus garden ecology in favor of an unlikely desert grassland—cow country, pard. You'll see some cholla, plenty of prickly pear, an occasional barrel, a forlorn saguaro or two, little more.

Incredibly, the drive in from the blacktop is *just* as the young Cactus Ed imagined it—*way past the end of the pavement . . . over hard, dry, rocky hills on a dim trail . . . under a harsh blue sky and a brilliant brassy sun . . . beyond the last of the windmills, up an old dry arroyo bed paved with stone and quiet colors . . . hoving always in the direction of the beautiful mountain.*

Dust-caked and butt-sore, we come at last to road's end and park the old beater in what passes for shade. After eating fresh Arizona oranges and tanking up on water, we hang packs on backs, stroll through an unlocked people portal beside the larger locked gate and follow the rocky lane to a well-kept old ranch complex—house, outbuildings, corral. The house easily predates Abbey's Babo fantasies and (as I'll bet he himself thought when first he saw it) fills his hideout bill just so.

There it is—silent, dark, empty-seeming now, almost hidden under the trees in the lee of the red cliff, its dust-colored walls, black eyeless windows—quiet, aware, motionless, waiting.

Two big beautiful horses eye us suspiciously as we stroll boldly through their domain. Nobody else at home.

Just past the ranch complex, a trail lines out along the dry gulch of Thomas Canyon, and we lean into its moderate uphill grade. Only nine o'clock on a mid-March morning but already a "brilliant brassy sun" sizzles like napalm on exposed skin. Soon enough, though, we come beneath big, shade-making trees—mostly evergreen oaks including especially Emory and the rare Mexican blue—with the odd walnut and spindly Mexican piñon pine tossed in for variety. So many trees that at the first crossing of the gulch we lose the faint trail beneath an ankle-deep litter of leaves. With semi-method we cast about, working up-canyon, relocate the way, move along.

In contrast to the cow-burnt *plana* of the valley below—where we camped last night and saw no wildlife of any kind, though one lonely coyote did "yodel wanly" from afar—the shaded riparian corridor of Thomas Canyon offers an abundance of food, cover, even water (at least here in the lower canyon) in modest pools ringed with cattails and what I call "piss willows" in honor of their distinctly uric aroma. Wildlife abounds.

Already we've seen ground squirrels, rabbits, lizards, some big unfamiliar rodent, and we've noted evidence of others—javelina-sized bites out of prickly pear pads, coyote scats and tracks in the dust, the hard brown pellet droppings of deer. Although he mused in his journals that *at times perhaps we'll live on the dry desert air, eating sunlight and drinking the miraculous blue*, Abbey and his little society of hermits would have had no trouble keeping themselves in wild meat hereabouts.

We cross the gulch a second time, alert lest we trod upon any of the Sonoran's plethora of poisonous residents. When Caroline spots a swarm of Apoidea buzzing angrily around a head-high hole in a big live oak alongside the trail ahead—having been forewarned that Sonoran bees are "Africanized"—we detour wide around. The bemused buzzers ignore us.

The higher we climb, the birdier it gets—a veritable "feathered landscape" (Terry Tempest Williams, poet). When a nervous covey of Gambel's quail scurries past just ahead, we fall into a traveling game of Name that Bird.

Most vocal and visible are the big, heavy-beaked Mexican jays, artful amalgams of raven and jay that thrive on the abundant mast in this nutty place. And twice we're blessed with flash-by glimpses of flame-red, sparrow-sized male vermilion flycatchers, among the most gorgeous of desert songsters. We hear more often than see the shy phainopeplas—big lean members of the flycatcher clan whose menfolk are glossy black with tuxedo tails and proudly crested heads. Look for phainos perched atop tall, isolated trees or cacti issuing their distinct single-note call: the Sonoran Desert anthem.

And so on—woodpeckers peck, thrashers thrash, flickers flick—at least until a pair of Harris hawks, resplendent and distinct with white-banded tails and chestnut wing and body markings, come shadowing low across the canyon, silencing and scattering the timid singers.

Far above the hawks, a swarm of swallows swirls gracefully on a right smart breeze eddying around Baboquivari massif. And hanging long and white from ledges and alcoves high on that stony visage, chalky stains like old men's beards mark the aeries of not just hawks, but eagles, ravens, even (we can suppose) that rare lovely falcon called *caracara*—the so-called "Mexican eagle" emblematic of that Nearby Faraway.

With the arrival of the hawks and the hushing of the songbirds, a liquid stillness floods the canyon. We stop and listen but hear only our own deep breathing. I look up—past trees and hawks and swallows and peak, into a flawless firmament. We've been roaming Baboland for days now, and are yet to hear or see a single stinkin' airplane.

One fat fly buzzes by, dissolving our pleasant trance. We hitch up our packs and carry on.

Our goal is a prominent notch in the ridge on the north shoulder of Baboquivari—the "drawn in at the middle" bit of O'odham fame, it would seem—where (we've been told) waits a cool, shaded, breezy campsite with a view. But no water. That must be humped all the long way up, providing this place with a built-in safeguard against overuse.

Gazing up from the ranch, the saddle didn't appear so very far, but we've been slogging for more than two hours now without a serious (sit-down) break and our goal appears not one slog closer. I've encountered this curious visual phenomenon before in the Sonoran, and lay it to the mirage-making qualities of desert light and landscape.

The trail grows increasingly steep, rocky and switchbacked as it ascends. Yet it's no worse than some "maintained" national forest trails I've hiked in the Rockies and Sierras, better than many and a lot less crowded (like, nobody).

We pass spear-leafed yucca by the dozens—Arizona and soaptree varieties, I presume—their erect penile flower stalks probing like flagstaffs at an unflawed sky. Grasses and forbs abound, though this is a lame spring for wildflowers—the winter was dry even by parched local standards—and Caroline is disappointed to spot only the odd clump of sand verbena, a few droopy stalks of sad red penstemon, a rare yellow cluster of wilted bloomers atop fish-hook barrel cactus.

The barrels, in conspiracy with mesquite, cholla, yucca, Engelmann and purple prickly pear, reach out to grab, stab and slash at our legs, making us glad we eschewed shorts in favor of pants. Alligator junipers have begun popping up among the hardwoods and piñons, growing bigger and more plentiful as we climb.

Off to our right now looms a deeply eroded rhyolite dike—a crumbling volcanic castle wall—gray-yellow rock stained lime green with lichens. To our left, lichens likewise beard the stony face of Old Man Baboquivari, enlivening his otherwise stark facade.

Noon approaches and we begin to droop. Already we've chugged a quart of water each and are wondering if we've brought enough. Moods are sinking when a tiny canyon wren flits by, gushing a joyful contrarian cascade of silvery notes that animate the arid atmosphere and revive our sagging spirits. How I love that little bird.

Directly above, a lone so-called white-throated raven (in fact merely gray-breasted) fights headlong into an invisible wind, muttering irritably to himself.

While I'm watching this spectacle in the sky, rather than the trail at my feet, a marble-sized stone shoots from beneath a clumsy boot and I go down hard, struggle to my feet (muttering irritably to myself), continue on.

And on.

Finally, after half a day of hiking, we mount Baboquivari's hirsute shoulder. I suppose an athletic young jock (or jockette), toting only the minimum of food and water and with a bee under his (or her) Bula cap, could make this hike—maybe four miles and three thousand vertical feet—in half the time. Good on him (or her). While it's no marathon, neither is it any cake walk and we've done well enough, Caroline and I. Perhaps too well. I mean—why rush it? Like life itself, rare is the destination that justifies a harried journey.

The saddle fulfills its promise—breezy and cool and deeply shaded. Plenty of room for two or even three small tents on fairly level packed earth. Long used (for millennia, no doubt), but little littered (a miracle these trashy days). A few minutes of local hunting and gathering should net plenty enough down-and-dead wood for a small evening conflagration. From here it's (mine to hope) an easy hike to the base of the mighty dome—should I decide, come morning, to attempt those last potentially killer thirteen-hundred-plus vertical feet.

This place is, in fact, the ideal approach camp for anyone planning to attack the peak from the east: a relaxed half-day up here, rest and enjoy . . . a full day to do the dome and return before dark . . . out the third day and (sigh) back to the "real" world.

Peering east from this vantage, you can see a hundred miles (it seems), out across the beef-bashed Altar Valley to the Coronado National Forest (likewise overgrazed and, consequently, mesquite infested). Seven distinct island ranges ring the Altar (they say), though you'd be hard pressed to separate and name them, even from such a fine observatory as this.

Feeling light as angels without our packs, we float on up the trail above the campsite, looking for a window through the trees from which to spy out the O'odham world lying westward and below. No such luck (can't see the desert for the trees). What we can see, however, is wild and rewarding—except, perhaps, for Kitt Peak at the northern terminus of the range, upon whose bald pate are visible two of the squadron of observatory domes perched there, glowing white and round like the eggs of reptilian invaders from Mars.

Directly below us rises yet another jagged broken castle wall of lichen-greened rhyolite. Beyond that and far, far below, a few patches of Indian Country come winking through, bearded over with some three hundred species of cacti. Down there, somewhere, hides old *I'itoi*, the O'odham god—who must be sleeping, since down there also, his six thousand Desert People are in pain. They still have their homeland, much of it, but like so very many indigenous peoples worldwide, they've lost their spiritual roots and, consequently, their health, perhaps their very souls.

A tangerine twilight stirs intermittent breezes, and what few bugs there were today—flies, gnats, killer bees—disappear with the sun. Sitting here staring into the winking flames of our little fire, my cholesterol-clogged old heart skips a beat with the thought that a reliable sighting of an errant Mexican jaguar—a *jaguar*—was made in Brown Canyon, *just* south of here, *just* last week. Not even the romantic young Abbey envisioned such a miracle.

The flames flicker and face to coals, the coals wink out and the night grows suddenly chill and dark, our only light a wan yellow rocker of quarter-moon.

The desert moon—there is magic for you . . . a bridge of ghostlight from here through space to the other world . . . a lonely moon above a lonely land.

A lonely land, indeed. And hauntingly quiet. Even the owls, coyotes and poor-wills are mute this idyllic spring night.

Morning.

Before abandoning this long-sought place—which, like so many cherished others, I may never see again (how are we to know?)—I opt to explore farther up the trail as it approaches and spirals westward

137

around the skyscraping vertical dome. Caroline, sensible as always, elects to stay in camp "to go for help if you don't come back." I've been cautioned against attempting the ascent alone, even the relatively "easy" class-four route. (The hard bit, as always, is getting back down.) But I'm carrying a fifty-foot length of stout nylon rope and I've got all day and a heartful of energy. We'll see.

And see we do, straight-away, when I hit serious snow, freezing me out, as it were, almost before I begin. On the hike up yesterday we spotted a few scattered patches of anomalous white tucked back in the shade of alcoves and dikes, remnants of a freak spring storm that blew through just over a week ago (with the errant jaguar). Now, up here in the abiding north-side shade, hard against the massif, the slippery damned stuff is everywhere. Soon the trail disappears entirely beneath deep, then deeper, ice-crusted drifts. The going gets increasingly treacherous and I (wisely, Caroline will concur) give it up—even as Abbey was forced by snow to abandon his premier Baboquivari attempt.

So be it.

Having reached the end of the trail (for now), I make a little speech—to myself, I suppose—then use my trusty hiking staff (an antique bamboo ski pole) to scratch two words and a clandestine symbol into the snow. A message for a friend who (who knows?) might just pass this way.

With my Baboquivari pilgrimage behind me, I return to camp, the ever-sweet Caroline . . . and whatever awaits us down the trail.

A CLANDESTINE FREEDOM

Lisa Couturier

Twenty years ago my family moved to the piedmont region of the Maryland countryside, where my parents built a house in a field of crushed cornstalks. The land we came to live on was part of a 110,000-acre agricultural preserve, some of which borders an isolated mountain called Sugarloaf Mountain. On weekend afternoons in our new country, my younger sister and I headed into the long, gold and rolling autumn land. It was a place bereft of people our age—fourteen and sixteen—and so we came home earlier than expected, our brown hair smelling of hay and chimney smoke.

My friendship with one person, Mr. Boyd, grew with the passing of many mornings. Early mornings, when I drove along the road leading out of our field and toward my high school of privilege in the city, I saw Mr. Boyd lingering in the purple light with jugs of water he'd filled from a stream. We began with waves of hello.

One winter afternoon when the corn had died, I walked through the gray, crisp and low-lying fields to Mr. Boyd's place to bring him Christmas cookies and three pairs of white socks (because I never saw him wear socks) for so graciously agreeing to be the subject of my junior-year photo essay. He invited me into the darkness of his one-room white house. It was a house passed on to him from his grandparents, who were born into slavery on the plantation land on which my parents built our home, and from his mother, who, he tried to remember, gave birth to him sometime in the 1890s. He guessed he was eighty-six.

Inside Mr. Boyd's house, I sat at a messy table wet from the water jugs on it, and near enough to a pail of liquid containing what I could smell

139

was Mr. Boyd's urine. I loaded my film by candlelight. He had no electricity, no running water, no bathroom. He lit a fire in his fireplace and apologized for the stacks of bean cans in a corner, for the piles of newspapers and old books, for the chill of his home. After a time, we took photos and ate cookies. The confectioners' sugar smeared on his dark cheeks. We talked of the deer in the woods behind his house and of the afternoon sun rolling down the flanks of Sugarloaf Mountain out his window.

Despite our good conversation, I felt misplaced. I was a white girl from the suburbs talking to a slave's descendant living in slave quarters. I had land and money but no rural skills. Mr. Boyd had rural skills but no land or money. Country life, I admitted to him, was not in my family tree. I knew nothing about soil or mountains, about crops, about selling eggs and pork on the roadside, about wild animals or the smell of my skin splashed with forest dust and sweat. He listened, sighed, said, "Take the long way home and, sooner or later, it will all echo in your body."

I did not know it on that day, but Mr. Boyd and I would remain friends for two years, until I left for college. He died while I was away. What follows is a good-bye letter to him, written now, eighteen years after last I saw him.

Dear Mr. Boyd,

You once insisted there was no freedom like the freedom Sugarloaf Mountain offered. I was young then and perhaps because I had not been confined, dominated, impeded, hampered, or restricted, I considered myself ineluctably free already. I would come to know Sugarloaf—its shady trails; its sharp outlines in the green air and its soft body muted in the gray rain; its awkwardness as one lone mountain rising out of farmland, like "the tallest kid in class everyone teases," you used to say. But freedom, to me at least, meant leaving the mountain and its surrounding rural farmland behind. Freedom was walking away, not walking within.

The day we hiked to the rural route, from where there was, and still is, an unobstructed view of the mountain, you spoke of freedom again. You recalled walking the several miles to Sugarloaf long ago, as a tribute to your grandparents who, tethered to their fields, could only dream of rising into the mountain air. Perhaps I responded with comments I thought empathic, something about abolition or the Civil War learned in a high school history course. In any case, you said I was born to have so much, you said I would search for freedom because I was privileged to do so, but that it would elude me unless I made a life on the piedmont by Sugarloaf. What kind of freedom was that, I laughed?

You promised then that we would go to the mountain together, promised to show me the freedom. But the hot mornings passed, the geese, the snows. Until finally it was simply that your legs were best suited to loitering in the flatter lands surrounding Sugarloaf. After you died, I had a dream you were homeless on your mountain, where you wandered like the Chinese mountain hermit and poet Han-shan, who centuries ago wrote, ". . . Already it seems like years and years. / Freely drifting, I prowl the woods and streams / And linger watching things themselves."

My hope was to hike Sugarloaf in a rain of fall's warm colors. But things didn't work out until a following spring when I piled my clan of left-wing college friends—idealists studying zoology, art, and journalism—into an old blue Pontiac, turned up the Neil Young cassette and headed for the mountain. They envisioned Sugarloaf as a twelve-hundred-foot-high peak surrounded by other mountains, rather than the monadnock it is. As we drove closer and closer to the mountain, it began to disappear into itself, to spread, as though lowering its limbs for our climb. We hiked seven miles along the Northern Peaks trail and the Mountain Loop that afternoon, imagining the ghosts of the mountains that once stood alongside Sugarloaf, the former sisters of an ancient higher landscape long since eroded into rolling farmland. Clinging in every dark or luminous niche along our hike was the mountain's blood—a life-blood, an alchemical blend of oak and cardinal, acorn, maple, chipmunk and rainwater, mushroom, moss, raccoon scat and red ant. Several fast hours later and nearing the top, we surfaced through lightning-stunted oak trees and gray boulders skinned with lichen, into the mountain's breath.

Back then I didn't have the experience to support what I am about to say, Mr. Boyd, and forgive me for what you may consider a certain sexual forthrightness. But I am remembering those evenings we watched the sun set behind the mountain, those evenings when I saw the silhouette of Sugarloaf drape feminine curves across the darkening sky. Later I read that the Chinese associate mountains with men—dry, hard, and bright; and they associate water with women—wet, soft, and dark. But being a woman now, and knowing a woman's body, its glens and rhythms, I must side with my initial image of the mountain as female. And I am tempted to embody it with a woman's ways—the mountain's topography as the arduous ascent of giving birth—pain, relief, pain, shock, pain, relief; the mountain's shape as the nursing breast.

But this is now, and I speak from a somewhat weathered self, as well as a more molded version of who you knew so long ago. Today, I go to Sugarloaf to inhale the yellowness of wet leaves in the way a mother lives off the sweet smell of her baby's skin. Or I go to the mountain to caress her wrinkled paths. In the days of my leftist friends, though, the purist pleasure was conquering the climb and savoring the aftertaste of stretched muscles and scratched bones. I still can picture my friend Smitty up there, in his mildly drugged state, attempting to envision Sugarloaf at the bottom of an ancient inland sea, a tidbit of knowledge passed from you to me to him. Meanwhile, Maureen spent the afternoon searching for any unlikely chestnuts, seedlings of the great trees that in your lifetime died away. Laura leapt between patches of the erosion-resistant white quartzite that caps Sugarloaf, looking like a butterfly flittering between bowls of sugar. Mark played his guitar in the tall breezes. And I looked eastward, toward our road, trying to spot your old house. But I did not feel freedom in the way I think you meant. I was free from school—because I'd skipped out on my responsibilities for a day. Though I remember you didn't equate escape with freedom.

Wind? Was your freedom in the wind, in the air, because it is limitless? Because air rushes into the rivers of our bodies offering, miraculously, life? Because it offers, invisibly, the sounds of the world? Because it offers, seamlessly, a blue fabric stitched with flying birds? Or did freedom come with standing high above the valley floor but just beneath your image of God, or Heaven? Was it in an immeasurable pleasure of being the tiniest bit closer to the sun? In college, when my biology professor lectured on energy and said sunlight flows through all living things before dispersing back into space, never to come our way again, I thought of you. Was freedom being part of the endless energy of the mountain, of the universe?

You had science books in your house, and poetry and fiction, some history. But philosophers, you believed, complicated the world. Most valuable was the book of the land. So we walked through pages of hills, words of trees. You underscored the smell of wet hay on rainy mornings and the froggy-wet woods by your house. When the soft chill of the night wrapped around our bodies like silk, we listened to the music of the spring peepers behind the old plantation mansion and spied on the great horned owl resting on a television antenna in the moonlight. How many times did we search with flashlights down by the stone bridge, Sugarloaf on the horizon, for the eyes of deer and fox stirring like restless red stars in pastures? Your book taught me to feel my body abandoned in the open spaces on which I lived, to feel my blood rush, to feel my senses heighten as some nocturnal creature myself. But back then the agricultural preserve with its strong mountain was more the setting of some novel or children's story than a place to become a person of some success. What chance did I stand there?

A philosopher I read in college, Norman O. Brown, had an interpretation of freedom. He described it as ". . . an invitation to the dance; a temptation, or irritation. No satisfying solutions; nothing to rest in; nothing to weigh us down." This definition was more concrete than yours, easier to follow. And so I did.

After college I moved away to New York City, traveled, and met men who declared freedom. Men like Eli, who took me twenty-five miles into the Atlantic on a rickety motorized rowboat to have a picnic on a barrier reef with a Central American fisherman, a dog and a chicken. Like Harold, who swam with my hand in his as we snorkeled around coral, searching for moray eel. Like Skye, who insisted we get out of our tent to sit on a log in a violent Vermont storm, while he made dinner and laughed, "Ahhh, rain, don't you love it!?" Like the Antarctic sailor in Patagonia who took me through ninety-mile-per-hour winds and shifting icebergs so we could chip ice off of a glacier for our vodka. Cheers. Like Carlos, who led me through a jungle of howler monkeys, convinced me to sit in their spray and wait, because soon, he promised, they would howl for us. These men split me open into the world. You told me to stay home.

Random images from my days on Sugarloaf coursed through me while I was away. Leaves scraping in the winds of an Ecuadorian rain shower announced the familiar roar of Sugarloaf's stormy canopy. And a condor flying the Chilean Andes cut the sky like the turkey vulture whose black shadow slid across my shoulders on top of our mountain. I missed our land then, remembering the astonishment of being momentarily subsumed by the great wings of a bird's solitary flight. Then, on a day on the other side of the world, I saw dwelling in drips of rain forest light all the sunspots Sugarloaf ever invented. Even a late-night walk home from work along the streets of New York took me back to the mountain. Muffled behind the harsh slaps of my heeled footsteps on city concrete, I heard my hiking boots resonating on Sugarloaf's trails—a gentle pat, a small echo, a tiny absorption of the body into the earth.

But life had been calling since long before my travels. The slick media, with its advertising, MTV and endless cable television stations depicted an increasingly self-interested, self-promoted, self-enriched idea of what it meant to be young and American. News events chronicled a conflicted and disappearing world. My Bohemian friends and I would jump into it all. We would be zoologists saving primates in Indonesia, journalists on the front line of injustice in Central America, photographers snapping images of vanishing wildlife in the Hebrides. We would find honor in rootlessness.

Fed by dreams of rescuing the larger world, I was oblivious to the possibility that Sugarloaf itself needed saving. I guess the land of one's childhood is akin to the room of one's childhood: you assume your treasures will always be there and are surprised to come home to find the room redecorated. Do not be afraid, Mr. Boyd, your mountain still stands. But the designation of the land surrounding the mountain as an agricultural preserve does not leave it invincible. Corn now grows in the air of the coal-burning power plant in Sugarloaf's valley. And it grows among radioactive soil particles that, despite community outrage and complaint, continue to leak from a nuclear production facility near the mountain's base. The most recent threat to Sugarloaf is a proposed highway that would cut through the preserve near the mountain. Meant to ease traffic congestion between Northern Virginia and rural Maryland, the road, should it be built, would ravage the preserve with development and yet more traffic. In the effort to ease, we ultimately dis-ease.

Mr. Boyd, you left me in a world drunken on the ideas of success, excess, progress.

Of course, I hopped on for the ride. Consumed with the heady bivouac that feminism provided me, I believed in the theory that freedom, liberation and personal success could best be found by forgoing certain human behaviors—namely marriage and motherhood, at least for a time. It would be negligent, unfair and arrogant to say I could've done without the privileges passed on to my generation by the feminists before us. But theory held up only until real life started, when, after years of hiking alone in the hilly walls of a city, I began stumbling again and again through the climb of a liberated self. Where were the permanent footholds? Where was a base camp? The red stars of animals' eyes? A child? A family? Where was the blood of the land? Rumi said, "Let yourself be silently drawn by the stronger pull of what you really love." Who wouldn't agree that that's the most difficult moment of a life—not to know what you love?

Mr. Boyd, almost thirteen hundred years ago the Japanese poet Yamanoue Okura spoke of the impermanence of human life. He wrote: "We are helpless in this world. / The years and months slip past / Like a swift stream, which grasps and drags us down. / A hundred pains pursue us, one by one."

I am beginning to understand those pains as a kind of weaning from innocence, perhaps pains irrefutably necessary to understanding the freedom you spoke of all those years ago. Because your freedom wasn't an easy freedom of wind on the mountain, or sun on a face. I'm guessing now it was a paradoxical freedom: that of being connected to the mountain, of being bound to Sugarloaf.

It was as though you imagined someone like myself to be living in a straight line, moving forward and gaining tenacity with each inch of escape into new space; while you imagined someone like yourself living in a circle, moving round and round, grounded in the same old territory. Ultimately, though, the straight line supports much less weight and is more easily broken. It is the circle that flows in an unending stream of energy. It is the circle that offers, in its familiarity with the circle before it, another layer of strength and thus a reciprocity and interdependence. There is no authentic life, and therefore no genuine freedom, conferred outside the circle of mountain, land and creature. The isolation of Sugarloaf, appearing to stand free itself, was a mirage. This was the teaching of our remote mountain.

And because I think it was not only the biology of Sugarloaf Mountain you had in mind, I believe your clandestine freedom paralleled something of what Thoreau thought when he wrote: "I love Nature partly because she is not a man, but a retreat from him. . . . If this world were all man, I could not stretch myself, I should lose all hope. He is restraint; she is freedom to me. He makes me wish for another world; she makes me content with this."

Dear Mr. Boyd, I see now—after having pursued a life of individualism, after having had a nomadic soul—that also you wished for me contentment. Thank you.

Finally, as you may have guessed, I had a child several years ago. I returned to Maryland because I believed my daughter should see the purple light of unbroken land in the morning; believed she should see hayfields swallowing deer and fox; believed she should have a community of not only people but of land and animals. Some days my child and I pass your old house on the way to visit her grandparents. She hides in the cornfields. The sun rolls down the flanks of Sugarloaf. I've taken the long way home, Mr. Boyd, but still I feel the land, our mountain, echoing in my body.

THE ROCKY MOUNTAIN FRONT

A. B. Guthrie Jr.

I am a resident, you might almost say a product, of the Rocky Mountain Front, "the Front," as we have come to call it. It is a strip of land just east of the Continental Divide and includes an edge of the plains, the higher benchlands, the foothills and then the great, jagged wall of the mountains. It starts just east of Glacier Park and includes on its outer rim the towns of Browning, Dupuyer, Bynum, Augusta, and Helena. The crow-flight distance is about 160 miles.

When we speak of the Front we are thinking not of the towns and the plains but of the western rises, the benches, the hills and the mountains that seem to stand guard over creature and land.

I know the Front well, particularly that section west of Choteau, where the Muddy and the Teton and Deep Creek flow, for I spent my young life in the town. I live now 25 miles to the west of it. Just four miles from our home rears my vision site of Ear Mountain. I use the term by extension. It was to the mountain that young Indian boys came, staying on top of it without food or water until, feverish and fanciful, they found their talismans, or medicine, in the form of bird or animal, thereafter held sacred. Don't think of them as foolishly superstitious. Superstition, as a philosopher remarked, is the other fellow's religion. I find my medicine just by looking.

Again to the west of us, three miles or less, runs the Old North Trail, which, it is surmised, travelers from Siberia followed after crossing the Bering land bridge to Alaska. One theory is that they merged with or became our American Indians. Well, maybe. Another is that they continued on to South America. Maybe again. The truth lies centuries beyond the backward reach of history. But there is no question that man came down the Front.

The trail is just one evidence of prehistory to be found on the Front. In late years 10 miles from our place, paleontologists have uncovered thousands of fossils of duck-billed dinosaurs—those of adults, infants, nests and eggs, all vestiges of the life of 70 million years ago. It perished, that life, seemingly all at once. Scientists incline to the belief that a great asteroid struck the earth and that the animals died from the dust and debris and especially from the cold that came with the blotting out of the sun. They wonder, too, about the classification of dinosaurs. They are commonly called reptiles, but the evidence suggests they were warm-blooded creatures that cared for their young, as reptiles are not and do not.

After the dinosaur came the mammal, notably the buffalo that included the Front in its range. If it weren't for obstacles in the way of sight, I could see a buffalo jump from our home. The bottom of that jump, where Indians butchered the dead and dying, has been mined and screened for arrowheads and mined and screened again, for it has been a rich source.

At the age of 86, living on the Front, I have come to feel a part of what has gone before, kin to dinosaur and buffalo and departed Indians that lived here. When I step out of doors and hear a small crunch underfoot I sometimes suspect I may be treading on the dusted bones of duckbill or bison or red man killed in the hunt.

But as I am part and brother of what went before, so am I related to the living creatures that inhabit the Front. They exist in great variety. That fact struck me again this past July when my wife, Carol, and I were returning from a meeting up the Teton canyon. It was night, but the long light of summer held on, and there in the middle of the road, magical, a mountain lion paused, then glided across into the bushes. A mountain lion! A creature so shy of man, so elusive, as to be rarely seen. Sometime travelers in the mountains hereabouts have never spotted one.

To find mountain lions you need dogs, and one day, I fear, hunters' dogs will find the scent of this one and tree it after a chase, and the hunters, following, will shoot it down and get their proud pictures in the paper along with their trophy.

I count out animals in my mind—bears, black and grizzly, deer, coyotes, badgers, beavers, raccoons, otters, minks, skunks, ground squirrels, three kinds of rabbit, sometimes an elk, rarely a wolf, maybe a moose, more rarely a mountain lion. An experienced guide once told me that the Front, at least part of the time, was home to virtually every Rocky Mountain creature.

Of these, bears get the most attention, particularly grizzly bears. The black bear is quite common and almost always harmless, and so people accept it, more or less. In our 12 years here, two have nosed around the house, hoping for garbage that we don't leave outside. The grizzly is a different proposition. Alarmed suddenly, chased or in the presence of imagined danger to its cubs, it is a fearsome animal.

Some people have criticized me for defending the grizzly. How wrong-headed was I to overlook the danger and discount the losses? All right. The passions of the moment pass and don't count in the long run. I stand by my convictions while tending to forget and forgive.

But while thinking of that great bear, the most memorable creature alive on this continent, this part of our lore and our heritage, I don't want it to disappear. Let him live.

Our visitors, in addition to the two black bears, include a badger. It ambles around the house, intent on some business of its own, and, unafraid, takes its flowing body down the bank to the river and is lost to sight. Deer are frequent presences in our backyard. Coyotes often sing at night. Once Carol spotted a wolf.

We are hosts now to five cottontails, a mixed blessing since they eat the plants in our ground-level flower boxes. We threaten to shoot them, but don't. Our impulses are contradictory. Last winter we heard a cry, that seldom-uttered, plaintive cry of the desperate, and we hurried to the back window to see. A cottontail was jumping, jumping to dislodge a little white death that swung from its neck. But no jumps could loosen that throat hold. The rabbit fell down and quivered and died, and the little white death fed on its blood. And our sympathies were with the pesky rabbit, not with the weasel.

The Bob Marshall Wilderness just west of the Front is great and needs no justification other than its being wilderness. Horseback riders and backpackers penetrate the miles of it to their great enjoyment. But what far more visitors see and appreciate is the Front. They come to it to picnic, to fish and to hunt and perhaps just to breathe the breath of free space. They can reach it easily, for there are roads to many spots. Men and women, residents of the Front towns and of the bigger ones farther east, come in numbers.

The situation may change. Some of the Front is privately owned. Far more is under the control of the Bureau of Land Management and the Forest Service. Much hinges on their decisions, for oil men and miners and timber cutters keep filing for permission to drill and blast and cut. In one instance I know of, drillers didn't wait for clearance. Activities like these frighten wild animals away, deface the land and in the case of timber felling give rise to floods.

Officials of counties like my own tend to line up with the despoilers, not without immediate reason, for counties are hard put these days, suffering from two years of dry weather and low prices for cattle and grains. Anything at all promising in the way of cash and jobs exerts its appeal. I believe, if reluctantly, that the officials are reflecting the convictions of the constituents.

They forget. They forget. As one man said of the Forest Service, they have no memory function. Without remembrance of the past, they are compelled to repeat it, as the philosopher Santayana said of history and civilizations. Few remember when the Teton River ran full, season to season. That was before clear-cutting and overgrazing and cultivation made a spring flood of it and a dry creek bed later.

Real estate developers threaten us, too. They regard every open space that may yield profit as an invitation to hammer and saw. Given opportunity and customers they would develop all the miles of the Front. That would be the end of it, of course.

We who live near the mountains tend to be protective of our environment. When it was proposed to sell cabin sites on about 150 acres along the south fork of the Teton, we filed suit. By we I mean ourselves, the Kenneth Gleasons, and the Wilderness Society. A few contributors helped us. The cabin sites, 37 of them, lay at an important entrance to the Bob Marshall Wilderness.

We proved in court that the contour of the acreage prevented effective septic disposal. We proved that the likelihood of finding water was remote. We proved that the State Board of Health, one of the defendants, had hardly investigated at all before giving the development approval.

Unaccountably, the judge, after accepting our contentions, found for the defendants.

We prepared to appeal and went so far as to have a transcript made. We didn't win the case then, so much as wear it out. Facing an appeal, the developers gave up, so advised, I would bet, by their attorneys, who felt that a reversal was sure.

It may sound as if I oppose every would-be cabin builder, as if, given the power, I would close the Front to all cabin seekers. That is not my position and not, I am sure, the position of other dwellers here. What's a cabin here and there, reasonably insulated by space? But 37 cabins on limited acreage! One building to about every four acres! Suburban cluster in our foothills!

I have fished most of the streams of the Front. I have hunted its covers for rabbits and grouse. From its beaver basins and lakes I have flushed mallards and bluebills, three kinds of teal and other waterfowl I made sure to identify. I have picnicked with family and friends. I have known all its weathers—the caress of spring, the frying heat of summer and the bite of cold when sundogs dog the sun. I can't say, with the naturalist John Burroughs, that always have goodness and joy waited on my comings and goings. It's enough that I have come out ahead.

I suppose people not of the Front think it odd of us, or at least eccentric, to live where we do, away from cities and the offerings of cities, away even from a small town where we could have close neighbors and take part in community activities. Maybe we are a bit strange, but I look to the north and the south, where foothills rise, east to the great roll of the high plains and west to the mountains and my vision site of Ear Mountain, and good medicine lies all around.

CREVASSE

Aliette Frank

The growth of the human mind is still high adventure; in many ways the highest adventure on earth.

—Anonymous

"You . . . you crazy? I ain't goin' down dat," says Ben, peering down into the ominous blackness that plunges at his feet. He throws his ice ax down, starts untying the rope connecting us together, and sits down on the ice, refusing to do anything. Meanwhile, I'm straddling what we on the Juneau Icefield, Alaska, call a "gaper": a large crevasse one never approaches without a line of protection. Ben has been invited here to the southern panhandle of Alaska, as one of the 30 students that participate each year in the Juneau Icefield Research Program (JIRP), a two-month summer research and expedition training program to conduct glaciological and arctic field studies. I attended this program three years ago, and have returned as one of the four guides leading the expedition part of the field work. Ben has been recruited as part of the student inner city contingent.

"Ben, you've got to hold me," I try to say diplomatically; inwardly, I'm screaming.

He says nothing, apparently unaware of the fact that although we're separate people, our fates are intertwined, and increasingly so the longer I stand here. I've been looking for an entrance to the crevasse so that we can go down to explore and gather the climatological data for our research to monitor climate change. The points of my crampons grip like teeth on either side of a linear depression in the ice, where a snowbridge from the recent dusting slightly covers the blackness beneath me. I probe my ice ax downward and it sinks up to its head through the weak ice.

"Ben, the ice is thin here—I need you to hold me if I fall."

"I don't wanna go down no crevasse," says Ben. He scoots himself around so his back faces me to tell me in body language that he couldn't care less.

I start estimating the leaping distance to safety. It is not that I do not trust Ben because he is not physically capable, but because his mental aspect needs a little work. We have been on the ice for over two weeks, and I and four other guides have taught him and the other scientists and researchers of JIRP the rules of safe glacier travel: self-arresting, crevasse rescue, roping up, and alpine survival skills.

"Fine," Ben finally says, turning to position himself to self-arrest me so I can make my way back across toward him. I cautiously maneuver across the weak points of the snowbridge, at the same time questioning my role as a guide. I am maneuvering on the fine line between selfishness and self-sacrifice. I safely cross to where Ben is and thankfully sit down. When my adrenaline slows, I have to fight my urge to lecture Ben on proper rope etiquette, but I must be kind, sure, and calm before him. I must give no indication that I question if he will make it for another two months across the ice where the conditions worsen and the need for mental control heightens. Our journey will take us to field stations and facilities scattered over about 1,000 square miles of ice.

"My pack's too heavy," says Ben, digging toward the base of his pack for his headphones, candy bars, card games, and a plethora of other weighty, inessential items—all the things I have come out here to escape. Out here, I thrill in the fresh perspective I gain outside the Ivy League scene at Dartmouth where I am a sophomore. There it is so easy to become wrapped up in constant stimulation and anxiety. I enjoy the seriousness of purpose that is sorely missing from the rest of my life that often seems overly influenced by gadgetry and material satiation. All gadgets out here are not for satiation, but for exploration: we use theodolites for surveying, gravity meters for force estimates, radiation instruments for meteorology, ice augers for ice coring, and the occasional kinepack of dynamite to detonate for geophysics measurements.

We sit on the frozen plateau in the utter stillness of the 1,500 square miles of blinding white ice that surrounds us. Apart from

Antarctica, Greenland, and Ellesmere Island, this remote country contains the largest fields of ice anywhere in the world. Except for the other JIRPers and a few daring climbers like Jon Krakauer, who climbed Devils Thumb—a craggy relief against the brilliant blue sky I can see to the south—this is a land untouched. Although it is only 25 air miles from the coastal rain forest of Juneau, it is a 10-hour hike in to the glaciers from Juneau and a 13-hour ski to the nearest camp.

I squint to see the buildings glinting in the sun, but cannot since the clouds are beginning to encroach from over the ocean in the west. The buildings should be perched on the windswept nunatak—the Greenland Eskimo word for an island of rock in a sea of ice—about 400 feet above us and the crevasse-riven Taku Glacier. They were constructed in the 1940s during an expedition that set out to look for a route so World War II icebreakers could access Russia through the Arctic. Steel cables are bolted deep in the rock, running over the roofs to tie the buildings down. The wind picks up, reminding me how the bitter gales and heavy snowfalls have been known to flatten tents, blow aluminum igloos down cliffs, splinter meteorological equipment shelters, sail roofs, and rip doors from buildings . . . including out-houses. With that thought, I figure we had better make a move.

"Come on Ben, don't you want to go down and see what it's like?"

"I don't wanna go down. I wanna go up," he says, pointing to the jumbled couloirs and rocky precipices of the Taku Towers, a series of five fanglike peaks jutting straight up from the ice. This makes no sense to me. Why would he want to go up instead of down? The Taku Towers stretch coal black against the sky, silhouetted by the approach-ing storm. The Towers are full of barren rock faces, pinnacled outcrop-pings, cold and wind. What does going up this mountain hold for Ben that going down in this crevasse does not? I have heard that Nature speaks in a foreign language, and often with a lisp. Perhaps Ben is speaking in metaphor. Maybe his subconscious sees more in this crevasse than I ever have in all my wild romping. Mountains have long been viewed as spiritual symbols, a parallel for life's challenges. The metaphors of our lives see mainly the upward part of organic motion. Achieving the summit of a mountain is tangible, concrete, immutable.

I figure after all this deep thinking, I had better refortify.

"Want some peanut butter?" I ask Ben, handing him a sandwich. We mostly live off peanut butter and pilot bread since all our food and supplies must be flown in by helicopter. The helicopters cannot carry much weight, and sometimes they come only every two weeks due to poor visibility. The pilot bread boxes make for excellent postcards. Ben snatches the treat and begins to munch. As he does, I watch him, intrigued.

Ben readjusts himself on the ice, looking very out of his element. Ben is from the "hoods" of New York City, boasting only ascents and descents of the stairs to his apartment. His body, uncarved from outdoor life, wrestles with his surroundings.

"I'm cold," Ben whines, flaking off the rime wreathing his facial hair, and the spicules of ice growing from his jacket. Our 4,000-foot elevation gives a climate like Point Barrow, Alaska, 335 miles north of the Arctic Circle. About 20 miles up glacier, where we will head to the next camp in a week or so, the 7,200-foot elevation can give conditions similar to the North Pole. In winter, thermometers have gone down to -87 degrees F. But the temperatures can be deceiving. Sun blisters up our noses, the bottoms of our tongues and inside our nostrils. The albedo, or sun's glare off the ice, greatly magnifies the effects of radiation. The sun also distorts our interpretation of space and distance.

Ben gazes perplexedly off at the enormity of the relentless tide of Taku Glacier that scours the bases of nameless peaks. Ice now covers about 10 percent of the earth's land area. But in the Pleistocene epoch, ice overspread 30 percent of the earth's land surface, with the southern edges of frozen North America reaching into Kentucky. A new Little Ice Age, which is where we are now, was in progress as early as six centuries ago.

Survey flags have been stretched across the Taku's corrugated tongue licking away from us. The flags have started to form a U-shape from the parabolic flow of the ice; the middle of the glacier flows more quickly than the sides, just like a river. The survey team is measuring the surface velocity of the glacier. Other teams are studying geology, ice physics, botanisty, arctic meteorology, glaciohydrology, and photogrammetry in search of a better understanding of these ice monsters.

Ben himself looks like he is searching for a better understanding, for reality, because what he has always known is not here. Instead of skyscrapers, there are impassible peaks; instead of car horns or sirens, there are sounds of calving glaciers. There is a feeling of insignificance not from crowds of people, but from the powerful mountains and the nothingness in between them. Indians called this vast whiteness "Home of the Spirits."

Then I realize that the reason Ben does not seem to want to go down is not so much because he struggles against the elements within nature, but he is struggling against the elements within himself. In its most common usage, "down" is nothing but a downer. Most of Ben's life has been spent going "downward." Growth and success have been inexorably caught in an ascensionist fantasy: Hebrews, Greeks, and Christians all give special value to heights, and our spiritually influenced compass of Western mortality tends to put better things up high and worse things down low. Each immigrant moved upward in social class as buildings moved upward with their elevators to move to expansive levels. Industrial refining of buried minerals—coal, iron, copper, oil—increased their economic value and the financial status of their owners simply by raising these basic materials from below to above. To be an adult is to be grown up. Failing computers are said to be "down," feeling blue is feeling "down." Darwin's thesis, *The Descent of Man*, became in our minds the ascent of man.

I walk to the edge of the crevasse and look down, trying to fathom what descending into a crevasse must mean if a mountain is something tangible, concrete, and immutable. The summit of the Taku Towers is there, shining like a brilliant pinnacle, light, fixed, a summit to guide his internal compass. Then I look back down to the crevasse: a dark void, a depthless unexplored place. Exploring this crevasse, the recesses of the glacier, is like exploring the recesses of the mind.

Ben crawls over to the lip next to me and peers down where the glacier drops off into an abyss of vertical ice.

"That muthuh's deep!" he says. The crevasses on the Juneau Icefield may extend down to about 125 feet. At that depth, the glacier's plastic flow heals the yawning cut.

"Why's it called a crevasse?" Ben asks.

"Crevasse means a fissure in a glacier," I say. Crevasses form when the glacier bends or stretches, and will break at the weakest point just like a rubber band. The greater the elevation change, the more stress and strain the ice experiences.

I point to the Taku Towers where it looks like heaven and earth meet, and say, "Mountains are made of crevasses. Going down in one is like going inside, seeing what the mountain is made of." I've come to realize that sometimes the most dangerous part of climbing mountains is confronting changing crevasses patterns. People I know who have climbed Everest often say that the most dangerous part of reaching the highest mountain on earth is the Khumbu Icefall. Climbers put ladders over the top—they never descend into them.

"Crevasses are constantly changing," I say as I clear away the cornice of the snowbridge, looking for a way into a place where the surface of the earth and its insides meet. I'd been down this particular crevasse two years ago when I came as a student in high school, but the changing climatic conditions sometimes make crevasses hard to find. Nourished by snowfall that often exceeds 100 feet a year, the Taku ranks as one of Alaska's largest and most active of the thousands of glaciers ranging along 900 miles of one of the world's stormiest coasts. Unlike a mountain of rock, whose change is measured in eons, a crevasse changes daily, finically dependent upon its environment: sun, heat, and precipitation. The very name of "Taku" is a reminder of change: the Indians say that it originally meant "the place where the geese sit down." Long ago, most recently 1750, the glacier crept across the head of its fiord, creating a 36-mile-long lake in the deep valley to the east. Some of these signs are visible on the valley sides as we look across the frozen sea. A crestal snowfield, called a neve, stretches six miles toward the rumpled peaks of the Coast Mountains, the boundary between Alaska and British Columbia. Today the Taku advances, but will likely soon retreat once again.

When the amount of snowfall is less than that which melts away, the glacier is considered to be in retreat (although it may still actually be moving forward). Glaciers wax and wane with solar activity: when the convulsions that cause sunspots wrack the sun, electrically charged particles stream earthward, converging over the magnetic poles. These particles increase the energy of the continental air mass, causing it to expand and nudge Alaska's usual storm track seaward. The influx of warming air lifts the line of maximum snowfall, always near 32 degrees F, up the mountain slopes, feeding high-level glaciers and starving those below. When the sun calms and the cooling continental air pulls back, the line of maximum snowfall descends to nourish lower glaciers.

Here, the glacier looks very malnourished. Heat has caused the surface ice to ablate, or melt, thereby exposing more of the crevasse. The conditions here are much worse now than I remember them to be two years ago. And with the recent dusting of snow creating a facade of surface stability, the remainder of our travel will be more difficult. But still, the mountains and glaciers here are magnificent to me not in spite of the crevasses, but precisely because of them.

Ben is still not impressed.

"Well, I've got to get the data, so I'll be back," I say, anchoring my rope so I can descend into the crevasse. We use an anchor, like a ski or ice ax in a T-trench, a trench dug deeply in the snow perpendicular to the weight it will hold. I reattach my prussiks so I can hang on the rope and ascend when I'm done gathering my data. Within a few minutes, I'm descending into the depths of nothingness while Ben waits on top, staring at a frozen halo arc, delicate prisms of crystals of fresh-fallen snow refracting the sun's slanting rays.

Down in the crevasse my hands quickly numb. They've been frozen many times, and the tips are often tinged blue, and have little feeling. I have come to learn that a lot of climbing mountains and living in alpine conditions is about enduring pain—not just the physical pain of continually pushing upward, lugging pounds to survive on your back, or even the mental pain of pushing through the physical pain. But it is also the pain of having time to think and reflect in places like this, within an exposed, barren landscape, where the ante of effort and concentration is deliberately raised to clear the mind of trivialities. The more improbable the situation and the greater the demands made, the more sweet is the release from all that tension.

Soon I am out in the blinding sun. Ben immediately greets me with, "I'm bleeding, I'm bleeding!" He's got a case of *Chrysophyta*. Next to him on the snow is red snow algae, one of the only living organisms on the icefield. Red pigment shields their chlorophyll from the sun's glare. They cluster in little red dots, coating the ice and absorbing solar heat. Underneath, the ice is cupped concavely in red "sun cups" that sometimes become deep enough to capsize vehicles.

Ben is more intrigued with the life on the surface. The snow algae, a few trees, and a few tenacious lichens surviving on nunataks a thousand years and longer add the only color to the black and whiteness out here. They can also reveal the age of rock through dendrochronology or lichenometry studies, which measure the diameters of the largest lichens to estimate when the ice receded, baring rock for the growth of plants.

"So you want to go down?" I ask Ben again. It's important to experience a crevasse when there's a choice to go inside, instead of falling into one unplanned. I remember the program director repeating, "Every year someone falls down a crevasse because they aren't paying attention and aren't listening to what they're trying to."

"No," Ben says emphatically, then wavers, "I don't wanna go alone, can't you come down too?"

"Sorry, only one person on the rope at a time," I say. If we were climbing a mountain, Ben could follow behind me in my footsteps, and if this were Everest, maybe even have to wait in line at the Hillary Step. But this is a solitary exploration, a solitude, like going in oneself for hours and meeting no one.

Ben stands above the abyss as if with a shyness before the unforeseeable past. White and gray bands from winter and summer months alternate all the way down. All the memories of the earth, the big events and the small, are recorded here in the stratigraphy of the ice. Bands form each year from layers of dust and pollen, often scalloped with surface irregularities produced by wind and sun. They separate one yearly snowfall from another: in the summer, there are more particles like pollen and dust in the air, so the ice is darker, whereas in the winter, the bands are lighter. Ben sees an unusually dark band that was created from a past volcanic eruption and inches himself over, holding tightly to the rope to begin descending. His eyes look like those of a child upon something unfamiliar, from out of the depth of one's own world, out of the expanse of one's solitude.

"Freaking amazing," he says. Suddenly his fear and inhibitions are transformed by the thought that down here, there is so much more, even more perhaps than he'd find ascending even the tallest mountain on earth that, if he were to "conquer," he'd stand on for only a few moments before his footprints would be washed away. The mentality of descending into a crevasse is not one of going up to "conquer," but rather, going inside to explore.

The Kabbalist Tree, as first elaborated in the 13th-century Spain, imagines the descending branches to be conditions of the soul's life, which becomes more and more manifest and visible as it descends. Buddha purposely left his palace so he could descend to the everyday world of those outside. Even the tallest trees send down roots as they rise toward light.

"There aren't any steps," he says.

"You have to kick them yourself," I answer.

Ben and the crevasse seem like two solitudes protecting and saluting each other. He descends farther just over the lip of the crevasse, so I can barely see the top of his head, but then he quickly pops up again. He tries to clamber back out onto the glacier's frozen hide.

"Ah, ah, there's nothing here . . . I'm claustrophobic," Ben says. Ben feels like he's being encroached upon and consumed by nothingness. It seems like there's nothing to spark any thought—no noise, no action. To have thoughts, he has to look inward. In solitude, away from stimulation, looking inward, is what led three great thinkers of the 20th century, Newton, Darwin, and Einstein, to their revelations. Newton was forced to take refuge in a country cottage, from the Bubonic plague in Cambridge. There, he explored his theories of physics, astronomy, and gravity. Darwin's voyage on the *Beagle* allowed him to ponder theories of evolution. Einstein was exiled from the academic world, and was forced to work in a patent factory, where he developed his theories on relativity.

"Take another look," I say to Ben. He begins descending past eons of time in milliseconds. "No way," he says, marveling at the amount of compression it must have taken to reduce the dirty layers to faint lines a few feet apart. This is a place where everything that seems forgotten on the outside is kept forever, frozen in time on the inside. And the inside is what matters, because the flow dynamics of the glacier depend on the solidarity of the material inside. Looking closely, he sees there are millions of crystals with intricate shapes. As the whole glacier moves through time, the crevasse changes form, sometimes distorts pieces of ice, crushing and disfiguring them through a complete metamorphosis.

Ben scratches the layers, becoming totally absorbed in the differences between the soft and the hard. There is a carapace of old snow, called firn, which forms a network of icy structures. These form a sort of skeleton with columns, walls, and floors of dense, granular ice. They are created when spring's meltwater percolates into the glacier's depths and refreezes.

"I hear something," says Ben. The faint sounds of water trickle far down below. Once the glacier warms to melting point, surface water no longer refreezes, but drains deep into the interior and runs off in subterranean tunnels, carrying erosional "rock flour" with it. This creates the milky streams that often flow from the terminus of a glacier. It's humbling to think that it will take this crevasse a century and a half before where we're sitting slides 30 miles down into the sea. Unless . . .

"A surge!" yells Ben. There is a shrieking of glass, unearthly sounds, and the rope grinds deeper into the lip of the crevasse, jerking Ben into a rude halt serenaded by madrigal creaks and percussive cracks. Avalanches or the unusual accruement of weight at high levels can cause the glacier to surge.

"I'm gonna fall!" Ben screams, as he too closely brushes with the enigma of mortality. He's frightened that if he falls, he might not be able to come up again. Going down is different than up, because when going up, you know how to get down since you've been there before, and you can always turn around.

The rope slowly settles, and Ben tries to regain his composure after he realizes that the glacier is not surging. There would have been an onslaught of booming ice, growling boulders crashing against other boulders, an orchestra of devastation. Ben hangs there for minutes, silent and motionless. It is perhaps a moment when something new has entered him, something unknown, where feelings grow mute in shy perplexity. Everything withdraws, a stillness comes. Perhaps there's a discovery not only in his intellect, but in his inmost consciousness and waking cognizance. He clings onto the sides of the crevasse, its realities and its metaphors that hardly anyone sees because they're always trying to go up instead of down, and yells up to me, "I had no idea what was down here."

FROM TRAVELS WITH WILLIAM BARTRAM

William Bartram

I waited two or three days at this post, expecting the return of an Indian who was out hunting. This man was recommended to me as a suitable person for a protector and guide to the Indian settlements over the hills; but upon information that he would not be in shortly, and there being no other person suitable for the purpose, rather than be detained, and perhaps thereby frustrated in my purposes, I determined to set off alone and run all risks.

I crossed the river at a good ford just below the old fort. The river here is just one hundred yards over. After an agreeable progress for about two miles over delightful strawberry plains, and gently swelling green hills, I began to ascend more steep and rocky ridges. Having gained a very considerable elevation, looking round, I enjoyed a very comprehensive and delightful view: Keowe, which I had but just lost sight of, appeared again, and the serpentine river speeding through the lucid green plain apparently just under my feet. After observing this delightful landscape, I continued on again three or four miles, keeping the trading path, which led me over uneven rocky land, crossing rivulets and brooks, and rapidly descending over rocky precipices; when I came into a charming vale, embellished with a delightful glittering river, which meandered through it, and crossed my road. On my left hand, upon the grassy bases of the rising hills, appeared the remains of a town of the ancients, as the tumuli, terraces, posts or pillars, old Peach and Plumb orchards, &c. sufficiently testify. These vales and swelling bases of the surrounding hills, afford vast crops of excellent grass and herbage fit for pasturage and hay; of the latter, Plantago Virginica, Sanguisorba, Geum, Fragaria, &c. The Panax quinquefolium, or Ginseng, now appears plentifully on the North exposure of the hill, growing out of the rich mellow humid earth amongst the stones or fragments of rocks.

Having crossed the vales, I began to ascend again the more lofty ridges of hills, then continued about eight miles over more gentle pyramidal hills, narrow vales and lawns, the soil exceedingly fertile, producing lofty forests and odoriferous groves of Calycanthus, near the banks of rivers, with Halesia, Philadelphus inodorus, Rhododendron ferrugineum, Azalea, Stewartia montana,* fol. ovatis acuminatis serratis, flor. niveo, staminum corona fulgida, pericarp. pomum exsuccum, apice acuminato dehiscens, Cornus Florida, Styrax, all in full bloom, and decorated with the following sweet roving climbers, Bignonia sempervirens, Big. crucigera, Lonicera sempervirens, Rosa paniculata, &c.

Now at once the mounts divide; and disclose to view the ample Occonne vale, encircled by a wreath of uniform hills; their swelling bases clad in cheerful verdure, over which, issuing from between the mountains, plays along a glittering river, meandering through the meadows. Crossing these at the upper end of the vale, I began to ascend the Occonne mountain. On the foot of the hills are ruins of the ancient Occonne town. The first step after leaving the verdant beds of the hills, was a very high rocky chain of pointed hills, extremely well timbered with the following trees: Quercus tinctoria, Querc. alba, Querc. rubra, Fraxinus excelsior, Juglans hickory various species, Ulmus, Tilia, Acer saccharinum, Morus, Juglans nigra, Juglans alba, Annona glabra, Robinia pseudacacia, Magnolia acuminata, Æsculus sylvatica, with many more, particularly a species of Robinia new to me, though perhaps the same as figured and slightly described by Catesby in his Nat. Hist. Carol. This beautiful flowering tree grows twenty and thirty feet high, with a crooked leaning trunk; the branches spread greatly, and wreath about, some almost touching the ground; however there appears a singular pleasing wildness and freedom in its manner

*This is a new species of Stewartia, unknown to the European botanists, and not mentioned in any catalogues.

of growth; the slender subdivisions of the branches terminate with heavy compound panicles of rose or pink coloured flowers, amidst a wreath of beautiful pinnated leaves.

My next flight was up a very high peak, to the top of the Occonne mountain, where I rested; and turning about, found that I was now in a very elevated situation, from whence I enjoyed a view inexpressibly magnificent and comprehensive. The mountainous wilderness which I had lately traversed, down to the region of Augusta, appearing regularly undulated as the great ocean after a tempest; the undulations gradually depressing, yet perfectly regular, as the squama of fish, or imbrications of tile on a roof; the nearest ground to me of a perfect full green; next more glaucous; and lastly almost blue as the ether with which the most distant curve of the horizon seemed to be blended.

My imagination thus wholly engaged in the contemplation of this magnificent landscape, infinitely varied, and without bound, I was almost insensible or regardless of the charming objects more within my reach: a new species of Rhododendron foremost in the assembly of mountain beauties; next the flaming Azalea, Kalmia latifolia, incarnate Robinia, snowy mantled Philadelphus inodorus, perfumed Calycanthus, &c.

This species of Rhododendron grows six or seven feet high; many nearly erect stems arise together from the root, forming a group or coppice. The leaves are three or four inches in length, of an oblong figure, broadest toward the extremity, and terminating with an obtuse point; their upper surface of a deep green and polished; but the nether surface of a rusty iron colour, which seems to be effected by innumerable minute reddish vesicles, beneath a fine short downy pubescence; the numerous flexile branches terminate with a loose spiked raceme, or cluster of large deep rose coloured flowers, each flower being affixed in the diffused cluster of a long peduncle, which, with the whole plant, possesses an agreeable perfume.

After being recovered of the fatigue and labour in ascending the mountain, I began again to prosecute my task, proceeding through a shady forest; and soon after gained the most elevated crest of the Occonne mountain, and then began to descend the other side; the winding rough road carrying me over rocky hills and levels, shaded by incomparable forests, the soil exceedingly rich, and of an excellent quality for the production of every vegetable suited to the climate, and seeming peculiarly adapted for the cultivation of Vines (Vitis vinifera), Olives (Oles Europea), the Almond tree (Amygdalus communis), Fig (Ficus carica), and perhaps the Pomegranate (Punica granatum), as well as Peaches (Amyg. Persica), Prunus, Pyrus, of every variety. I passed again steep rocky ascents, and then rich levels, where grew many trees and plants common in Pennsylvania, New-York and even Canada, as Pinus strobus, Pin. sylvestris, Pin. abies, Acer saccharinum, Acer striatum, s. Pennsylvanicum, Populus tremula, Betula nigra, Juglans alba, &c.; but what seems remarkable, the yellow Jessamine (Bignonia sempervirens), which is killed by a very slight frost in the open air in Pennsylvania, here, on the summits of the Cherokee mountains associates with the Canadian vegetables, and appears roving with them in perfect bloom and gaiety; as likewise Halesia diptera, and Hal. tetraptera, mountain Stewartia, Styrax, Ptelea, Æsculus pavia; but all these bear our hardest frosts in Pennsylvania. Now I enter a charming narrow vale, through which flows a rapid large creek, on whose banks are happily associated the shrubs already recited, together with the following; Staphylæa, Euonimus Americana, Hamamelis, Azalea, various species, Aristolochia frutescens, s. odoratissima, which rambles over the trees and shrubs on the prolific banks of these mountain brooks. Passed through magnificent high forests, and then came upon the borders of an ample meadow on the left, embroidered by the shade of a high circular amphitheatre of hills, the circular ridges rising magnificently one over the other. On the green turfy bases of these ascents appear the ruins of a town of the ancients. The upper end of this spacious green plain is divided by a promontory or spur of the ridges before me, which projects into it: my road led me up into an opening of the ascents through which the glittering brook which watered the meadows ran rapidly down, dashing and roaring over high rocky steps. Continued yet ascending until I gained the top of an elevated rocky ridge, when appeared before me a gap or opening between other yet more lofty ascents, through which continued as the rough rocky road led me, close by the winding banks of a large rapid brook, which at length turning to the left, pouring down rocky precipices, glided off through dark groves and high forests, conveying streams of fertility and pleasure to the fields below.

The surface of the land now for three or four miles is level, yet uneven, occasioned by natural mounds or rocky knobs, but covered with a good staple of rich earth, which affords forests of timber trees and shrubs. After this, gently descending again, I travelled some miles over a varied situation of ground, exhibiting views of grand forests, dark detached groves, vales and meadows, as heretofore, and producing the like vegetable and other works of nature; the meadows, affording exuberant pasturage for cattle, and the bases of the encircling hills, flowering plants, and fruitful strawberry beds: observed frequently ruins of the habitations or villages of the ancients. Crossed a delightful river, the main branch of Tugilo, when I began to ascend again, first over swelling turfy ridges, varied with groves of stately forest trees; then ascending again more steep grassy hill sides, rested on the top of mount Magnolia, which appeared to me to be the highest ridge of the Cherokee mountains, which separate the waters of Savanna river from those of the Tanase or greater main branch of the Cherokee river. This running rapidly a North-West course through the mountains, is joined from the North-East by the Holstein; thence taking a West course yet amongst the mountains, receiving into it from either hand many large rivers, leaves the mountains immediately after being joined by a large river from the East, becomes a mighty river by the name of Hogehege, thence meanders many hundred miles through a vast country consisting of forests, meadows, groves, expansive savannas, fields and swelling hills, most fertile and delightful, flows into the beautiful Ohio, and in conjunction with its transparent waters, becomes tributary to the sovereign Mississippi.

This exalted peak I named mount Magnolia, from a new and beautiful species of that celebrated family of flowering trees, which here, at the cascades of Falling Creek, grows in a high degree of perfection: I had, indeed, noticed this curious tree several times before, particularly on the high ridges betwixt Sinica and Keowe, and on ascending the first mountain after leaving Keowe, when I observed it in flower, but here it flourishes and commands our attention.

This tree,* or perhaps rather shrub, rises eighteen to thirty feet in height; there are usually many stems from a root or source, which lean a little, or slightly diverge from each other, in this respect imitating the Magnolia tripetala; the crooked wreathing branches arising and subdividing from the main stem without order or uniformity, their extremities turn upwards, producing a very large rosaceous, perfectly white, double or polypetalous flower, which is of a most fragrant scent; this fine flower sits in the centre of a radius of very large leaves, which are of a singular figure, somewhat lanceolate, but broad towards their extremities, terminated with an acuminated point, and backwards

---

*Magnolia auriculata.

they attenuate and become very narrow towards their bases, terminating that way with two long narrow ears or lappets, one on each side of the insertion of the petiole; the leaves have only short footstalks, sitting very near each other, at the extremities of the floriferous branches, from whence they spread themselves after a regular order, like the spokes of a wheel, their margins touching or lightly lapping upon each other, form an expansive umbrella superbly crowned or crested with the fragrant flower, representing a white plume; the blossom is succeeded by a very large crimson cone or strobile, containing a great number of scarlet berries, which, when ripe, spring from their cells, and are for a time suspended by a white silky web or thread. The leaves of those trees which grow in a rich, light humid soil, when fully expanded and at maturity, are frequently above two feet in length, and six or eight inches where broadest. I discovered in the maritime parts of Georgia, particularly on the banks of the Alatamaha, another new species of Magnolia, whose leaves were nearly of the figure of those of this tree, but they were much less in size, not more than six or seven inches in length, and the strobile very small, oblong, sharp pointed, and of a fine deep crimson colour; but I never saw the flower. These trees grow straight and erect, thirty feet or more in height, and of a sharp conical form much resembling the Cucumber tree (Mag. acuminata) in figure.

The day being remarkably warm and sultry, together with the labour and fatigue of ascending the mountains, made me very thirsty and in some degree sunk my spirits. Now past mid-day, I sought a cool shaded retreat, where was water for refreshment and grazing for my horse, my faithful slave and only companion. After proceeding a little farther, descending the other side of the mountain, I perceived at some distance before me, on my right hand, a level plain supporting a grand high forest and groves: the nearer I approached, my steps were the more accelerated from the flattering prospect opening to view. I now entered upon the verge of the dark forest, charming solitude! as I advanced through the animating shades, observed on the farther grassy verge a shady grove; thither I directed my steps. On approaching these shades, between the stately columns of the superb forest trees, presented to view, rushing from rocky precipices under the shade of the pensile hills, the unparalleled cascade of Falling Creek, rolling and leaping off the rocks: the waters uniting below, spread a broad glittering sheet over a vast convex elevation of plain smooth rocks, and are immediately received by a spacious bason, where trembling in the centre through hurry and agitation, they gently subside, encircling the painted still verge; from whence gliding swiftly, they soon form a delightful little river, which continuing to flow more moderately, is restrained for a moment, gently undulating in a little lake: they then pass on rapidly to a high perpendicular steep of rocks, from whence these delightful waters are hurried down with irresistible rapidity. I here seated myself on the moss-clad rocks, under the shade of spreading trees and floriferous fragrant shrubs, in full view of the cascades.

At this rural retirement were assembled a charming circle of mountain vegetable beauties; Magnolia auriculata, Rhododendron ferrugineum, Kalmia latifolia, Robinia montana, Azalea flammula, Rosa paniculata, Calycanthus Floridus, Philadelphus inodorus, perfumed Convalaria majalis, Anemone thalictroides, Anemone hepatica, Erythronium maculatum, Leontice thalictroides, Trillium sessile, Trillium cesnum, Cypripedium, Arethusa, Ophrys, Sanguinaria, Viola uvularia, Epigea, Mitchella repens, Stewartia, Halesia, Styrax, Lonicera, &c. Some of these roving beauties stroll over the mossy, shelving, humid rocks, or from off the expansive wavy boughs of trees, ending over the floods, salute their delusive shade, playing on the surface; some plunge their perfumed heads and bathe their flexile limbs in the silver stream; whilst others by the mountain breezes are tossed about, their blooming tufts bespangled with pearly and chrystaline dew-drops collected from the falling mists, glistening in the rainbow arch. Having collected some valuable specimens at this friendly retreat, I continued my lonesome pilgrimage. My road for a considerable time led me winding and turning about the steep rocky hills; the descent of some of which were very rough and troublesome, by means of fragments of rocks, slippery clay and talc: but after this I entered a spacious forest, the land having gradually acquired a more level surface: a pretty grassy vale appears on my right, through which my wandering path led me, close by the banks of a delightful creek, which sometimes falling over steps of rocks, glides gently with serpentine meanders through the meadows.

After crossing this delightful brook and mead, the land rises again with sublime magnificence, and I am led over hills and vales, groves and high forests, vocal with the melody of the feathered songsters; the snow-white cascades glittering on the sides of the distant hills.

It was now afternoon; I approached a charming vale, amidst sublimely high forests, awful shades! Darkness gathers around; far distant thunder rolls over the trembling hills: the black clouds with august majesty and power, move slowly forwards, shading regions of towering hills, and threatening all the destruction of a thunder storm: all around is now still as death; not a whisper is heard, but a total inactivity and silence seem to pervade the earth; the birds afraid to utter a chirrup, in low tremulous voices take leave of each other, seeking covert and safety: every insect is silenced, and nothing heard but the roaring of the approaching hurricane. The mighty cloud now expands its sable wings, extending from North to South, and is driven irresistibly on by the tumultuous winds, spreading its livid wings around the gloomy concave, armed with terrors of thunder and fiery shafts of lightning. Now the lofty forests bend low beneath its fury; their limbs and wavy boughs are tossed about and catch hold of each other; the mountains tremble and seem to reel about, and the ancient hills to be shaken to their foundations: the furious storm sweeps along, smoaking through the vale and over the resounding hills: the face of the earth is obscured by the deluge descending from the firmament, and I am deafened by the din of the thunder. The tempestuous scene damps my spirits, and my horse sinks under me at the tremendous peals, as I hasten on for the plain.

The storm abating, I saw an Indian hunting cabin on the side of a hill, a very agreeable prospect, especially in my present condition; I made up to it and took quiet possession, there being no one to dispute it with me except a few bats and whip-poor-wills, who had repaired thither for shelter from the violence of the hurricane.

Having turned out my horse in the sweet meadows adjoining, and found some dry wood under shelter of the old cabin, I struck up a fire, dried my clothes, and comforted myself with a frugal repast of biscuit and dried beef, which was all the food my viaticum afforded me by this time, excepting a small piece of cheese which I had furnished myself with at Charleston, and kept till this time.

The night was clear, calm and cool, and I rested quietly. Next morning at day-break I was awakened and summoned to resume my daily task, by the shrill cries of the social night hawk and active merry mock-bird. By the time the rising sun had gilded the tops of the towering hills, the mountains and vales rang with the harmonious shouts of the pious and cheerful tenants of the groves and meads.

I observed growing in great abundance in these mountain meadows, Sanguisorba Canadensis and Heracleum maximum; the latter exhibiting a fine show, being rendered conspicuous even at a great distance, by its great height and spread, vast pennatifid leaves and expansive umbels of snow-white flowers. The swelling bases of the surrounding hills fronting the meadows presented for my acceptance the fragrant red strawberry, in painted beds of many acres surface, indeed I may safely say, many hundreds.

After passing through this meadow, the road led me over the bases of a ridge of hills, which as a bold promontory dividing the fields I had just passed, form expansive green lawns. On these towering hills appeared the ruins of the ancient famous town of Sticoe. Here was a vast Indian mount or tumulus and great terrace, on which stood the council-house, with banks encompassing their circus; here were also old Peach and Plumb orchards; some of the trees appeared yet thriving and fruitful. Presently after leaving these ruins, the vale and fields are divided by means of a spur of the mountains pushing forward: here likewise the road forked; the left-hand path continued up the mountains to the Overhill towns: I followed the vale to the right hand, and soon began to ascend the hills, riding several miles over very rough, stony land, yielding the like vegetable productions as heretofore; and descending again gradually, by a dubious winding path, leading into a narrow vale and lawn, through which rolled on before me a delightful brook, water of the Tanase. I crossed it and continued a mile or two down the meadows; when the high mountains on each side suddenly receding, discovered the opening of the extensive and fruitful vale of Cowe, through which meanders the head branch of the Tanase, almost from its source, sixty miles, following its course down to Cowe.

I left for a little while, the stream passing swiftly and foaming over its rocky bed, lashing the steep craggy banks, and then suddenly sunk from my sight, murmuring hollow and deep under the rocky surface of the ground. On my right hand the vale expands, receiving a pretty silvery brook of water which came hastily down from the adjacent hills, and entered the river a little distance before me. I now turn from the heights on my left, the road leading into the level lawns, to avoid the hollow rocky grounds, full of holes and cavities, arching over the river through which the waters are seen gliding along: but the river is soon liberated from these solitary and gloomy recesses, and appears waving through the green plain before me. I continued several miles, pursuing my serpentine path, through and over the meadows and green fields, and crossing the river, which is here incredibly increased in size, by the continual accession of brooks flowing in from the hills on each side, dividing their green turfy beds, forming them

171

into parterres, vistas, and verdant swelling knolls, profusely productive of flowers and fragrant strawberries, their rich juice dying my horses feet and ancles.

These swelling hills, the prolific beds on which the towering mountains repose, seem to have been the common situations of the towns of the ancients, as appears from the remaining ruins of them yet to be seen, and the level rich vale and meadows in front, their planting grounds.

Continue yet ten or twelve miles down the vale, my road leading at times close to the banks of the river, the Azalea, Kalmia, Rhododendron, Philadelphus, &c. beautifying his now elevated shores, and painting the coves with a rich and cheerful scenery, continually unfolding new prospects as I traverse the shores: towering mountains seem continually in motion as I pass along, pompously raising their superb crests towards the lofty skies, traversing the far distant horizon.

The Tanase is now greatly increased from the conflux of the multitude of rivulets and brooks, descending from the hills on either side, generously contributing to establish his future fame, already a spacious river.

The mountains recede, the vale expands; two beautiful rivulets stream down through lateral vales, gliding in serpentine mazes over the green turfy knolls, and enter the Tanase nearly opposite to each other. Straight forward the expansive green vale seems yet infinite: now on the right hand a lofty pyramidal hill terminates a spur of the adjacent mountain, and advances almost into the river; but immediately after doubling this promontory, an expanded wing of the vale spreads on my right, down which came precipitately a very beautiful creek, which flowed into the river just before me; but now behold, high upon the side of a distant mountain overlooking the vale, the fountain of this brisk-flowing creek; the unparalleled waterfall appears as a vast edifice with crystal front, or a field of ice lying on the bosom of the hill.

I now approach the river at the fording place, which was greatly swollen by the floods of rain that fell the day before, and ran with foaming rapidity; but observing that it had fallen several feet perpendicular, and perceiving the bottom or bed of the river to be level, and covered evenly with pebbles, I ventured to cross over; however I was obliged to swim two or three yards at the deepest channel of it, and landed safely on the banks of a fine meadow, which lay on the opposite shore, where I immediately alighted and spread abroad on the turf my linen, books, and specimens of plants, &c. to dry, turned out my steed to graze, and then advanced into the strawberry plains to regale on the fragrant, delicious fruit, welcomed by communities of the splendid meleagris, the capricious roe-buck, and all the free and happy tribes, which possess and inhabit those prolific fields, who appeared to invite, and joined with me in the participation of the bountiful repast presented to us from the lap of nature.

I mounted again, and followed the trading path about a quarter of a mile through the fields, then gently ascended the green beds of the hills, and entered the forests, being a point of a chain of hills projecting into the green vale or low lands of the rivers. This forest continued about a mile, the surface of the land level but rough, being covered with stones or fragments of rocks, and very large, smooth pebbles of various shapes and sizes, some of ten or fifteen pounds weight: I observed on each side of the road many vast heaps of these stones, Indian graves undoubtedly.*

After I left the graves, the ample vale soon offered on my right hand, through the tall forest trees, charming views, which exhibited a pleasing contrast, immediately out of the gloomy shades and scenes of death into expansive, lucid, green, flowery fields, expanding between retiring hills, and tufty eminences, the rapid Tanase gliding through, as a vast serpent rushing after his prey.

My winding path now leads me again over the green fields into the meadows, sometimes visiting the decorated banks of the river, as it meanders through the meadows, or boldly sweeps along the bases of the mountains, in surface receiving the images reflected from the flowery banks above.

Thus was my agreeable progress for about fifteen miles, since I came upon the sources of the Tanase, at the head of this charming vale: in the evening espying a human habitation at the foot of the sloping green hills, beneath lofty forests of the mountains on the left hand, and at the same time observing a man crossing the river from the opposite shore in a canoe and coming towards me, I waited his ap-

---

*At this place was fought a bloody and decisive battle between these Indians and the Carolinians, under the conduct of general Middleton, when a great number of Cherokee warriors were slain, which shook their power, terrified and humbled them, insomuch that they deserted most of their settlements in the low countries, and betook themselves to the mountains as less accessible to the regular forces of the white people.

proach, who hailing me, I answered I was for Cowe; he entreated me very civilly to call at his house, adding, that he would presently come to me.

I was received and entertained here until next day with the most perfect civility. After I had dined, towards evening, a company of Indian girls, inhabitants of a village in the hills at a small distance, called, having baskets of strawberries; and this man, who kept here a trading house, being married to a Cherokee woman of family, was indulged to keep a stock of cattle, and his helpmate being an excellent house-wife, and a very agreeable good woman, treated us with cream and strawberries.

Next morning, after breakfasting on excellent coffee, relished with bucanned venison, hot corn cakes, excellent butter and cheese, sat forwards again for Cowe, which was about fifteen miles distance, keeping the trading path which coursed through the low lands between the hills and the river, now spacious and well beaten by travellers, but somewhat intricate to a stranger, from the frequent collateral roads falling into it from villages or towns over the hills. After riding about four miles mostly through fields and plantations, the soil incredibly fertile, arrived at the town of Echoe, consisting of many good houses, well inhabited. I passed through, and continued three miles farther to Nucasse, and three miles more brought me to Whatoga. Riding through this large town, the road carried me winding about through their little plantations of Corn, Beans, &c. up to the council-house, which was a very large dome or rotunda, situated on the top of an ancient artificial mount, and here my road terminated. All before me and on every side, appeared little plantations of young Corn, Beans, &c. divided from each other by narrow strips or borders of grass, which marked the bounds of each one's property, their habitation standing in the midst. Finding no common high road to lead me through the town, I was now at a stand how to proceed farther; when observing an Indian man at the door of his habitation, three or four hundred yards distance from me, beckoning me to come to him, I ventured to ride through their lots, being careful to do no injury to the young plants, the rising hopes of their labour and industry; crossed a little grassy vale watered by a silver stream, which gently undulated through; then ascended a green hill to the house, where I was cheerfully welcomed at the door, and led in by the chief, giving the care of my horse to two handsome youths, his sons. During my continuance here, about half an hour, I experienced the most perfect and agreeable hospitality conferred on me by these happy people; I mean happy in their dispositions, in their apprehensions of rectitude with regard to our social or moral conduct. O divine simplicity and truth, friendship without fallacy or guile, hospitality disinterested, native, undefiled, unmodifyed by artificial refinements!

My venerable host gracefully and with an air of respect, led me into an airy, cool apartment; where being seated on cabins, his women brought in a refreshing repast, consisting of sodden venison, hot corn cakes, &c. with a pleasant cooling liquor made of hommony well boiled, mixed afterwards with milk; this is served up, either before or after eating, in a large bowl, with a very large spoon or ladle to sup it with.

After partaking of this simple but healthy and liberal collation, and the dishes cleared off, Tobacco and pipes were brought; and the chief filling one of them, whose stem, about four feet long, was sheathed in a beautiful speckled snake skin, and adorned with feathers and strings of wampum, lights it and smoaks a few whiffs, puffing the smoak first towards the sun, then to the four cardinal points, and lastly over my breast, hands it towards me, which I cheerfully received from him and smoaked; when we fell into conversation. He first enquired if I came from Charleston? if I knew John Stewart, Esq., how long since I left Charleston? &c. Having satisfied him my answers in the best manner I could, he was greatly pleased; which I was convinced of by his attention to me, his cheerful manners, and his ordering my horse a plentiful bait of corn, which last instance of respect is conferred on those only to whom they manifest the highest esteem, saying that corn was given by the Great Spirit only for food to man.

I acquainted this ancient prince and patriarch with the nature and design of my peregrinations, and that I was now for Cowe, but having lost my road in the town, requested that I might be informed. He cheerfully replied, that he was pleased I was come in their country, where I should meet with friendship and protection, and that he would himself lead me into the right path.

After ordering my horse to the door, we went forth together, he on foot, and I leading my horse by the bridle; thus walking together near two miles, we shook hands and parted, he returning home, and I continuing my journey for Cowe.

This prince is the chief of Whatoga, a man universally beloved, and particularly esteemed by the whites for his pacific and equitable disposition, and revered by all for his exemplary virtues, just, moderate, magnanimous and intrepid.

He was tall and perfectly formed; his countenance cheerful and lofty, and at the same time truly characteristic of the red men, that is, the brow ferocious, and the eye active, piercing or fiery, as an eagle. He appeared to be about sixty years of age, yet upright and muscular, and his limbs active as youth.

After leaving my princely friend, I travelled about five miles through old plantations, now under grass, but which appeared to have been planted the last season; the soil exceeding fertile, loose, black, deep and fat. I arrived at Cowe about noon. This settlement is esteemed the capital town: it is situated on the bases of the hills on both sides of the river, near to its bank, and here terminates the great vale of Cowe, exhibiting one of the most charming natural mountaneous landscapes perhaps any where to be seen; ridges of hills rising grand and sublimely one above and beyond another, some boldly and majestically advancing into the verdant plain, their feet bathed with the silver flood of the Tanase, whilst others far distant, veiled in blue mists, sublimely mounting aloft with yet greater majesty lift up their pompous crests, and overlook vast regions.

The vale is closed at Cowe by a ridge of mighty hills, called the Jore mountain, said to be the highest land in the Cherokee country, which crosses the Tanase here.

On my arrival at this town I waited on the gentlemen to whom I was recommended by letter, and was received with respect and every demonstration of hospitality and friendship.

I took my residence with Mr. Galahan the chief trader here, an ancient respectable man, who had been many years a trader in this country, and is esteemed and beloved by the Indians for his humanity, probity, and equitable dealings with them; which, to be just and candid I am obliged to observe (and blush for my countrymen at the recital) is somewhat of a prodigy; as it is a fact, I am afraid too true, that the white traders in their commerce with the Indians, give great and frequent occasions of complaint of their dishonesty and violence: but yet there are a few exceptions, as in the conduct of this gentleman, who furnishes a living instance of the truth of the old proverb, that "Honesty is the best policy"; for this old honest Hibernian has often been protected by the Indians, when all others round about him have been ruined, their property seized, and themselves driven out of the country or slain by the injured, provoked natives.

Next day after my arrival I crossed the river in a canoe, on a visit to a trader who resided amongst the habitations on the other shore.

176

After dinner, on his mentioning some curious scenes amongst the hills, some miles distance from the river, we agreed to spend the afternoon in observations on the mountains.

After riding near two miles through Indian plantations of Corn, which was well cultivated, kept clean of weeds, and was well advanced, being near eighteen inches in height, and the Beans planted at the Corn-hills were above ground; we left the fields on our right, turning towards the mountains, and ascending through a delightful green vale or lawn, which conducted us in amongst the pyramidal hills, and crossing a brisk flowing creek, meandering through the meads, which continued near two miles, dividing and branching in amongst the hills. We then mounted their steep ascents, rising gradually by ridges or steps one above another, frequently crossing narrow fertile vales as we ascended: the air felt cool and animating, being charged with the fragrant breath of the mountain beauties, the blooming mountain cluster Rose, blushing Rhododendron, and fair Lily of the valley. Having now attained the summit of this very elevated ridge, we enjoyed a fine prospect indeed; the enchanting Vale of Keowe, perhaps as celebrated for fertility, fruitfulness and beautiful prospects, as the Fields of Pharsalia or the Vale of Tempe; the town, the elevated peaks of the Jore mountains, a very distant prospect of the Jore village in a beautiful lawn, lifted up many thousand feet higher than our present situation, besides a view of many other villages and settlements on the sides of the mountains, at various distances and elevations; the silver rivulets gliding by them, and snow white cataracts glimmering on the sides of the lofty hills; the bold promontories of the Jore mountain stepping into the Tanase river, whilst his foaming waters rushed between them.

After viewing this very entertaining scene, we began to descend the mountain on the other side, which exhibited the same order of gradations of ridges and vales as on our ascent; and at length rested on a very expansive, fertile plain, amidst the towering hills, over which we rode a long time, through magnificent high forests, extensive green fields, meadows and lawns. Here had formerly been a very flourishing settlement; but the Indians deserted it in search of fresh planting land, which they soon found in a rich vale but a few miles distance over a ridge of hills. Soon after entering on these charming, sequestered, prolific fields, we came to a fine little river, which crossing, and riding over fruitful strawberry beds and green lawns, on the sides of a circular ridge of hills in front of us, and going round the bases of this promontory, came to a fine meadow on an arm of the vale, through which meandered a brook, its humid vapours bedewing the fragrant strawberries which hung in heavy red clusters over the grassy verge. We crossed the rivulet; then rising a sloping, green, turfy ascent, alighted on the borders of a grand forest of stately trees, which we penetrated on foot a little distance to a horse-stamp, where was a large squadron of those useful creatures, belonging to my friend and companion, the trader, on the sight of whom they assembled together from all quarters; some at a distance saluted him with shrill neighings of gratitude, or came prancing up to lick the salt out of his hand, whilst the younger and more timorous came galloping onward, but coyly wheeled off, and fetching a circuit stood aloof; but as soon as their lord and master strewed the crystaline salty bait on the hard beaten ground, they all, old and young, docile and timorous, soon formed themselves in ranks, and fell to licking up the delicious morsel.

It was a fine sight: more beautiful creatures I never saw; there were of them of all colours, sizes and dispositions. Every year, as they become of age, he sends off a troop of them down to Charleston, where they are sold to the highest bidder.

Having paid our attention to this useful part of the creation, who, if they are under our dominion, have consequently a right to our protection and favour, we returned to our trusty servants that were regaling themselves in the exuberant sweet pastures and strawberry fields in sight, and mounted again. Proceeding on our return to town, continued through part of this high forest skirting on the meadows: began to ascend the hills of a ridge which we were under the necessity of crossing; and having gained its summit, enjoyed a most enchanting view; a vast expanse of green meadows and strawberry fields; a meandering river gliding through, saluting in its various turnings the swelling, green, turfy knolls, embellished with parterres of flowers and fruitful strawberry beds; flocks of turkies strolling about them; herds of deer prancing in the meads or bounding over the hills; companies of young, innocent Cherokee virgins, some busy gathering the rich fragrant fruit, others having already filled their baskets, lay reclined under the shade of floriferous and fragrant native bowers of Magnolia, Azalea, Philadelphus, perfumed Calycanthus, sweet Yellow Jessamine and cerulean Glycine frutescens, disclosing their beauties to the fluttering breeze, and bathing their limbs in the cool fleeting streams; whilst other parties, more gay and libertine, were yet collecting strawberries, or wantonly chasing their companions, tantalizing them, straining their lips and cheeks with the rich fruit.

The sylvan scene of primitive innocence was enchanting, and perhaps too enticing for hearty young men long to continue idle spectators.

In fine, nature prevailing over reason, we wished at least to have a more active part in their delicious sports. Thus precipitately resolving, we cautiously made our approaches, yet undiscovered, almost to the joyous scene of action. Now, although we meant no other than an innocent frolic with this gay assembly of hamadryades, we shall leave it to the person of feeling and sensibility to form an idea to what lengths our passions might have hurried us, thus warmed and excited, had it not been for the vigilance and care of some envious matrons who lay in ambush, and espying us, gave the alarm, time enough for the nymphs to rally and assemble together. We however pursued and gained ground on a group of them, who had incautiously strolled to a greater distance from their guardians, and finding their retreat now like to be cut off, took shelter under cover of a little grove; but on perceiving themselves to be discovered by us, kept their station, peeping through the bushes; when observing our approaches, they confidently discovered themselves, and decently advanced to meet us, half unveiling their blooming faces, incarnated with the modest maiden blush, and with native innocence and cheerfulness, presented their little baskets, merrily telling us their fruit was ripe and sound.

We accepted a basket, sat down and regaled ourselves on the delicious fruit, encircled by the whole assembly of the innocent jocose sylvan nymphs: by this time the several parties, under the conduct of the elder matrons, had disposed themselves in companies on the green, turfy banks.

My young companion, the trader, by concessions and suitable apologies for the bold intrusion, having compromised the matter with them, engaged them to bring their collections to his house at a stipulated price: we parted friendly.

And now taking leave of these Elysian fields, we again mounted the hills, which we crossed, and traversing obliquely their flowery beds, arrived in town in the cool of the evening.

WHITE MOUNTAINS

William O. Douglas

We are old friends—the White Mountains and I. They are mostly New Hampshire's, though their eastern edge lies in Maine. The bulk of them—about 680,000 acres—are in the White Mountain National Forest. The White Mountains—50 miles or more in depth and width—are rounded and heavily forested, except for the domes. The ridges are undulating and now and then severely notched. They have over eighty lakes or ponds, most of which have fish. Mount Washington (6288 feet) is the highest peak and the best-known. Mount Carrigain (4680 feet) is closer to the center of the range. There are forty-six peaks over 4000 feet high; and the area is threaded with about 1700 miles of trails, many of which are too steep and rocky for burros, not to mention horses.

For many Summers I fished the dark blue waters that lie in the wooded valleys south of the mountains. Lake Wentworth was one of my favorites. It is today one of the best small-mouthed-bass ponds in New Hampshire. I knew it so well I could find my way across it in a fog without striking a reef. After months of searching, I found the deep springs where the bass congregate on hot days. Sunapee was another familiar friend. The flashing of one of its golden trout coming to the surface through waters teeming with fingerlings had the brilliance of sunsets. As I traveled this lake country I kept seeing the peaks of the White Mountains to the north. Those distant views were like magnets. I turned to them, hiking the lower ridges, where the white pines and red maples grow, and falling in love with the wild tumble of mountains that are northern New Hampshire.

The Great Stone Face I knew as a boy from books. Later I saw it from Franconia Notch and from the steep trail that leads through Eagle Notch to the Greenleaf Hut (4288 feet), constructed by the Appalachian Mountain Club. The Great Stone Face—now secured by bolts and cables against collapse—shows serenely on calm, bright days in Profile Lake. I came on intimate terms with Chocorua peak—sharp-pointed and standing in splendid isolation above an azure lake by the same name. I liked to lie on the edge of meadows lined with wild blackberries and brightly dotted with tall yellow cinquefoil, violets, and Indian paintbrush, and watch fleecy white clouds pass over Chocorua.

East and northeast weather is apt to bring rain that lasts three days. Violent storms often come from the south and southwest. While hiking the ridges, I learned that when thunder seems to come from all directions, a severe electrical storm has arrived and it's time to go for cover *at once*. Electric storms that break over these mountains send forked fingers into the woods and bring torrential rains. The clearing winds come out of the west or northwest. They make up into great blows with fresh and bracing air. Cumulus clouds race overhead, providing spectacular backdrops.

The valleys and lower ridges—once filled with white pine, balsam fir, and red spruce—were heavily logged last century and this. The hardwoods came in after the logging, and by the time I first explored the lower woods, maples, beech, yellow birch, and paper birch were dominant. The understory is not dense. Blister sedge is often knee-high along the trails. Deeper in shade are skunk currants and blueberry bushes. A large percentage of the ground cover is made up of ferns—hay-scented ferns, lady ferns, and long beech ferns. The aspen (which is known locally as popple), the striped maple (moosewood), mountain ash, scarlet elderberry, and hobblebush leave an open effect. The brooks that tumble over granite boulders have nothing but clear, cold water that one can drink to this day. There are trout in their pools. Willow, alder, and maples often lock limbs to cover the streams, making it difficult for a fly fisherman. Yet one who likes to use his arms as well as legs in walking can do so safely in these mountain ravines. There are no rattlesnakes to worry about, and only an occasional garter snake.

The banks of the creeks in June are thick with bright bunchberries (Canadian dogwood). In open places the white petals of wild raspberries are on display and, less conspicuous, those of the cloudberry

(*Rubus Chamaemorus*). Tiny white bluets appear in unexpected places. Shaded banks are robed with oxalis, whose shamrock-shaped leaves, when crushed, are excellent for removing pine or fir resin from the hands. And the granite rocks are almost always thickly covered with soft moss.

Patience and unhurried exploration of the ravines and ridges are necessary if one is really to know the White Mountains. There is always some rich reward—an eastern brook trout in a white-water pool; a white mat of tiny sandwort; a patch of the yellow mountain avens standing in isolated splendor. It may be paper birches against the dark green of balsam and spruce, with a blue sky overhead. Those who know the north woods associate whitebark birch with other bright memories—bass, pickerel, and trout; trees dripping after a rain; blueberries on an open slope; the swish of paddles in dark water; loons calling after a storm; the crackle of a yellow-birch fire; and tall tales over a campfire. A hairy woodpecker is at work on a beech. The call of a red-eyed vireo is heard in a ravine. The song of the hermit thrush rises above the roar of a falls. There are Virginia deer and black bear in these woods. Beaver, once almost extinct, came back with the hardwoods. The fisher—fierce member of the weasel family—roams these woods, looking for its choice food—the porcupine; and when that animal is in short supply, it turns to red squirrels, chipmunks, and grouse. The fisher is apparently approaching its golden age. Once there were so many porcupines in and around Pinkham Notch, it was called "Porky Gulch." Today one seldom sees a porcupine. Red squirrels also seem to be on the decline. One June when George Hamilton, of the Appalachian Mountain Club, Paul Doherty, of New Hampshire's Conservation Department, and I hiked the 50-odd miles from Wildcat range, overlooking Carter Notch in the east, to Lonesome Lake above Franconia Notch in the west, we heard no squirrels and saw but one.

I had known the White Mountains some years before I climbed Mount Washington. Even in Summer its rounded dome is usually hidden in clouds. It is the place where our nation's worst storms brew. One bright October day when I took the Raymond Path out of Glen House, there was not a single cloud. Mount Washington towered 4000 feet above me. The maples were red, the birch yellow, the beech bronze. Every leaf was turned; not a one had fallen. The woods were silent; not a breath of air stirred. Never had I seen the north woods so brilliant. It must have been the kind of day Thoreau wrote about.

"I do not see why," he said, "since America and her autumn woods have been discovered, our leaves should not compete with the precious stones in giving names to color."

The Raymond Path is a long, swinging one of gentle grade that eventually comes into the Tuckerman Trail, not far below the present shelter. I went up the massive head wall at the end of Tuckerman Ravine that rises almost sheer for about 1200 feet. This great cirque gouged out by some ancient glacier is usually heavy with snow into June. This October day there was no snow; and only a trickle of water was coming down. The mountain ash, paper birch, and mountain alder that grow there were bright and gay. As I climbed, I reached the zone where all trees are dwarf. Balsam and spruce were hardly three feet high. Dwarf birch made streaks of bright yellow against the dark evergreens. The tiny mountain cranberry was in fruit; and I saw a few tiny bilberries. Loveliest of all was a mountain ash, hardly two feet high, that was turning port. When I topped the head wall and came to the barren rock fields that stretch up to the summit, a strong wind was blowing. The balsam fir and black spruce were prostrate and spread out into thick flat mats. There were black spiders among the granite boulders. I saw one junco in a stand of balsam; and I heard more calling. On Bigelow Lawn—the rocky slope on the south flank of Washington—the wind picked up in velocity. It had the sting of sleet and snow in it, although the day was bright. I stopped to rest as I began the final 300-foot climb to the top. Bigelow Lawn is a mass of polygons. Some call them frost boils. The working of frost, the freezing and thawing of water, pushes and moves the rocks. They end up forming polygons. Some polygons may have nothing but bare soil in the center. The more developed ones have a center of sedges, grasses, or rushes. At times the crowberry, mountain cranberry, and bilberry take possession. I was to learn on later trips that this austere and wind-blown slope can produce an arctic garden that is bright and gay. This October it was dull and drab. The wind was a gale; I almost lost my hat. In a few minutes I was chilled through, for I was dressed too lightly for Mount Washington weather.

I had known that there was a cog railroad up the west side of Washington, finished in 1869, and an auto road up the east side, finished in 1861. I also knew there was a restaurant and hotel there. But I was not prepared for the shock I experienced on my arrival. A man who was 50 pounds overweight and smoking a cigar greeted me and cast aspersions on my character for walking up, when there were commercial enterprises which, for a fee, could have saved me the effort. At least a hundred other people were inside the Summit House. I went among them, visiting and talking about the mountain. Not a one of them had walked up. Not a one knew about the polygons on Bigelow Lawn, or cared about the mountain cranberry, prostrate black spruce, or dwarf bilberries that work hard to survive in this bit of the arctic transplanted in New Hampshire.

I was sad as I retraced my steps down the mountain. These people seemed to be little interested in the world around them. They had little concern for the earth which held so many secrets it had become sacred to me. Those people represent the America that had grown soft and flabby and overfed and perhaps a bit callous.

It was dusk when I reached my car. A strong wind was now whirling colored leaves. The chill of Fall was in the air. As I drove south I put the White Mountains behind me. The crowd on Mount Washington that had come by car and train made me turn my back. Years passed before I returned; and my return made me realize how much I had missed in the intervening years. For when I came back I put the cog railway and auto road aside, turned to peaks other than Mount Washington, and learned that the White Mountains have some of the best hiking trails in America.

Some are long, swinging ones that lead up the ridges. Others come up the valleys or ravines to mount a head wall or follow wild, broken terrain, dropping 1000 feet, only to regain them after many ups and downs. However one travels, there are several zones to traverse—the hardwood forests sprinkled with red spruce and balsam fir that usually lie under 3500 feet; the next 1000-foot zone, where the slopes are thick with dwarf birch and mountain ash standing head-high; and the alpine zone above 4500 feet, where prostrate black spruce, balsam fir, birch, mountain ash, willow, and many arctic plants grow. These zones are only approximations, as they vary on different slopes, depending on wind and moisture.

The great cirques that mark the White Mountains are in the dwarf-birch and mountain-ash zone. They are glacial products—bowl-shaped basins and deep, round-bottomed valleys with semicircular, precipitous head walls. The continental glaciers coming down from the northwest reached high on the Presidential Range. There are still striae to be seen. Many smooth, rounded knobs, known as sheepbacks, were shaped by the glaciers. Some ledges are capped by perched boulders brought from distant parts. Many of these were probably deposited from the slow-melting ice sheet after it had lost its motion. Smoothly polished pebbles of whitish quartzites and drab slates were brought from faraway places and deposited high in the White Mountains. All indications are that the glaciers were at least 5000 feet thick. Some glaciers were probably valley glaciers, not part of the continental ice sheet. Some cirques—like King Ravine on the north of Mount Madison—are filled with granite debris. Rocks as large as houses provide obstacles for the hiker. Trails go around and over these rocks. Sometimes there are subterranean trails that wind under them. Deep caves (both in King Ravine and in Carter Notch) retain snow and ice all Summer long. The air from these caves is a cool, refreshing updraft on a warm day.

Granite rocks in the hardwood zone are moss-covered. In the dwarf-birch zone the lichens take over. Gray ones—that are very slippery when wet—are impregnated in the rock. The gray lichens are soon joined by yellow ones, black ones, and red ones, until near the top the whole rock field is gay. There are flaky black ones known as "tripe of the rocks." One of the brightest is a gray lichen known as reindeer moss (Cladonia rangiferina) often growing in other moss.

Many kinds of warblers and thrushes call as one walks the lower woods in June. Juncos, ruffed grouse, and spruce grouse are higher in the dwarf-birch and mountain-ash zone. The farther one climbs, the more he hears the purple finch—New Hampshire's state bird—and the white-throated sparrow. On one hike the fog had moved in so thickly as we reached the top that I could not see my companions, George T. Hamilton and Paul Doherty, at a distance of 25 feet. But through the fog came the fast, lively notes of the purple finch, and, even louder, the song of the white-throated sparrow, saying as plain as can be, "Old Sam Peabody, Peabody, Peabody."

Timber line is never higher than 5500 feet in the White Mountains, and usually lower. The tops have only prostrate trees that supply little wood for the camper. One who sleeps out must bring his own fuel, shelter, and warm clothes. For great storms come all of a sudden on these ridges, changing pleasant 70° temperature to freezing or even lower. Summer temperatures range from 20° F. to 71° F. on the summits; and Summer winds mount as high as 100 miles an hour. In recent years, winds 150 miles an hour or more have been recorded at the weather observatory atop Mount Washington. The highest wind ever recorded blew 234 miles an hour on that mountain. That was on April

12, 1934. The reason for these high winds is, apparently, the sheer eastern wall. East winds hit the summit without having been slowed down by any intervening peaks. These low temperatures and high winds have caused people to die of exposure. When fog is added, the mountains become treacherous. Then it is easy to miss the cairns that mark the trails and to end up lost and facing the danger of death by exposure or by falling over cliffs. The Appalachian Mountain Club has seven huts, managed by George T. Hamilton and spaced at convenient intervals across these mountains. The huts have lessened the risks of the range and increased the pleasures of hiking. The Appalachian Mountain Club and the Forest Service also have over fifty shelters in the White Mountains, lean-tos or cabins in sheltered areas and close to good water. The huts, however, furnish dormitories as well as food for those who want to travel light.

The first of these huts was built at Madison in 1888; and it is called Chez Belle by the hut men. It is my favorite hut because of the refuge it offered when, dead tired, I first saw it on a foul night. By the 1930s six others were either built or acquired. By the 1960s the seven were furnishing about 7000 lodgings during the Summer months. They open in mid-June and close in mid-September. They are manned by high school and college men, carefully selected for physical fitness and qualities of leadership. Only a few positions are open each year, as hut men usually return Summer after Summer. The senior is hut master who posts a roster of work each day. Everyone takes turns cooking, cleaning, and washing dishes. Every hut man packs supplies from a base camp up the mountain to the hut, making several trips a week. Fifty to 70 pounds is the normal pack at the start of the season. As the hut men get into condition, the packs increase in weight—80 pounds being normal. At Madison the Valleyway Trail rises 3600 feet in 3.6 miles. Bringing a pack of 100 pounds up in three hours is good time. In the 1960 season a new record was set at Madison: an average of 96 pounds per trip. At Greenleaf, where the trail rises 2700 feet in 2.5 miles, Bill Emerson of Concord (Massachusetts) High School brought up a load of 166 pounds in four and a half hours. It is not unusual for hut men to pack in nearly a ton of supplies during a season. Burros supplement the hut men and help at peak periods. But during a season the hut men bring up nine tenths of all supplies.

The list of ex–hut men is a distinguished one—Thomas G. Corcoran, Washington, D.C., lawyer; Edmund Ware Smith, *Ford Times*; De-long Monahan, Providence Mutual Life Insurance Company; Robert Monahan, Dartmouth College; George Campbell, Baltimore & Ohio Railroad Company; Grosvenor Campbell, U.S. Steel Corporation; Dr. Arthur Watkins, Boston General Hospital; Dr. Millett Morgan, Dartmouth College; Dr. Richard Hodge, Western Reserve Medical School; Dr. Stuart K. Harris, Boston University, are a few of them.

Hut men, past and present, have been a happy, wholesome lot with a unique *esprit de corps*. The ordeal of back-packing is a challenge. There is a satisfaction in doing the impossible and making it to the top under a great load on one's own. An unofficial proposal was made to eliminate all packing by substituting helicopters. I talked with hut men about it. At Madison I discussed the problem with Doug Kirkwood, who then was finishing college at Middlebury. He shook his head at the idea of helicopters.

"Then the romance would go out of the huts," he said. "Backpacking brings a deep sense of achievement."

I knew what he meant. It was the old story of man against the mountain—a contest won by heart and will power alone. Yet I think there is more to it than that. G. M. Trevelyan has a line that fits the young man's mood. "And to the young who have no pain, who have not yet kept watch on man's mortality, nature is a joy responding to their own, haunting them like a passion." All who have done backpacking in the mountains know that there is a reward understandable only in terms of romance. Those are bright moments that march with the man from his youth to old age.

Three of the huts—Madison (4825 feet), Lakes of the Clouds (5000 feet), and Greenleaf (4288 feet)—lie above the tree line and know the full force of the storms. They are also often wrapped in fog for days at a time. The trails leading to them are marked by rock cairns closely placed and topped, wherever possible, by a piece of white quartz that is apt to show through the foulest weather. Lakes of the Clouds offers the best prospect for botanizing, as the arctic wildflowers seem to flourish with sphagnum moss in the damp areas between this hut and nearby Mount Monroe. The Lakes suffers, however, from its proximity to Mount Washington. Autos and the railroad bring people to the summit; and the Lakes, which lies 1000 feet lower, to the south, is an easy hike of not much over a mile. Yet the Lakes fills up with hikers too and, businesswise, is the busiest.

Madison and Greenleaf are much more difficult to reach. One who rides to the summit of Mount Washington has a good six-mile hike along the sky line before he comes to Madison. En route he skirts Jefferson (5715 feet), Adams (5798 feet), and Madison (5563 feet)— all barren, rocky, and wind-blown. Two other huts—Carter (3600 feet) and Lonesome (2743 feet) that are about 50 miles apart—are located on lakes where square-tail trout cruise. Like Zealand (2700 feet) and Galehead (3800 feet), they are in the timber zone. Black spruce, paper birch, and mountain ash fringe those mountain gardens. Carter Lake is one of the highest bodies of water in New England that has trout and, as this is written, the second highest in the eastern states that has beaver.

The varying hare, white in the Winter and brown in the Summer, is on some of the ridges. Colored butterflies seem to be everywhere. The alpine barrens are filled with botanical wonders. In June the tiny mountain cranberry (cowberry) is apt to have some of last year's fruit to offer the inquisitive. Some top areas show mostly sedges and rushes. Others—better protected from the wind—have several varieties of grasses. The spring beauty and blue violets are found in damp spots. The goldthread (so named for its long bright yellow rootstocks) shows delicate white petals. Alpine saxifrage and the cassiope or heather show tiny white flowers. Solomon's seal is present, and a close kin known as twisted stalk. Club moss in the shape of tiny pine trees grows in damp places. Mountain heath, *Phyllodoce coerulea*, shows purplish, urn-shaped flowers. A dwarf shadbush grows in high areas, as do the Greenland sandwort and several species of dwarf willow that are low and thickly matted. The willow leaves are minute; only the white fluffy catkins, hardly an inch long, make it familiar. In damp spots there is bog kalmia with leathery leaves, *Kalmia polifolia*, a miniature form of the swamp laurel common in the Cascades. Its star-shaped flowers are reddish-purple. On foggy days its neatly cupped blossoms are filled with dew. The anthers on some are bent back and held by their tips in pits in the petals. When an insect disturbs the anthers they whip up, spraying the intruder with pollen. Sphagnum moss is thickly matted in moist spots. Alpine flowers favor it as a seedbed. An exciting discovery is the wine-leaf cinquefoil (*Potentilla tridentata*), a tiny white sprite flourishing in dampness. Even more colorful are pinkish-white beds of arctic diapensia (*Diapensia lapponica*) hugging the ground and sometimes covering the lee side of rocks with a thick mantle.

I learned on my wanderings along these alpine barrens that the White Mountains have some of the arctic plants that I met in the Brooks Range of northeast Alaska.

On one moist shoulder I found cotton grass, *Eriophorum opacum*, cousin to that I had known in Alaska.

Near the Lakes of the Clouds I found the *Rhododendron lapponicum*, or rosebay, that paints the Brooks Range cerise. Here were the selfsame low-bush blueberries that I had found in Alaska—the cowberry and the bog bilberry too.

These soils on the ridge tops of the White Mountains, like arctic soils, are low in nitrogen. These ridges, like the arctic, do not have the warmth of the sun necessary to convert chemicals into protoplasm. Even summer temperatures are low. Though thick fogs lay over the ridges, making them very moist, winds that are cold and whistling dehydrate plants faster than they can absorb water from the soil. Since arctic conditions are duplicated, arctic plant life flourishes.

Sedges grow better than grass on the more exposed slopes. Blueberries creep up on the lee side of rocks. The hard-cutting wind turns their branches back when they reach the edges of the rocks as if it were a mower.

All prostrate plants on top the Presidential Range face disaster in Winter if the snow does not cover them. When they lay exposed, they get frostbitten and desiccated. Most of the water escapes through small openings in the undersurface of the leaves. Labrador tea has a mat of hair over the undersurface of its leaves which helps slow up the loss of water. The leaves of some plants have edges that are rolled to cover the undersurfaces. Others are not so well protected. One skimpy layer of snow may set the growth back thirty years or more. This is marginal land for plant growth. The ecological balance is delicate. The Presidential Range, like the arctic, is a fragile domain that needs man's tender care.

One night when I was at the Lakes of the Clouds, I went out on the slopes of Mount Monroe with Paul Doherty to watch the sun set over Bretton Woods in the distance. With a map, Paul helped me realize how deeply indebted this generation is to earlier generations of professors from Harvard, Massachusetts Institute of Technology, and Tufts, who made this range their laboratory. They formed the Appalachian Mountain Club and were its early leaders. The trails, cols, ravines, and slopes are named mostly for them. They were the first to discover the ceaseless wonders of this bit of the arctic transplanted in New England. It was their interest in the marvels of nature, their reverence for God's creations, that largely made this a dedicated place.

As I was busy examining the dainty pinkish bloom and tiny leaves of the cowberry (*Vaccinium Vitis-idaea*), the wind suddenly picked up and reached gale proportions. It had the chill of frost and ice in it. No man dressed as lightly as I was could have lived very long in that blast. That night I first appreciated why unsuspecting people have died of exposure on Summer days atop the Presidential Range and how useful the A.M.C. hut system is.

While there are great sights to behold and interesting discoveries to make on the wind-blown slopes of the Presidential Range, the wooded ridges and ravines have the most powerful pull on me. They were all lumbered at one time or other. No matter the pitch of the slopes, logging roads traversed them at long, gentle grades. The outline of those old roads—tier on tier—can be seen on many of the hillsides, in spite of the new growth that has taken possession. There is a great regenerative power in New England. Precipitation, sunshine, and temperatures combine to reproduce ground cover quickly. The softwoods—spruce, fir, and hemlock—are generally the climax forest at the higher altitudes. But generalizations are dangerous. The softwoods come in where the soil is skimpy or not well drained. The hardwoods—birch, beech, maple—need rich soil that is well drained. As one sits on a ridge, viewing the broad expanse of rounded ridges and soft gentle valleys, it is apparent that there are not many zones where softwoods begin and hardwoods end. There generally is a mixture that adds variety and zest to the trails.

The section between Crawford Notch on the east and Franconia on the west is for me a wonderland. The trails are strictly up and down. Altitude slowly gained is quickly lost; the descent is no sooner finished than a new ascent is made. One who starts the day at 3600 feet and ends at 3800 feet will climb, in all, 3000 feet or more. There are pieces of trails as smooth as garden walks. They are, however, the exception. White Mountain trails are often sheer steps, where balsam fir or birch are the handrails. Their roots are treacherous footing when wet. The roots of the birch seem more gnarled, more tenacious, more firm than any of the others. When I see them, I think of the lines of Edgar A. Guest:

> Man thinks he knows what nature wills.
> But much he plants the winter kills,
> While far away from human care

And on a cliff by storms swept bare,
Denied the commonest of needs,
A birch tree silently succeeds!

The granite rocks are covered with blankets of moss sufficiently thick and moist as to make excellent seedbeds. Seeds germinate there, forming seedlings that for years can be as easily plucked from the moss as a carrot can be pulled from the garden. Given time, the tree sends its roots over the granite rock and down on several sides. The mature tree has the entire rock in its grasp, its roots embracing it tightly. There are tree frogs and toads in abundance where the ground is moist. As one climbs, he finds stands of mazzard cherry (*Prunus Avium*), and if he comes in mid-June, they usually are in bloom. Various species of the serviceberry make streaks of white against the delicate greens of late Spring. Mountain maple are shaped into a lovely shrub. As the black spruce diminishes in size, it seems to acquire distinction. Perhaps it is due to the tiny purple cones that now are conspicuous and give the tree the quality of royalty.

The lower woods are filled with meadow rue that in places grows nearly knee-high. It is known locally as quicksilver, by reason of its silvery sheen when submerged in water. It has tiny purple flowers, some upright, some drooping, depending on the sex. The starflower seems ever-present. It is a bright forest sprite. We have its cousin in the Cascades. The White Mountain species is *Trientalis borealis*. The slightly pointed leaves are five to ten in number. From the center of the leaf whorl rises a simple six-petal white flower. This flower that loves moisture and shade is a constant June companion in the lower woods.

The higher trails in June are lined with bunchberry, which hug the ground, making great white scatter rugs. The dwarf red blackberry (*Rubus pubescens*) is an occasional companion. On shady trails the Canada bead-ruby (*Maianthemum canadense*) grows, showing a delicate raceme of white flowers above two bright waxy leaves. Here are masses of tiny white bluets and, in lesser quantities, the white-starred cucumber-root medeola, named after Medea, the sorceress, for its imagined medicinal virtues. The coarse orange hawkweed with its hairy stems (sometimes called devil's paintbrush) and a large-leafed plant called Indian poke are constant companions. The white bloom of the broadleaf meadowsweet spirea (*Spiraea latifolia*) seems to be everywhere. The bead lily (*Clintonia borealis*), with greenish-yellow flowers, appears in unexpected places. With it grows the painted trillium.

Labrador tea appears higher up among the rocks, its creamy-white blossoms brightening acres of granite. The mountain cranberry, with tiny waxen leaves and pinkish blossoms, keeps it company. The yellow mountain avens brightens moss-covered granite ledges.

One who hikes these trails in June risks wet weather. But the thick beds of bunchberry, the sedate bead lily, and the showy Labrador tea make mile after mile bright and gay even on dark days.

By mid-June the grouse have hatched their young. The spruce grouse is a lovely creation in mottled reddish golden-brown. White shows when the tail is opened. There are red marks over the eyes. On one hiking trip, George Hamilton and I once had a spruce-grouse hen charge us over and again while her chicks found cover. Then she took to the woods, and in a few minutes we heard her calling her brood much as a chicken does. The birds are numerous in the Zealand-Galehead area. The purple finch and white-throated sparrow are almost constant companions. The Winter wren is present. Warblers and robins serenade. The haunting song of the hermit thrush is heard over and over. Occasionally a Bicknell's thrush offers a solo. Juncos and black-capped chickadees scold. The hairy woodpecker stakes out his domain. The northern yellowthroat and cedar waxwing add to the chorus.

Deer tracks are conspicuous. Bobcat scat is common, and occasionally the print of his paw is as distinct as handwriting. Once Paul Doherty and I thought we saw the track of the fisher. We were not certain, however. These fierce hunters are hard to see; and they apparently avoid the traveled trails.

The White Mountains are rich in sphagnum moss, and the wonders it works are evident in the shallow ponds. Eagle Lake, about three miles from Franconia Notch and just below Greenleaf hut, is such a place. The water at no place is over six feet deep, and water lilies cover the bottom in the shallower portions. Sphagnum moss flourishes along the shore line. This matriarchal moss retains a lot of water and forms a seedbed for many flowers—orchids, pitcher plants, sundews, cotton grass. It is glorious moss that fashions a floating shelf which moves forward a little every year. As the shelf grows thicker and firmer, bog bilberries, bog kalmia, and other members of the heath family come in and form a thick mat. Before long the floor is firm enough to permit spruce and fir to grow in dwarf form. Thus sphagnum moss starts the cycle that converts water into land.

While I had seen sphagnum moss all the way from Alaska's Brooks Range to Maine's Mount Katahdin, it was in the White Mountains that I learned what a blessing sphagnum moss can be to the hiker. One June day George Hamilton and I were hiking from Galehead to Greenleaf. The first part of the trip—to Garfield and down to Garfield Pond—had an abundance of drinking water. Small creeks were cold and crystal-clear. Elizabeth Spring had water 38° F. As we climbed Mount Lafayette I discovered one of the loveliest of God's creations. Water dripping over moss-covered granite at the base of paper birches formed a trail-side pool lined with bunchberries in bloom and fringed with moss. A pink lady's-slipper, mirrored in the water, stood in solitary splendor. Goldthread, rooted in sphagnum moss, formed a small white mat. The creeping pearlberry—with alternate oval leaves—sent long streamers through the moss. This pool held no more than a few gallons. Yet it showed the full glory and grandeur of New Hampshire. It had the music of falling water, the freshness of wet moss, the splendor of delicate flowers, the restful greenness of the northland.

This was our last drinking water. Now the trail headed up the northern ridge of Mount Lafayette. Not a breath of air stirred. Black flies appeared in numbers. Our packs weighed heavily this hot afternoon. Shortly before we left the timber we stopped by a gigantic granite boulder to rest. The rock wore a thick mantle of sphagnum moss. No water was in sight. But a handful of the moss, when squeezed, produced a cupful. We thoroughly doused our heads and necks. The cool water was as refreshing as a shower. My old friend—sphagnum moss— did me a new favor this warm, windless day.

The White Mountains, which offer unique hiking trails in a unique wilderness, are the solace and comfort of three million people today. The number who will turn to them, seeking refuge from civilization, will increase in the years immediately ahead. Today the White Mountains are within a day's drive by car for over forty million people. By the end of this century that number will double, and the trails, ponds, shelters, campgrounds, and huts will be increasingly used. With our mounting population, every ridge, every crag, every wooded ravine will have increased value.

Great conflicts are in the making. Industry—which once cut every square mile of these majestic woodlands—is waiting for the cycle of growth to be completed. The machines are waiting to chew up the new forests, especially those machines that make pulp out of wood and by their stench make some places in northern New Hampshire almost unlivable. The wheels of factories must turn to keep life coursing in the veins of our complex society. Yet people do not live by bread alone. They need the great sanctuaries of the hills if they are to be kept whole. Long-range planning with a view to the health as well as the employment of people must be made. Today the White Mountains can be ravished by the machines or preserved as wilderness, depending on the will of the men in the Forest Service. None of these valleys and ranges is preserved by law for recreation alone or for industrial use alone. The Forest Service operates under the motto of "multiple use." Dedication of each section of land to as many uses as possible is a constructive policy so far as many areas go. But if applied to some sections it means the end of the woodland wilderness. In the old days, cutting of lumber was mostly a Winter operation, the logs being taken out on narrow-gauge railroads or rivers. Today lumbering operations are on a different scale. Bulldozers permanently deface a valley or hillside; and the permanent roads that are built become arteries of travel and highways of erosion. To cut a section of land today means its perpetual dedication to uses which can be served by the automobile. Forestry and picnic grounds, forestry and campgrounds are therefore compatible. But roads are the antithesis of wilderness. There is none where roads and autos penetrate. There is no wildness where the roar of motors is heard.

Preservation of wilderness often means a *single use*, exclusive of all others. Lyle F. Watts, former Chief Forester, was among the first to proclaim that there will be times when an area must be "devoted to one dominant use," including wilderness preservation. And Congress, in the Multiple Use Act of 1960, stated, "The establishment and maintenance of areas of wilderness are consistent with" its notions of multiple use. Yet the idea of "multiple use," as sometimes applied by the Forest Service, is at war with keeping inviolate the bits of wilderness that remain in our national forests.

These days the Forest Service states that "Wilderness is a recognized and important use of national forest law." But it is often niggardly in putting the concept into effect. The primitive areas, where saws, axes, and roads are barred, are usually confined to the peaks and basins above the line where merchantable timber grows. There are exceptions. In the White Mountains the Forest Service has set aside *one* area where no roads and no cutting can take place. It is known as the Great Gulf. One sees the Great Gulf best from Mount Jefferson. It lies

2500 feet below the trail. It is a deep, bowl-like wooded ravine, with Spaulding Pond near its head—a pond that Paul Doherty has stocked with trout. It is thickly wooded, untouched by man, pristine in beauty and wonders. A wild or wilderness area that is established by the Forest Service gives some assurance of administrative protection. But their boundaries do not protect them against mining. The line marking the boundaries does not protect a wilderness area against dams or reservoirs. The Forest Service has no power to prevent those projects from being constructed. The wilderness area offers no protection for wild life. The Forest Service has no control over wild-life populations. That power is vested in the states.

The Forest Service has dedicated men making plans for the White Mountains. Lee Kelley is one; Richard Goodrich is another. I have been with them on the trails; they know the spiritual values in these mountains; they know that dollars are not all-important. Yet Forest Service men come and go. Some unconsciously favor the lumber interests. Since they may go with those companies on retirement, they are not going to alienate those interests in their early years. Moreover, their education has emphasized, not conservation and recreation, but the conversion of God's wilderness into board feet of lumber.

Forestry schools, in their curricula, place their greater weight on the commercial aspects. The usual product of a forestry school is known as a "saw log forester." There are exceptions. But the emphasis in forestry education is underlined by the fact that about three fourths of the graduates enter the lumber industry. Finally, the wild areas and primitive areas established by the Forest Service can be reclassified and opened to commercial projects by a decision within the federal bureaucracy. What is classified as wilderness today can be logged tomorrow—if a few men in Washington, D.C., so decide.

The oncoming generation will inherit either wilderness or mountains chewed up by machines, depending on the social philosophy and outlook of a few men in the Forest Service. This is not right. Those who love wilderness as man's refuge need more protection than the whim or caprice of a bureaucracy. The sacred precincts should be locked and barred against all machines and against all encroachments by civilization. They need to be protected, not by mere administrative orders that can be changed at will, but by laws as enduring as we can make them.

The heart of the White Mountains need this protection. Even with most of this area saved and set aside, there will be hardly room enough in the decades ahead for all who want to lose themselves in the tangled wildwood and search out the mysteries of life in the sphagnum moss of the deep woods.

Paul Doherty, George Hamilton, and I were discussing this problem as we left Madison Hut by the Valleyway Trail that leads to Randolph. After we had dropped 1000 feet on a rocky trail, portions of which are built like a staircase, we came to a mixed forest, now seventy years or so old, where hemlock and spruce are reaching kingly proportions alongside of yellow birch, rock maple, and beech as handsome as man could desire. The forest was so lush that the boughs locked overhead. A few beams of direct sunshine reached the forest floor, but not many. The woods were lighted indirectly. A soft emerald glow infused them and gave an air of mystery to this sanctuary.

Paul stood by a beech, fondling it as a man would a horse or a dog he loves. This beech was a lovely creation. This is the tree that once furnished nuts for the great flocks of passenger pigeons which filled our skies. Beech bark was one of the earliest writing materials man used. Our word "book" derives, indeed, from the Anglo-Saxon "beece," for beech. Virgil put the tradition in these words:

> Or shall I rather the sad verse repeat
> Which on the beech's bark I lately writ?

The one we stopped to admire had nobility. Its gray bark ran to every branchlet. This was a tree of elegance and grace—a true patrician of the north woods. Paul ran his hand over its smooth bark and said, "It would be a crime to turn the loggers in here."

"People need these woods as badly as they need the wind-swept tops," George added.

The entire wilderness problem had been neatly summed up in those simple words. These two outdoorsmen made articulate what is unexpressed in the minds of millions of people who also love wildness for the music and wonders it provides and the skill with which it unravels care. Yet if our wilderness values are to be saved and perpetuated, all those of like mind must make conservation a great passion in their lives and become organized and vocal. They must be prepared to oppose the most powerful lobbies that Washington, D.C., has ever known.

$\mathcal{B}$ELLY OF THE $\mathcal{I}$NDIAN

Sue Marsh

$\mathcal{S}$heep Mountain. The Sleeping Indian, to people in Jackson Hole. A long block of limestone unraveling under the Wyoming sky, the mountain looks uncannily like a sharp-nosed chief in a Mutual-of-Omaha war bonnet, lying flat on his back with his arms folded over his chest. Among mortals, a sense of expectation stirs as he dozes with one ear cocked toward the rising sun. Someday the Sleeping Indian may wake and walk among us.

From the Sleeping Indian, a horizon full of mountains unfolds, ridge upon ridge of transparent blue. This is how the world once looked, a wild and tumbled land. As a Jackson Hole landmark, the high massif of Sheep Mountain is second only to the Teton Range. When I return from journeys its outline tells me I am home. But a nickname like the Sleeping Indian attempts to blunt the mountain's fearsome spires. It suggests a familiarity and gentleness that is not there.

In the summer of 1996, the ungentle Indian made its claim on an Air Force cargo plane. With another two hundred feet under their wings, the crew would have escaped.

A month before the plane crashed, I left behind the sultry heat of July and climbed five thousand feet into the Sleeping Indian's coat-snapping wind. There I crawled through turf and talus to photograph ground-hugging wildflowers: three-inch mats of forget-me-not with flowers like startled violet eyes; a council of alpine sunflowers with out-sized heads saluting the sunrise; a cascade of purple saxifrage, with long-tongued trumpets draped across knots of tiny leaves. The dark

199

rocks where the flowers grew ticked quietly around me as they warmed under the sun. Eye-level with the ladybugs, I pressed my belly against the belly of the Indian. The stones shifted slightly and short grasses flattened beneath me. For a moment, the mountain and I changed contours, each to fit the other.

There are many ways to climb the Sleeping Indian. A hunter's trail scales the south side. Abandon the trail at the highest fringe of whitebark pines and follow the boulder-strewn trace of a rivulet. The slope levels off into a ramp of shattered dolomite where no wildflower or willow grows higher than a hand. When you reach the widest bulge along the crest, you are standing on the belly of the Indian.

This is where the plane crashed.

One morning after the disaster, I walked to the park north of Jackson and stared across the valley to the Sleeping Indian. It was near the end of August and the mountain's alpine tundra was cured to a brassy tan. A smudge like Lenten ashes ran up its beveled grade. In the early haze the scar might have been only a vague shadow, except I knew there was nothing up there to cast a shadow—no ravine or cliff on that broad, golden slope. I wanted to look away, but the scar kept tugging at my gaze. My eyes worried it like my tongue would probe a broken tooth. The size and shape of a football field, it looked like a big trap door. I imagined the door falling open at the plane's approach, giving to a secret passage Was the C-130 still flying around in the belly of the Indian like a moth inside a lampshade?

The Sleeping Indian, stony guardian of the Gros Ventre Range, cradle of alpine flower, foil for wind and catcher of early snows, now wore the brand of death. Nine strangers who never saw the wildflowers had become a part of it. The night the plane crashed, the moon was new and the stars were blotted by smoke from distant forest fires. To the pilot the Sleeping Indian was only another blank sector of the sky until the trap door in its belly yawned open.

One evening I came home to find a bulging burlap sack on the front porch. Because I worked in the national forest that included the Sleeping Indian, a friend thought I'd want to know what she had found. A note read, "Multiply this by a thousand. It's a mess up there."

I opened the parcel. It was filled with charred paper and torn metal. I pulled each of the larger pieces out and arranged them in a row as if on an examining table, and took inventory. A government-issue cardboard box, five by six inches. Its plain black lettering read: BATTERY, NON-RECHARGEABLE LITHIUM/SO$_2$, ITEM #BA-5590/U. 1 EACH.

Manufactured in July of 1992; due for testing the following August. The box, unopened, was still inside its unscorched plastic wrapper. The battery was gone. In a plastic sleeve I found the table of contents for a pre-flight checklist. Missing from the list was this: Watch for Indians made of stone, which might toss in their sleep or reach into the sky to grab unsuspecting aircraft.

Most of the other items I could only identify by comparing them to something familiar. A scrap of woven fiberglass mesh. It looked like the kind my husband draped over the blades of our canoe paddles to reinforce them. A three-inch square of green plastic honeycomb. It looked like a coarse pot scrubber. A twisted shard of heavy-gauge aluminum, painted battleship gray on one side and lime-green on the other. It looked like . . . No familiar object came to mind, only the sad remains of a wrecked airplane.

I cradled the flotsam, artifacts from a grave. Unlike the routine litter of plastic Coke bottles and beer cans I packed out of the wilderness, these scraps begged for consecration. They did not belong to me. But I didn't want to take them back and put them on the mountain, where perhaps they most belonged. With the solemnity of laying a wreath on the earth, I lowered them into the garbage.

A valley legend claims the Sleeping Indian stirs once every hundred years. The last time, in 1925, fifty million cubic yards of rock flew down the north slope to create Slide Lake. On the day when I lay taking pictures against the belly of the Indian, I imagined a heartbeat deep within the mountain. Was it just a loose rock shifting under my weight, or did the Indian stir again, restless for a sojourn?

Before the plane crash, I believed I knew the Sleeping Indian, with its familiar twists of trail, its flowered incline leading to the sky. But I am limited by my senses and a trained, rational mind. These feeble tools tell me the mountain is not really an Indian asleep, but a block of limey sediment that formed on the ocean floor eons ago, turned to stone, and heaved itself eleven thousand feet above the sea. Such a story is no less fantastic than that of a sleeping mountain that wakes every hundred years. But it is science, the religion of our times. Under its influence I am like the blind man with the elephant, aware of one view of the world, insisting that is all there is to know.

But there is more to know. We repeat its legends and predict the weather by its moods. We lay our own narratives at its feet, of walks and wildflowers, of metamorphism and orogeny, of evenings spent

201

watching the war bonnet glow like an ember in the setting sun. Now we have added the story of miscalculation and sudden death. The mountain does not discriminate among these tales; it gathers all of them into its secret trap doors.

The Sleeping Indian is more generous than I am. I resist the story of death now superimposed upon the wildflowers and sunsets, memories that once seemed to make the mountain mine. I will never look at it the way I did before thirty thousand gallons of jet fuel burned all night where the Arctic willows grew, before the Air Force helicopter lifted off the mountain in a cloud of dust, carrying the largest piece of wreckage away—the airplane's tail.

Even now that the black scar has healed and the trap door has closed, the mountain holds the story. That certain Douglas fir with a strip of bark six inches wide peeled away by lightning, the outcrop where bright clumps of Draba splash sun-yellow across the limestone, the whitebark pine grooved by a bear's claws—they all comprehend the change. Where that rivulet choked by dark talus leads to the ridge from the trail, my eye will scan the bare slope above, drawn by the knowledge I wish I did not have. But only a few scorched patches of willow remain. Buttercups bloom around them. Twisted scraps of metal are already buried in the mountain turf, as if the Indian wished to consume the evidence.

The lingering scent of jet fuel betrays the crash site. My nose brings information that does not track with what I see from the Sleeping Indian, and the first whiff of it makes me glance around— what's this? But there is nothing out of place. Off to the north, the tilted hills of rust and lavender fan away from the Gros Ventre River. The ripples on Blue Miner Lake glint like a shattered mirror from behind a fringe of trees far below. The smaller, higher lakes, tucked under the pinnacles of the mountain's north face, are pools of turquoise devouring slabs of ice. The Tetons cut the usual ragged skyline to the west and mats of alpine flowers bloom underfoot. There is no tale among my cherished stories of this mountain to explain the smell.

Jet fuel on a mountaintop, a dizzying, sickening stench, writing a new chapter in the story of the Sleeping Indian. It feels as though the mountain has been taken away from me, my stories erased. It feels as though the mountain has agreed to this. I realize the mountain was never mine at all.

Still I persist in my quest to make the mountain mine, to describe it in ways that make it seem less fearsome. The new, unwelcome chapter reminds me I have failed. How do I go on living in such a world, where a mountain with an affectionate nickname can become a poster of death and reek of jet fuel years later? How do I find hope and optimism and faith in the coming day? There is just this: I watch that mountain. I abide with it and follow its familiar paths, watch the same light that falls across its face at sundown evening after evening, year after year. Eventually I see the scorched scars healing, its buttercups multiplying, the willow growing back. The smell of jet fuel is fainter than it was the year before.

Tragedies come and go, while the mountain endures. Through stories I grasp for a thread of that durability, as if tying them to something as permanent as the Sleeping Indian will save me from my own tragic end. But the mountain evades my grasp. Sometimes it wakes and shifts. It allows the tale of untimely death to settle in beside stories of beauty and inspiration like a patch of saxifrage in a talus slope.

I know one face of the Sleeping Indian, the one described by science and natural history. I want to know the one that waits to waken, to brush itself off and stand, its limestone war bonnet shedding talus, its trap doors falling open. I once felt the mountain's heartbeat as I lay in a carpet of purple saxifrage. If I could so easily believe the sea floor lithified and thrust itself into the sky, why not believe the Indian had hidden an airplane in its pocket? Why not believe it could get up and walk away?

Now it is October, month of the Hunter's Moon, month of summer passing into winter. On the spine of a low, bare ridge a squall whips at my back, vanguard of the first winter storm. At the farthest knob, the ridge drops away into the canyon of Flat Creek. Sheltered in a cluster of square boulders, I gaze across a mile of vacant air to the frost-encrusted Indian. It wraps itself in snow, ready to sleep through winter like a bear. I watch for signs of wakefulness, but the mountain turns out to be only a mountain after all. Just as I glimpse the Indian of legend, the one that might stir at any moment, it settles into a deep and permanent sleep.

Mist brims over the canyon of Flat Creek and shrouds the knuckled ridge where I stand. It fills my lungs with its thick, cold breath. It rises and spreads until it wraps the world, all except a final band of sunlight that clings to the mountainside above.

The valley disappears under the storm, but on the belly of the Indian the patch of light remains. It falls across that high, wild slope, a searchlight homing in on the trap door where the plane crashed. The light grows brighter, defiant against the spinning shreds of cloud that close around it like a cat's eye. I pull my gaze away and turn into the wind toward home.

I hurry along the ridge, then I glance over my shoulder one last time. The Indian is gone.

Thinking Like a Mountain

Aldo Leopold

A deep chesty bawl echoes from rimrock to rimrock, rolls down the mountain, and fades into the far blackness of the night. It is an outburst of wild defiant sorrow, and of contempt for all the adversities of the world.

Every living thing (and perhaps many a dead one as well) pays heed to that call. To the deer it is a reminder of the way of all flesh, to the pine a forecast of midnight scuffles and of blood upon the snow, to the coyote a promise of gleanings to come, to the cowman a threat of red ink at the bank, to the hunter a challenge of fang against bullet. Yet behind these obvious and immediate hopes and fears there lies a deeper meaning, known only to the mountain itself. Only the mountain has lived long enough to listen objectively to the howl of a wolf.

Those unable to decipher the hidden meaning know nevertheless that it is there, for it is felt in all wolf country, and distinguishes that country from all other land. It tingles in the spine of all who hear wolves by night, or who scan their tracks by day. Even without sight or sound of wolf, it is implicit in a hundred small events: the midnight whinny of a pack horse, the rattle of rolling rocks, the bound of a fleeing deer, the way shadows lie under the spruces. Only the ineducable tyro can fail to sense the presence of absence of wolves, or the fact that mountains have a secret opinion about them.

Aldo Leopold

My own conviction on this score dates from the day I saw a wolf die. We were eating lunch on a high rimrock, at the foot of which a turbulent river elbowed its way. We saw what we thought was a doe fording the torrent, her breast awash in white water. When she climbed the bank toward us and shook out her tail, we realized our error: it was a wolf. A half-dozen others, evidently grown pups, sprang from the willows and all joined in a welcoming mêlée of wagging tails and playful maulings. What was literally a pile of wolves writhed and tumbled in the center of an open flat at the foot of our rimrock.

In those days we had never heard of passing up a chance to kill a wolf. In a second we were pumping lead into the pack, but with more excitement than accuracy: how to aim a steep downhill shot is always confusing. When our rifles were empty, the old wolf was down, and a pup was dragging a leg into impassable slide-rocks.

We reached the old wolf in time to watch a fierce green fire dying in her eyes. I realized then, and have known ever since, that there was something new to me in those eyes—something known only to her and to the mountain. I was young then, and full of trigger-itch. I thought that because fewer wolves meant more deer, that no wolves would mean hunters' paradise. But after seeing the green fire die, I sensed that neither the wolf nor the mountain agreed with such a view.

Since then I have lived to see state after state extirpate its wolves. I have watched the face of many a newly wolfless mountain, and seen the south-facing slopes wrinkle with a maze of new deer trails. I have seen very edible bush and seedling browsed, first to anaemic desuetude, and then to death. I have seen every edible tree defoliated to the height of a saddlehorn. Such a mountain looks as if someone had given God a new pruning shears, and forbidden Him all other exercise. In the end the starved bones of the hoped-for deer herd, dead of its own too-much, bleach with the bones of the dead sage, or molder under the high-lined junipers.

I now suspect that just as a deer herd lives in mortal fear of its wolves, so does a mountain live in mortal fear of its deer. And perhaps with better cause, for while a buck pulled down by wolves can be replaced in two or three years, a range pulled down by too many deer may fail of replacement in as many decades.

So also with cows. The cowman who cleans his range of wolves does not realize that he is taking over the wolf's job of trimming the herd to fit the range. He has not learned to think like a mountain. Hence we have dustbowls, and rivers washing the future into the sea.

We all strive for safety, prosperity, comfort, long life, and dullness. The deer strives with his supple legs, the cowman with trap and poison, the statesman with pen, the most of us with machines, votes, and dollars, but it all comes to the same thing: peace in our time. A measure of success in this is all well enough, and perhaps is a requisite to objective thinking, but too much safety seems to yield only danger in the long run. Perhaps this is behind Thoreau's dictum: In wildness is the salvation of the world. Perhaps this is the hidden meaning in the howl of the wolf, long known among mountains, but seldom perceived among men.

Magic at Ruth Lake

Rick Bass

I'm going to tell you about some mountains in northern Utah.

But first, you've got to promise never to visit them. They're my mountains; I adopted them. They are the most majestic mountains in America—the wildest, freest, coldest, oldest, windiest, mountain wildflowerest, mule deerest mountains there are.

Fittingly, they run north–south, the way other North American mountain ranges run. To the north lies a great green sprawl of northern coniferous forests, and beyond that the haze of Wyoming wheatgrass prairie. Beyond that, a few more insignificant rocks, rivers, and mountains such as the Tetons, the Snake, and the Yellowstone, and beyond that, Canada.

The closer you get to Canada, the more things'll eat your horse.

I tell you what—I'll do this. I'll tell you how to get to these mountains if you promise not to ever go up there while I'm visiting them. I live in Mississippi, wretched Mississippi (the "M" stands for "Mosquitoes"), and I only get up there three times a year. They are a huge mountain range; with work, there is room for both of us. I drive an orange Volkswagen Rabbit. If you see it parked by the side of the road, keep moving and don't look back. Pretend you never saw it. Natty Bumpo says git.

Except that sometimes I do this: in times of financial liberty, I fly into Salt Lake City (coach fare) and rent a car (subcompact) and drive into the mountains in the little red rent-a-car. Sometimes it is blue, though. Once it was yellow.

I pick the brightly colored little rent-cars because they stand out so well against the violet sky once I get above treeline, once I get up into the tundra and alpine meadows above 12,500 feet.

So I will do this: so that you will know it is my car, so that you can steer plenty clear of me, I'll put a pretty fair-sized rock on the hood of the car. A rock that you cannot help but see. It will be like an old Indian signal, like a trail sign: Do Not Enter.

I'll put an old rag under the rock so it doesn't scratch the paint.

Now I'll tell you about my adopted mountains. They cover many thousands of square miles, and have places in them with names like this: Moon Lake, Laughing Coyote Uplift. Wolf Tooth Creek, Spirit Lake, and the Lost Elk Caves. Lake of the Gods, and the Screaming River. Blue Hole.

Spirit Lake is, I suppose, as good a place as any to fall in love with someone.

Thunderstorms are spectacular and beautiful up in the jagged rocky peaks. They get about two per year.

They are the oldest mountains our country has; if we—and I'm considering getting a bill started in Congress—ever decided to have a National Mountain Range, this would have to be them. They're Precambrian, before Life; they've almost always been here.

Also, there's lots of bald eagles. Hiking down a narrow rushing stream, sometimes you spook them up out of dead trees. They fly off with great strong wingbeats. It is really something you should see, the way they fly.

There are a lot of dead trees up high in this mountain range. Big, dead trees, as if size and strength and age are no insurance against the winters.

I am presently trying to learn to use understatement in my writings. I believe this is a good point to practice.

Winters are harsh.

The only way into these mountains is through one of two roads. One gravelly frost-heaved road gingerly and innocently skates its way up through the western quarter of the range, going (most of the time) north–south. The other one delicately skirts the northern boundaries.

It, too, is a two-laner. It's a bad place to have a busted water hose, a bad place to have a flat. There are no gas stations, there are no cafés. There is nothing that is not beautiful.

I've been up there and been snowed on in July, and August. Snowed on hard.

The two little skeins of roads that lead into the area usually close up in early November, but sometimes late October. The area sleeps undisturbed, protected under a sheet of snow and ice for as many as seven to eight months each year. It seems to me that all this ice and snow and beauty sleep preserves it, and resculpts it a little, and makes it a little more awesome each spring.

Except that spring sometimes does not come until the Fourth of July.

And yes, it does have glaciers.

It is mind-boggling to pick up a slab of rock and find in it an ancient brachiopod, a fossil of one of the earliest, most primitive sea creatures ever known, and realize that these mountains in the heartland of the United States of America were once a coastline.

Sometimes, it really makes me quite dizzy.

There's got to be a strange and long-lost history about the place; sometimes, working my way through a narrow niche in a sheer cliff wall between two wild and empty valleys, threading my way down a talus slope as a snow-dusting August storm comes rolling in low and foggy, rolling in to meet me, then sometimes I will begin crying for no reason. A terrible sadness wrenches from me, and I have to get away from the place and down to one of the meadows below me before the feeling is gone.

Other times, I start to laugh almost uncontrollably. I lean back against a tree in one of the forests and feel the rough hard texture of the bark pressing against my back and the warm forest pine straw beneath me, and for many minutes the woods will roar with great hearty booming laughs: my laughs. Laughs the likes of which Jackson, Mississippi, has never heard.

They are magic mountains.

You would not believe the alpenglow in the evenings.

The sunrises are pretty neat, too.

Once, while hiking down a dark and narrow corridor of a game trail, with dense tall sweet-smelling Doug firs and blue spruce on either side, and little mountain primroses for a carpet beneath me, I looked up to see someone standing in the trail ahead of me. In the shadows. It was just a silhouette.

Only it wasn't a someone; it was a doe mule deer. I stopped, and then walked closer. She did not run.

I got to within thirty or forty yards of her before she turned and ran down the trail.

I do believe it was the first time she had ever seen a human.

There are lots of good things about these mountains, but the best are the lakes.

There are lots of lakes.

Little lost slipper-sized things, they are cold and blue and clear and have lily pads around the shore and lots of fish in them.

The fish are quite tasty. The water is delicious. In November, when snow clouds come rolling in in the mornings, you can sit down on the shoreline, crouched behind a boulder or a tree, and see ducks, mallards mostly, come whistling in to splash down on the lakes.

From September to April there is ice on the ponds. Halloween weekends are the best; they are almost always frozen over by then, with a good smooth soft white blanket of snow to boot, and it is fun to go tramp words out in the middle of one of the little lens-shaped lakes. There is just one after the other after the other—they lie in chains, one- to ten-acre depressions in the glacial slickrock, usually at the base of steep cirques and cliffs.

I once spent two weeks in the summer traveling from lake to lake, fishing with spoons and spinners. I came out of the woods on the east end of the range sunburned, bearded, and twenty pounds heavier, and still I had not resolved which way I liked Utah trout best: broiled on a hot flat rock, or deep fried in bacon grease for breakfast. Toward the end of the trip I ran out of bacon grease; it was a shame, too, because I had almost been ready to make my decision.

It is clear to me that my only option is to go back and try it again. Start from scratch. I will bring more bacon grease this time.

I mentioned that these are magic mountains. They are. The rocks are magic, the lakes are magic, the wind and snow and trees are magic . . . they will all talk to you, if you listen right.

A farm boy from Indiana, of all places, taught me to listen. He was a friend of Ken's and mine, my first year up at school, up at Utah State. I had applied to U.S.U. because it was the campus closest to the mountains I had seen in the movie *Jeremiah Johnson*.

He had applied to U.S.U. because once he had gone fishing for an afternoon in one of the little mountain lakes while driving cross-country through the area with his cousin. Surely you will agree with me that it takes a great deal of magic to do that, to make a farmboy from Indiana and a city boy from Texas apply to a school two thousand miles away from home just because of a one-day fishing trip and a two-hour movie, respectively.

Once they get into you, they are as jealous as a lover; they will never let you look at other mountains again, and you will never want to.

When you are away from them, they will be all you think about. Weeks, months, even years will be measured in terms of how long you've been away, and how long it is till you return.

Now you see why I am hesitant to give you their name. Their beauty is a curse as well as a blessing. No one ever forgets them.

The farm boy's name was Rob. Rob Samuelson. His family was from Sweden, and he said *ja* instead of yeah. He had played basketball for the state high school 4-A champions in Indiana and could carry a seventy-five-pound backpack up a steep trail all day long and then sing songs around the campfire until dawn. He played the guitar. His favorite food was Dinty Moore beef stew. He would actually giggle whenever he smelled it cooking, simmering in the campfire, with fir branches snapping and aspen logs popping at night.

Also, I forgot to tell you this about these mountains: at night, there are more stars over them than anywhere else in the world, it is a fact. A tall man can jump up and almost reach them. Rob used to try, quite often.

"Too much Dinty Moore," I would tell him when he missed. He weighed 245 pounds.

We were freshmen, and had been in Utah three days when we made our first trip into the, into these, mountains. We drove up maple-studded Logan Canyon, wound around royal blue Bear Lake, breezed down into the dusky sage country of southwestern Wyoming, and suddenly, there we were, at the north entrance.

They sprawled across the southern horizon like a jagged chain of bluish snow-tipped biceps. Big biceps.

We stopped the car and got out and looked at them. We were still fifty miles off, and they looked huge. It was cold and still out; it was evening, and there was chill in the air. There was no traffic. We watched them, stunned, as if waiting for them to do something—move toward us to greet us? break into song and dance? take a bow?—but when they did not, we got cold and got back in the car and hurried on.

Once we reached the forested regions and started up the switchbacks, we zipped up our down jackets to stay warm and rolled the windows down so we could smell the trees.

Surely our mere graduating from high school did not merit this reward; there had to be some catch. We were incredulous. A herd of mule deer, all does, ran across the road in front of us, panicked, darted back off the road, and ran along the woodline beside us for a while, wild-eyed, before slipping back into the woods.

It was the first time in my life I had ever seen mule deer; I could not believe my good fortune. It was like a graduation present, like a much-thought-over birthday gift. I was eighteen.

No one should live to be eighteen without seeing these mountains. It should be a national law.

We drove past little turnouts for trucks and sightseers; we groaned up peaks and idled down passes. There were no side roads, no logging roads, just wild country, and mountains, and lakes.

Grandaddy Lake. Mirror Lake. Lost Pine Lake.

Ruth Lake. ¼ Mile.

We stopped at the Ruth Lake trail. It was getting late. There was a place by the wooden trail sign that was big enough for two or three cars to pull off onto; there was a ridge. The cliffs behind us, on the other side of the road, were beginning to glow. It frightened me; I thought something was wrong with them.

I had never seen alpenglow before.

We chocked the car tires with rocks and slipped our packs on and hurried up the trail like prisoners let out of jail. We did not look back.

When you visit these mountains, bring a down coat or parka, and gloves, and heavy socks and a ski cap, no matter what time of year it is.

The ground felt hard and frozen under our boots; our breath came in shallow bursts of exhaled cloud vapor, and our nostril hairs froze together when we inhaled. It was turning colder; the sun was going down. The air tasted delicious. I felt quite dizzy; quite giddy. I felt like I never wanted to leave these mountains.

Ahead of me, Rob hurried along the trail. He was in a hurry to get to Ruth Lake. He had not eaten since lunch. He had a whole case of Dinty Moore beef stew in his pack.

I'm not even going to tell you how beautiful Ruth Lake was, you wouldn't believe it. We came around a corner and suddenly there it was, in the middle of the forest. A cow elk and calf on the other end of the lake looked up in alarm and whirled and galloped off across a little meadow before disappearing into the trees. Long after they were gone we could still hear timber crashing and hooves striking rock.

It was not a big lake, but standing beside it, we felt tiny. We were awed by its beauty, not its size. A cold wind was gusting across the water, dancing toward us; it made our noses tingle and our cheeks flush. Rob took his pack off and began scouting for firewood. There was plenty to be found. There are lots of live trees in these mountains, but there are a lot of dead ones too.

It is a very old place. The Precambrian outcroppings are at least two billion years old. We sat down in a grove of trees by the lake's edge and listened to and smelled the stew simmering, and listened to the breezes, and watched the lake, and for a little while, the stars. It was very cold. Coals would pop and crackle, and sparks would float up into the night. The stew was good. After we had finished it we watched the fire and talked about what we were going to study. When we went to bed, the stars were gone; there were gray slippers of clouds tumbling down out of the taller mountains like frost-fog boiling out of an open freezer. When we woke up in the morning, it was snowing. I went bonkers. I had never seen snow before.

Rob was playing basketball that year, and I football; we had to be back by noon. He packed while I ran around in the snow and threw snowballs and slid in it and ate it and kicked it like sand. Then we hiked out. There was fog everywhere; it was still snowing.

There were lots of animal tracks out. I took care not to step in them. The tallest of the late-season meadow flowers poked up through the snow. I guessed there to be a foot of snow on the ground. Rob said it was an inch and a half. I fell down several times.

It was sunny and dry back down in the valley, back on campus; no snow had fallen. No one believed us when we told them it had snowed up in the mountains.

Of course, if anyone had asked us how to get to Ruth Lake, we would have given them the wrong directions.

We were already making plans for next week.

I've been all over northern Utah since then, all over these mountains in all types of seasons and weather: the Upper Fork of the Weber River, discovered by trapper Pete Skene Ogden, that lucky devil, and other places too.

Jim Bridger used to live in these mountains, over on the eastern flanks, near where Fort Bridger used to be. And there's King's Peak, the highest point in Utah—13,528 feet. I've been to all of these places in my adopted mountains, over and over. There's still one thing I always do once each year, though: I always make one special overnight trip to Ruth Lake, and I always pitch my tent down in the trees by the water's edge and build a fire in the same place and watch the lake by moonlight and listen to the wind. I always bring a can of Dinty Moore beef stew and, silently, I toast Rob with a Sierra Club cup full of crystal-cold lake water.

It is still always my best trip of the year.

$\mathcal{V}$OLCANOES

David Rains Wallace

$\mathcal{V}$olcanoes ultimately express the ambiguities that bless and curse the [Central American] land bridge: rich coasts and hurricanes, sheltered valleys and earthquakes. Except for the earthquakes, they make its biggest surprises. Huge cinder cones accumulate in a few generations or blast into nothingness too quickly for flight, and ash deposits from such explosions blanket about 400,000 square kilometers, reaching far out into the Pacific. Fertile with erupted minerals, volcanic soils have supported rich civilizations for over three millennia, but cones provoke an endemic anxiety which seventeenth-century Englishman Thomas Gage expressed in describing two of them, Agua and Fuego: "That of water hanging on the south side, almost perpendicularly over the city; the other of fire standing lower. . . . That of water . . . yields a goodly prospect to the sight, being almost all the year green . . . but the other . . . is unpleasing and more dreadful to behold. . . . Thus is Guatemala seated in the midst of a paradise on one side and a hell on the other."

Central America's highest mountain, 4,220-meter Tajumulco volcano, looms directly east of the high Cuchumatanes, and the two awesome heights form a kind of demon portal for the Pan-American Highway. I passed through this obliviously in 1971, but encountered the active volcanic zone a little farther south, at Lake Atitlán, where an ancient cone has collapsed to form a caldera ringed with basalt cliffs and younger cones. One of my hitchhiking rides called it "the most beautiful place in the world," and it was certainly spectacular, but the thing that struck me about Atitlán was an apparent discrepancy of scale. To my unaccustomed eye, its cones looked more like the rear-projected backgrounds of movies than real mountains. They seemed too high to believe.

Volcanic disasters have been horribly real, however. One of Atitlán's cones exploded ten times in the nineteenth century, and "unpleasing" Volcán Fuego has erupted fifty times since 1524. Girolamo Benzoni described how a landslide and flood from Volcán Agua, the *less* threatening cone Thomas Gage mentioned, destroyed Guatemala's first capitol in 1541. "Soon after midnight there began to arise from that mountain so great and so terrible a quantity of water and with such an impetus and fury, as to precipitate rocks of incredible size, carrying along and destroying whatever it met with in its course; and there were heard in the air cries and lamentations and frightful noises." A dose of riding rickety, overcrowded buses around the highlands, and the sense of ever-impending disaster that conveyed, cured my initial incredulity about Guatemalan volcanoes. Perhaps because the country around them is so high and steep, they never seemed safely distant as they might have, however deceptively, on a lowland plain. It seemed they might slide downhill anytime, as they have in the past.

Guatemala's volcanoes are the highest in Central America because they stand on a twenty-million-year-old plateau accumulated as eruptions spewed lava and ash 2,000 meters deep over 10,000 square kilometers. The plateau also covers western Honduras and eastern El Salvador, and I got a sense of its massiveness where it looms above the breezy Salvadoran town of Metapán. Because it isn't near an active fault, Metapán gets fewer earthquakes than most Central American towns, so it has some of the oldest churches. This makes it seem anachronistic, which is typical of the volcanic plateau, a region that remains remote although the Spanish settled it in the early 1500s. With black vultures on its slaughterhouse roof and bats emerging from downtown eaves at dusk, Metapán probably was much the same in 1993 as in 1893.

The peak that marks the plateau's south edge, 2,418-meter Montecristo, has some of El Salvador's last virgin forest and was one of its two functioning national parks when I was there, but getting up it wasn't easy. First I had to walk five kilometers from town to the park entrance because there was no other transportation. Even walking wasn't encouraged, since it had been a guerrilla zone during the recent civil war. When I got to the entrance, I found another reason why walking *to* the park wasn't encouraged. My permit had a provision I'd overlooked: *"No se permiten caminatas dentro del parque"*—no walking in the park. I had to wait until a vehicle would pick me up. Luckily, some meteorologists soon came along on their way to examine a weather station abandoned since the war's beginning, and I got a spine-jarring ride in the back of their pickup with the ranger assigned to accompany them. He had worked in the park before the guerrillas took it over, then had returned, but wasn't happy about the situation. Poaching was common because the staff didn't have the equipment to stop it. The local police poached. When I asked why I couldn't walk in the park, he said it was because of the danger of assault.

As the truck banged up increasingly steep switchbacks of red and white volcanic dust and mud, I was glad I hadn't walked. I'd never have made it in a day. The trees at the top had seemed close from Metapán, but Metapán didn't look at all close from the plateau slopes, in fact, it soon disappeared. Above about 2,000 meters, we were climbing in the clouds. Four kilometers from the station the road got too muddy even for a 4-wheel drive, and we walked the rest of the way through huge, epiphyte-covered trees. Birds I'd never seen before flew among them: bushy-crested jays, dark blue like North American Steller's jays, but bigger, with yellow eyes. They made squeaky, murmuring sounds, stealthily feeding on grubs in the branches. The station was in a steep pasture, but the clouds obscured everything more than a few meters away, so I didn't see the plateau top at all on that trip.

In the rest of northern Central America, volcanoes rise above lower lands, like central El Salvador's Valle de las Hammacas. One cinder cone there, 1,870-meter Izalco, has grown from a cornfield in the last two centuries. A local clergyman told John Lloyd Stephens it had been "a small orifice . . . puffing out . . . pebbles," in 1798. By 1840, it was so high that the fire of its eruptions were visible from far out to sea, a growth that excited Stephens to a semierotic enthusiasm. "The sight was fearfully grand," he wrote. "The crater had three orifices . . . and after a report, deep in the huge throat of the third appeared a light blue vapor and then a mass of thick black smoke, whirling and struggling out in enormous wreaths, and rising in a dark, majestic column, lighted for a moment by a sheet of flame." Izalco kept this up almost continuously until 1957, when entrepreneurs who shared Stephens's enthusiasms built a hotel with bedrooms overlooking it. Then it stopped, although when I saw it in 1993 it remained bare of trees, a gargantuan slag heap above the fields.

Salvador's volcanic past has been even more active. Like Guatemala's Atitlán, its Lake Ilapongo is an ancient caldera whose explosion about eighteen hundred years ago destroyed an area 3,000 kilometers square and expelled the region's population for centuries. Thick layers of pumice called "tierra blanca" cover ruins from that period. A later explosion created a miniature Pompeii at a place called Ceren, entombing a clay-walled farmstead which yielded traces of a flock of domestic ducks and a Maya book. Ilopango remains active, periodically extruding domes that could explode, and more Cerens undoubtedly lie in El Salvador's future. Surrounded by live volcanoes and built on volcanic calderas, its towns made me feel not just under volcanoes, as in Guatemala, but *in* them.

The active zone changes in Nicaragua. Volcanoes there rise from the Depression's level floor and thus seem preternaturally high. When I drove north from Managua one morning in 1993 with Jacinto Cedeño of the Nicaraguan National Park Service, I had to crane my neck to see their tops through his pickup's windshield. Each cone or cluster of cones stood isolated, gargantuan, like a receding file of Goya colossi. One would loom over the horizon, stand obdurately for awhile, then disappear, replaced by another.

Cedeño had invited me along while he did some park business near Cosiguina, the northernmost Nicaraguan volcano, which is also its first nature reserve, established by the Somoza government in the 1950s. Cosiguina is unimpressive now, low and tree-covered, only 870 meters high. In 1836, it stood at almost 3,000 meters when it exploded with the biggest bang in Central American history, which, John Lloyd Stephens wrote, "startled the people of Guatemala four hundred miles off." Just hearing about the explosion excited Stephens to an apocalyptic vision: "The cone of the volcano was gone . . . a mountain and field of lava ran down to the sea; a forest as old as creation had entirely disappeared, and two islands were formed in the sea; shoals were discovered in one of which a large tree was fixed upside down; one river was completely choked up, and another formed, running in an opposite direction . . . wild beasts, howling, left their caves in the mountains, and ounces, leopards, and snakes fled for shelter to the abodes of men."

The country around Cosiguina still looked disaster-stricken. The only modern homesteads were big export *fincas*, apparently abandoned, their fields overgrown with orange sunflowers. Everybody else seemed to live in palm-thatched huts dotted about the savanna.

Cedeño, a portly, patient man, said it was *"tierra maliosa."* The people were withdrawn, distrustful. He'd had come to dispute with a *finca* heir who'd returned from living in England during the Contra War, and wanted some forest land from the government. They argued a long time, standing outside a tumbledown worker's barracks, while orange-chinned parakeets and ladder-backed woodpeckers squabbled in the trees above them.

"La lucha para la tierra," Cedeño sighed, getting back in the truck. The struggle for the land. We drove south again to the beachfront resort of Jiquilillo. I was scouting locations for an ecotourism guidebook, but a *maremoto,* a tsunami, had swept through the resort the year before, and it looked like it. The wave had buried the asphalt beachfront road in a sandbar and stranded houses out in the surf. "This used to be a very popular place," Cedeño said. "Lots of people came out from Managua for the weekend." Smoke billowed from Volcán San Cristobal, the next peak south of Cosiguina, as we continued south toward Managua. A perfect 1,780-meter cone, Cristobal is Nicaragua's highest, and its cap had shone white as snow when we'd driven past it in the morning, but that had been only the mist and smoke that usually hangs there. It glowed red in the twilight. When we stopped for gas in Léon, the station attendant told us there had been an earthquake about an hour earlier, just about when we were driving along the devastated Jiquillio beach. It had been a deep one out at sea, probably the kind that had caused the previous year's tsunami, but we hadn't felt a thing.

Perhaps the most awesome Nicaraguan volcano is the twin one of Concepción and Maderas in Lake Nicaragua. The lake can be as rough and dark as the sea, and the two cones, Maderas black with forest, Concepción gray with cinders, appear fantastically high from its surface. Their scale seems incongruous with the historical world of towns and ferryboats, as though the backdrop for a Jurassic diorama of plesiosaurs and ichthyosaurs has fallen over the horizon by mistake. All I saw in the way of dinosaur relatives while crossing to Omotepe was a flock of cormorants, but they looked antediluvian enough beneath the cones. "The lake is too large to be called beautiful," wrote Thomas Belt, "and its large extent and the mere glimpses of its limits and cloud-capped peaks appeal to the imagination rather than to the eye."

Concepción and Maderas are visible from far to the south in Costa Rica, where their starkness looks even stranger. Southern Central America's volcanic zone, where new oceanic land replaces old continental land, is very different from the north's. Indeed, volcanoes change so quickly below the Costa Rican border that they seem to have a kind of national identity. Compared to Guatemala's lowering cones and Nicaragua's looming ones, Costa Rica's seem amorphous, almost understated, although there is one remarkable exception. The huge cone of Arenal in north central Costa Rica exploded so violently in 1968 that cannonading boulders covered 12 square kilometers with impact craters, and glowing clouds filled the sky. The eruption killed seventy-eight people, and lesser eruptions continued through the early 1970s. When I was in the adjacent Cordillera de Tilaran in the late 1980s, Arenal's occasional rumbles shook the ground like sonic booms.

More typically Costa Rican is Volcán Rincón de la Vieja northwest of Arenal. It looks impressively volcanic from the Guanacaste coastal plain, and has ejected jets of ash as recently as the 1950s and '60s. When I camped at Rincón's foot in 1990, however, the cone seemed to fade into the dense forest that covered its lower slopes, and trees even obscured the fumaroles and other infernal devices that welled up at the base. Living gumbo limbos grew over mudpots that periodically flung boiling glop four meters in the air, and strangler figs enclosed fissures that steamed sulfur like a mineral bath.

The big volcanoes of Costa Rica's Cordillera Central—Poás, Irazú, Turrialba—seem even more cryptic, clumped together in cordilleras so massive that the active craters are obscured. It's not that they aren't dangerous. Volcán Poás near San José expelled an 8,000-meter smoke plume which blanketed most of the Valle Central with ash in 1910, and did similar things in 1952, 1974, and 1978. When I was there in 1990, the farm around it had been declared a disaster area because of poisonous fumes and acid rain. Poás has the potential to become as explosive as Cosiguina. Yet my first sight of its active crater was anticlimactic. One moment, I was walking through a gently sloping meadow of ragwort and blueberry bushes, the next I was standing before what might have been an open-pit sulfur mine dug out of the forested ridge. There were great heaps of yellow ash and steaming green lakes, but less sense that this was an opening to internal fires than in Nicaragua.

Inactive craters seem mere lakes buried in elfin forest, and their cones may be hard to recognize as volcanoes, they are so heavily covered with clouds and plants. At an extinct cone called Volcán Cacao in northwest Costa Rica, I embarrassed myself by referring to some "sandstone" outcrops when talking to a geologist. The brown, granular stone of the outcrops was volcanic ash, of course, not sedimentary sandstone, but in the damp forest it was hard to remember that the mountain had once been smoking and barren. Much of Cacao never has been mapped because continual cloud cover prevents aerial photographs.

I'm not the only one who has been fooled by Costa Rican vulcanism. Early geologist Miguel Obregon thought he'd found an active volcano at a hill called Barra Honda on the Pacific coast's Nicoya Peninsula because vertical holes on the top issued sulfurous fumes and rumblings. In 1937, ornithologist Alexander Skutch recognized the holes as "sink-holes, such as one finds in many calcareous formations, rather than volcanic vents," but also described inexplicable volcanolike features. "From this cavern issued a gas with an unpleasant odor, which was neither that of hydrogen sulphide nor that of sulphur dioxide. From the depths of the cavity came a continuous fine, shrill whistle, as of gas escaping under pressure from a narrow orifice." Skutch's guide told him that the gas came out of one vent "with sufficient volume and force to sway the boughs of trees." Skutch speculated that roosting bats in the limestone caves might be causing the noises and smells, but couldn't think of any reason why "so much gas issued from them." A cave explorer told me that the gases might in fact have come from thermal vents under the limestone, but when I visited Barra Honda in 1990, I found neither smells, noises, gas or bats, only a juvenile mottled owl teetering on a branch above one cave's mouth.

The final surprise of Central America's active volcanoes is that they suddenly stop. No active volcanoes occur south of Volcán Irazu in central Costa Rica, and even inactive ones disappear from the Talamanca mountains. There are volcanoes in western Panama, but they are inactive. The southernmost, El Valle, last erupted about forty thousand years ago. The most impressive is Volcán Barú, a peak which, although quiescent, seems a kind of sum of Central American volcanoes. Like Guatemalan and Salvadoran volcanoes, Barú looms over a plateau broken by deep gorges—the gorge of the Rio Caldera just east of it is one of the most dizzying I've seen. Like Nicaraguan volcanoes, Barú is isolated and brooding, its summit often capped by cloud. Like Costa Rican ones, it lacks a classic cone shape, and might seem nonvolcanic if it didn't have seven craters at its top and hot springs at its bottom.

Like all the others, Barú has attracted a large human population with its fertile ash. I met a Guaymi man in the Caldera Gorge who was staring up at the cliffs, which are fluted with basalt blocks so regularly shaped they might have been hand-carved. When asked what he was looking at, he said he was thinking how to grow vegetables up there.

THE $\mathscr{D}$EVILS $\mathscr{T}$HUMB

Jon Krakauer

$\mathscr{B}$y the time I reached the interstate I was having trouble keeping my eyes open. I'd been okay on the twisting two-lane black-top between Fort Collins and Laramie, but when the Pontiac eased onto the smooth, unswerving pavement of I-80, the soporific hiss of the tires began to gnaw at my wakefulness like ants in a dead tree.

That afternoon, after nine hours of humping 2 × 10s and pounding recalcitrant nails, I'd told my boss I was quitting: "No, not in a couple of weeks, Steve; right now was more like what I had in mind." It took me three more hours to clear my tools and other belongings out of the rust-stained construction trailer that had served as my home in Boulder. I loaded everything into the car, drove up Pearl Street to Tom's Tavern, and downed a ceremonial beer. Then I was gone.

At 1 A.M., thirty miles east of Rawlins, the strain of the day caught up to me. The euphoria that had flowed so freely in the wake of my quick escape gave way to overpowering fatigue; suddenly I felt tired to the bone. The highway stretched straight and empty to the horizon and beyond. Outside the car the night air was cold, and the stark Wyoming plains glowed in the moonlight like Rousseau's painting of the sleeping gypsy. I wanted very badly just then to be that gypsy, conked out on my back beneath the stars. I shut my eyes—just for a second, but it was a second of bliss. It seemed to revive me, if only briefly. The Pontiac, a sturdy behemoth from the Eisenhower years, floated down the road on its long-gone shocks like a raft on an ocean swell. The lights of an oil rig twinkled reassuringly in the distance. I closed my eyes a second time, and kept them closed a few moments longer. The sensation was sweeter than sex.

A few minutes later I let my eyelids fall again. I'm not sure how long I nodded off this time—it might have been for five seconds, it might have been for thirty—but when I awoke it was to the rude sensation of the Pontiac bucking violently along the dirt shoulder at seventy miles per hour. By all rights, the car should have sailed off into the rabbitbrush and rolled. The rear wheels fishtailed wildly six or seven times, but I eventually managed to guide the unruly machine back onto the pavement without so much as blowing a tire, and let it coast gradually to a stop. I loosened my death grip on the wheel, took several deep breaths to quiet the pounding in my chest, then slipped the shifter back into drive and continued down the highway.

Pulling over to sleep would have been the sensible thing to do, but I was on my way to Alaska to change my life, and patience was a concept well beyond my twenty-three-year-old ken.

Sixteen months earlier I'd graduated from college with little distinction and even less in the way of marketable skills. In the interim an off-again, on-again four-year relationship—the first serious romance of my life—had come to a messy, long-overdue end; nearly a year later, my love life was still zip. To support myself I worked on a house-framing crew, grunting under crippling loads of plywood, counting the minutes until the next coffee break, scratching in vain at the sawdust stuck *in perpetuum* to the sweat on the back of my neck. Somehow, blighting the Colorado landscape with condominiums and tract houses for three-fifty an hour wasn't the sort of career I'd dreamed of as a boy.

Late one evening I was mulling all this over on a barstool at Tom's, picking unhappily at my existential scabs, when an idea came to me, a scheme for righting what was wrong in my life. It was wonderfully uncomplicated, and the more I thought about it, the better the plan sounded. By the bottom of the pitcher its merits seemed unassailable. The plan consisted, in its entirety, of climbing a mountain in Alaska called the Devils Thumb.

The Devils Thumb is a prong of exfoliated diorite that presents an imposing profile from any point of the compass, but especially so from the north: its great north wall, which had never been climbed, rises sheer and clean for six thousand vertical feet from the glacier at its base. Twice the height of Yosemite's El Capitan, the north face of the Thumb is one of the biggest granitic walls on the continent; it may well be one of the biggest in the world. I would go to Alaska, ski across the Stikine Icecap to the Devils Thumb, and make the first ascent of its notorious nordwand. It seemed, midway through the second pitcher, like a particularly good idea to do all of this solo.

Writing these words more than a dozen years later, it's no longer entirely clear just *how* I thought soloing the Devils Thumb would transform my life. It had something to do with the fact that climbing was the first and only thing I'd ever been good at. My reasoning, such as it was, was fueled by the scattershot passions of youth, and a literary diet overly rich in the works of Nietzsche, Kerouac, and John Menlove Edwards—the latter a deeply troubled writer/psychiatrist who, before putting an end to his life with a cyanide capsule in 1958, had been one of the preeminent British rock climbers of the day.

Dr. Edwards regarded climbing as a "psycho-neurotic tendency" rather than sport; he climbed not for fun but to find refuge from the inner torment that characterized his existence. I remember, that spring of 1977, being especially taken by a passage from an Edwards short story titled "Letter From a Man":

> So, as you would imagine, I grew up exuberant in body but with a nervy, craving mind. It was wanting something more, something tangible. It sought for reality intensely, always if it were not there . . .
> But you see at once what I do. I climb.

To one enamored of this sort of prose, the Thumb beckoned like a beacon. My belief in the plan became unshakeable. I was dimly aware that I might be getting in over my head, but if I could somehow get to the top of the Devils Thumb, I was convinced, everything that followed would turn out all right. And thus did I push the accelerator a little closer to the floor and, buoyed by the jolt of adrenaline that followed the Pontiac's brush with destruction, speed west into the night.

You can't actually get very close to the Devils Thumb by car. The peak stands in the Boundary Ranges on the Alaska–British Columbia border, not far from the fishing village of Petersburg, a place accessible only by boat or plane. There is regular jet service to Petersburg, but the sum of my liquid assets amounted to the Pontiac and two hundred dollars in cash, not even enough for one-way airfare, so I took the car as far as Gig Harbor, Washington, then hitched a ride on a northbound seine boat that was short on crew. Five days out, when the *Ocean Queen* pulled into Petersburg to take on fuel and water, I jumped ship, shouldered my backpack, and walked down the dock in a steady Alaskan rain.

Back in Boulder, without exception, every person with whom I'd shared my plans about the Thumb had been blunt and to the point: I'd been smoking too much pot, they said; it was a monumentally bad idea. I was grossly overestimating my abilities as a climber, I'd never be able to hack a month completely by myself, I would fall into a crevasse and die.

The residents of Petersburg reacted differently. Being Alaskans, they were accustomed to people with screwball ideas; a sizeable percentage of the state's population, after all, was sitting on half-baked schemes to mine uranium in the Brooks Range, or sell icebergs to the Japanese, or market mail-order moose droppings. Most of the Alaskans I met, if they reacted at all, simply asked how much money there was in climbing a mountain like the Devils Thumb.

In any case, one of the appealing things about climbing the Thumb—and one of the appealing things about the sport of mountain climbing in general—was that it didn't matter a rat's ass what anyone else thought. Getting the scheme off the ground didn't hinge on winning the approval of some personnel director, admissions committee, licensing board, or panel of stern-faced judges; if I felt like taking a shot at some unclimbed alpine wall, all I had to do was get myself to the foot of the mountain and start swinging my ice axes.

Petersburg sits on an island, the Devils Thumb rises from the mainland. To get myself to the foot of the Thumb it was first necessary to cross twenty-five miles of salt water. For most of a day I walked the docks, trying without success to hire a boat to ferry me across Frederick Sound. Then I bumped into Bart and Benjamin.

Bart and Benjamin were ponytailed constituents of a Woodstock Nation tree-planting collective called the Hodads. We struck up a conversation. I mentioned that I, too, had once worked as a tree planter. The Hodads allowed that they had chartered a floatplane to fly them to their camp on the mainland the next morning. "It's your lucky day, kid," Bart told me. "For twenty bucks you can ride over with us. Get you to your fuckin' mountain in style." On May 3, a day and a half after arriving in Petersburg, I stepped off the Hodads' Cessna, waded onto the tidal flats at the head of Thomas Bay, and began the long trudge inland.

The Devils Thumb

&c&c&c&c

The Devils Thumb pokes up out of the Stikine Icecap, an immense, labyrinthine network of glaciers that hugs the crest of the Alaskan panhandle like an octopus, with myriad tentacles that snake down, down to the sea from the craggy uplands along the Canadian frontier. In putting ashore at Thomas Bay I was gambling that one of these frozen arms, the Baird Glacier, would lead me safely to the bottom of the Thumb, thirty miles distant.

An hour of gravel beach led to the tortured blue tongue of the Baird. A logger in Petersburg had suggested I keep an eye out for grizzlies along this stretch of shore. "Them bears over there is just waking up this time of year," he smiled. "Tend to be kinda cantankerous after not eatin' all winter. But you keep your gun handy, you shouldn't have no problem." Problem was, I didn't have a gun. As it turned out, my only encounter with hostile wildlife involved a flock of gulls who dive-bombed my head with Hitchcockian fury. Between the avian assault and my ursine anxiety, it was with no small amount of relief that I turned my back to the beach, donned crampons, and scrambled up onto the glacier's broad, lifeless snout.

After three or four miles I came to the snowline, where I exchanged crampons for skis. Putting the boards on my feet cut fifteen pounds from the awful load on my back and made the going much faster besides. But now that the ice was covered with snow, many of the glacier's crevasses were hidden, making solitary travel extremely dangerous.

In Seattle, anticipating this hazard, I'd stopped at a hardware store and purchased a pair of stout aluminum curtain rods, each ten feet long. Upon reaching the snowline, I lashed the rods together at right angles, then strapped the arrangement to the hip belt on my backpack so the poles extended horizontally over the snow. Staggering slowly up the glacier with my overloaded backpack, bearing the queer tin cross, I felt like some kind of strange *Penitente*. Were I to break through the veneer of snow over a hidden crevasse, though, the curtain rods would—I hoped mightily—span the slot and keep me from dropping into the chilly bowels of the Baird.

The first climbers to venture onto the Stikine Icecap were Bestor Robinson and Fritz Wiessner, the legendary German-American alpinist, who spent a stormy month in the Boundary Ranges in 1937 but failed to reach any major summits. Wiessner returned in 1946 with Donald Brown and Fred Beckey to attempt the Devils Thumb, the nastiest looking peak in the Stikine. On that trip Fritz mangled a knee during a fall on the hike in and limped home in disgust, but Beckey went back that same summer with Bob Craig and Cliff Schmidtke. On August 25, after several aborted tries and some exceedingly hairy climbing on the peak's east ridge, Beckey and company sat on the Thumb's wafer-thin summit tower in a tired, giddy daze. It was far and away the most technical ascent ever done in Alaska, an important milestone in the history of American mountaineering.

In the ensuing decades three other teams also made it to the top of the Thumb, but all steered clear of the big north face. Reading accounts of these expeditions, I had wondered why none of them had approached the peak by what appeared, from the map at least, to be the easiest and most logical route, the Baird. I wondered a little less after coming across an article by Beckey in which the distinguished mountaineer cautioned, "Long, steep icefalls block the route from the Baird Glacier to the icecap near Devils Thumb," but after studying aerial photographs I decided that Beckey was mistaken, that the icefalls weren't so big or so bad. The Baird, I was certain, really was the best way to reach the mountain.

For two days I slogged steadily up the glacier without incident, congratulating myself for discovering such a clever path to the Thumb. On the third day, I arrived beneath the Stikine Icecap proper, where the long arm of the Baird joins the main body of ice. Here, the glacier spills abruptly over the edge of a high plateau, dropping seaward through the gap between two peaks in a phantasmagoria of shattered ice. Seeing the icefall in the flesh left a different impression than the photos had. As I stared at the tumult from a mile away, for the first time since leaving Colorado the thought crossed my mind that maybe this Devils Thumb trip wasn't the best idea I'd ever had.

The icefall was a maze of crevasses and teetering seracs. From afar it brought to mind a bad train wreck, as if scores of ghostly white boxcars had derailed at the lip of the icecap and tumbled down the slope willy-nilly. The closer I got, the more unpleasant it looked. My ten-foot curtain rods seemed a poor defense against crevasses that were forty feet across and two hundred fifty feet deep. Before I could finish figuring out a course through the icefall, the wind came up and snow began to slant hard out of the clouds, stinging my face and reducing visibility to almost nothing.

In my impetuosity, I decided to carry on anyway. For the better part of the day I groped blindly through the labyrinth in the whiteout, retracing my steps from one dead end to another. Time after time I'd think I'd found a way out, only to wind up in a deep blue cul de sac, or stranded atop a detached pillar of ice. My efforts were lent a sense of urgency by the noises emanating underfoot. A madrigal of cracks and sharp reports—the sort of protests a large fir limb makes when it's slowly bent to the breaking point—served as a reminder that it is the nature of glaciers to move, the habit of seracs to topple.

As much as I feared being flattened by a wall of collapsing ice, I was even more afraid of falling into a crevasse, a fear that intensified when I put a foot through a snow bridge over a slot so deep I couldn't see the bottom of it. A little later I broke through another bridge to my waist; the poles kept me out of the hundred-foot hole, but after I extricated myself I was bent double with dry heaves thinking about what it would be like to be lying in a pile at the bottom of the crevasse, waiting for death to come, with nobody even aware of how or where I'd met my end.

Night had nearly fallen by the time I emerged from the top of the serac slope onto the empty, wind-scoured expanse of the high glacial plateau. In shock and chilled to the core, I skied far enough past the icefall to put its rumblings out of earshot, pitched the tent, crawled into my sleeping bag, and shivered myself to a fitful sleep.

Although my plan to climb the Devils Thumb wasn't fully hatched until the spring of 1977, the mountain had been lurking in the recesses of my mind for about fifteen years—since April 12, 1962, to be exact. The occasion was my eighth birthday. When it came time to open birthday presents, my parents announced that they were offering me a choice of gifts: According to my wishes, they would either escort me to the new Seattle World's Fair to ride the Monorail and see the Space Needle, or give me an introductory taste of mountain climbing by taking me up the third highest peak in Oregon, a long-dormant volcano called the South Sister that, on clear days, was visible from my bedroom window. It was a tough call. I thought the matter over at length, then settled on the climb.

To prepare me for the rigors of the ascent, my father handed over a copy of *Mountaineering: The Freedom of the Hills,* the leading how-to manual of the day, a thick tome that weighed only slightly less than a bowling ball. Thenceforth I spent most of my waking hours poring over its pages, memorizing the intricacies of pitoncraft and bolt placement, the shoulder stand and the tension traverse. None of which, as it happened, was of any use on my inaugural ascent, for the South Sister turned out to be a decidedly less than extreme climb that demanded nothing more in the way of technical skill than energetic walking, and was in fact ascended by hundreds of farmers, house pets, and small children every summer.

Which is not to suggest that my parents and I conquered the mighty volcano: From the pages and pages of perilous situations depicted in *Mountaineering: The Freedom of the Hills*, I had concluded that climbing was a life-and-death matter, always. Halfway up the South Sister I suddenly remembered this. In the middle of a twenty-degree snow slope that would be impossible to fall from if you tried, I decided that I was in mortal jeopardy and burst into tears, bringing the ascent to a halt.

Perversely, after the South Sister debacle my interest in climbing only intensified. I resumed my obsessive studies of *Mountaineering*. There was something about the scariness of the activities portrayed in those pages that just wouldn't leave me alone. In addition to the scores of line drawings—most of them cartoons of a little man in a jaunty Tyrolean cap—employed to illustrate arcana like the boot-axe belay and the Bilgeri rescue, the book contained sixteen black-and-white plates of notable peaks in the Pacific Northwest and Alaska. All the photographs were striking, but the one on page 147 was much, much more than that: it made my skin crawl. An aerial photo by glaciologist Maynard Miller, it showed a singularly sinister tower of ice-plastered black rock. There wasn't a place on the entire mountain that looked safe or secure; I couldn't imagine anyone climbing it. At the bottom of the page the mountain was identified as the Devils Thumb.

From the first time I saw it, the picture—a portrait of the Thumb's north wall—held an almost pornographic fascination for me. On hundreds—no, make that thousands—of occasions over the decade and a half that followed I took my copy of *Mountaineering* down from the shelf, opened it to page 147, and quietly stared. How would it feel, I wondered over and over, to be on that thumbnail-thin summit ridge, worrying over the storm clouds building on the horizon, hunched against the wind and dunning cold, contemplating the horrible drop on either side? How could anyone keep it together? Would I, if I found myself high on the north wall, clinging to that frozen rock, even attempt to keep it together? Or would I simply decide to surrender to the inevitable straight away, and jump?

The Devils Thumb

∼∽∼∽∼∽

I had planned on spending between three weeks and a month on the Stikine Icecap. Not relishing the prospect of carrying a four-week load of food, heavy winter camping gear, and a small mountain of climbing hardware all the way up the Baird on my back, before leaving Petersburg I paid a bush pilot a hundred and fifty dollars—the last of my cash—to have six cardboard cartons of supplies dropped from an airplane when I reached the foot of the Thumb. I showed the pilot exactly where, on his map, I intended to be, and told him to give me three days to get there; he promised to fly over and make the drop as soon thereafter as the weather permitted.

On May 6 I set up a base camp on the Icecap just northeast of the Thumb and waited for the airdrop. For the next four days it snowed, nixing any chance for a flight. Too terrified of crevasses to wander far from camp, I occasionally went out for a short ski to kill time, but mostly I lay silently in the tent—the ceiling was too low to sit upright—with my thoughts, fighting a rising chorus of doubts.

As the days passed, I grew increasingly anxious. I had no radio, nor any other means of communicating with the outside world. It had been many years since anyone had visited this part of the Stikine Icecap, and many more would likely pass before anyone did so again. I was nearly out of stove fuel, and down to a single chunk of cheese, my last package of ramen noodles, and half a box of Cocoa Puffs. This, I figured, could sustain me for three or four more days if need be, but then what would I do? It would only take two days to ski back down the Baird to Thomas Bay, but then a week or more might easily pass before a fisherman happened by who could give me a lift back to Petersburg (the Hodads with whom I'd ridden over were camped fifteen miles down the impassable, headland-studded coast, and could be reached only by boat or plane).

When I went to bed on the evening of May 10 it was still snowing and blowing hard. I was going back and forth on whether to head for the coast in the morning or stick it out on the icecap, gambling that the pilot would show before I starved or died of thirst, when, just for a moment, I heard a faint whine, like a mosquito. I tore open the tent door. Most of the clouds had lifted, but there was no airplane in sight. The whine returned, louder this time. Then I saw it: a tiny red-and-white speck, high in the western sky, droning my way.

A few minutes later the plane passed directly overhead. The pilot, however, was unaccustomed to glacier flying and he'd badly misjudged the scale of the terrain. Worried about winding up too low and getting nailed by unexpected turbulence, he flew a good thousand feet above me—believing all the while he was just off the deck—and never saw my tent in the flat evening light. My waving and screaming were to no avail; from that altitude I was indistinguishable from a pile of rocks. For the next hour he circled the icecap, scanning its barren contours without success. But the pilot, to his credit, appreciated the gravity of my predicament and didn't give up. Frantic, I tied my sleeping bag to the end of one of the crevasse poles and waved it for all I was worth. When the plane banked sharply and began to fly straight at me, I felt tears of joy well in my eyes.

The pilot buzzed my tent three times in quick succession, dropping two boxes on each pass, then the airplane disappeared over a ridge and I was alone. As silence again settled over the glacier I felt abandoned, vulnerable, lost. I realized that I was sobbing. Embarrassed, I halted the blubbering by screaming obscenities until I grew hoarse.

I awoke early on May 11 to clear skies and the relatively warm temperature of twenty degrees Fahrenheit. Startled by the good weather, mentally unprepared to commence the actual climb, I hurriedly packed up a rucksack nonetheless, and began skiing toward the base of the Thumb. Two previous Alaskan expeditions had taught me that, ready or not, you simply can't afford to waste a day of perfect weather if you expect to get up anything.

A small hanging glacier extends out from the lip of the icecap, leading up and across the north face of the Thumb like a catwalk. My plan was to follow this catwalk to a prominent rock prow in the center of the wall, and thereby execute an end run around the ugly, avalanche-swept lower half of the face.

The catwalk turned out to be a series of fifty-degree ice fields blanketed with knee-deep powder snow and riddled with crevasses. The depth of the snow made the going slow and exhausting; by the time I front-pointed up the overhanging wall of the uppermost *bergschrund,* some three or four hours after leaving camp, I was whipped. And I hadn't even gotten to the "real" climbing yet. That would begin immediately above, where the hanging glacier gave way to vertical rock.

The rock, exhibiting a dearth of holds and coated with six inches of crumbly rime, did not look promising, but just left of the main prow was an inside corner—what climbers call an open book—glazed with frozen melt water. This ribbon of ice led straight up for two or three hundred feet, and if the ice proved substantial enough to support the picks of my ice axes, the line might go. I hacked out a small platform in the snow slope, the last flat ground I expected to feel underfoot for some time, and stopped to eat a candy bar and collect my thoughts. Fifteen minutes later I shouldered my pack and inched over to the bottom of the corner. Gingerly, I swung my right axe into the two-inch-thick ice. It was solid, plastic—a little thinner than I would have liked but otherwise perfect. I was on my way.

The climbing was steep and spectacular, so exposed it made my head spin. Beneath my boot soles, the wall fell away for three thousand feet to the dirty, avalanche-scarred cirque of the Witches Cauldron Glacier. Above, the prow soared with authority toward the summit ridge, a vertical half-mile above. Each time I planted one of my ice axes, that distance shrank by another twenty inches.

The higher I climbed, the more comfortable I became. All that held me to the mountainside, all that held me to the world, were six thin spikes of chrome-molybdenum stuck half an inch into a smear of frozen water, yet I began to feel invincible, weightless, like those lizards that live on the ceilings of cheap Mexican hotels. Early on a difficult climb, especially a difficult solo climb, you're hyperaware of the abyss pulling at your back. You constantly feel its call, its immense hunger. To resist takes a tremendous conscious effort; you don't dare let your guard down for an instant. The siren song of the void puts you on edge, it makes your movements tentative, clumsy, herky-jerky. But as the climb goes on, you grow accustomed to the exposure, you get used to rubbing shoulders with doom, you come to believe in the reliability of your hands and feet and head. You learn to trust your self-control.

By and by, your attention becomes so intensely focused that you no longer notice the raw knuckles, the cramping thighs, the strain of maintaining nonstop concentration. A trance-like state settles over your efforts, the climb becomes a clear-eyed dream. Hours slide by like minutes. The accrued guilt and clutter of day-to-day existence—the lapses of conscience, the unpaid bills, the bungled opportunities, the dust under the couch, the festering familial sores, the inescapable prison of your genes—all of it is temporarily forgotten, crowded from your thoughts by an overpowering clarity of purpose, and by the seriousness of the task at hand.

At such moments, something like happiness actually stirs in your chest, but it isn't the sort of emotion you want to lean on very hard. In solo climbing, the whole enterprise is held together with little more than chutzpa, not the most reliable adhesive. Late in the day on the north face of the Thumb, I felt the glue disintegrate with a single swing of an ice axe.

I'd gained nearly seven hundred feet of altitude since stepping off the hanging glacier, all of it on crampon front-points and the picks of my axes. The ribbon of frozen melt water had ended three hundred feet up, and was followed by a crumbly armor of frost feathers. Though just barely substantial enough to support body weight, the rime was plastered over the rock to a thickness of two or three feet, so I kept plugging upward. The wall, however, had been growing imperceptibly steeper, and as it did so the frost feathers became thinner. I'd fallen into a slow, hypnotic rhythm—swing, swing; kick, kick; swing, swing; kick, kick—when my left ice axe slammed into a slab of diorite a few inches beneath the rime.

I tried left, then right, but kept striking rock. The frost feathers holding me up, it became apparent, were maybe five inches thick and had the structural integrity of stale cornbread. Below was thirty-seven hundred feet of air, and I was balanced atop a house of cards. Waves of panic rose in my throat. My eyesight blurred, I began to hyperventilate, my calves started to vibrate. I shuffled a few feet farther to the right, hoping to find thicker ice, but managed only to bend an ice axe on the rock.

Awkwardly, stiff with fear, I started working my way back down. The rime gradually thickened, and after descending about eighty feet I got back on reasonably solid ground. I stopped for a long time to let my nerves settle, then leaned back from my tools and stared up at the face above, searching for a hint of solid ice, for some variation in the underlying rock strata, for anything that would allow passage over the frosted slabs. I looked until my neck ached, but nothing appeared. The climb was over. The only place to go was down.

Heavy snow and incessant winds kept me inside the tent for most of the next three days. The hours passed slowly. In the attempt to hurry them along I chain-smoked for as long as my supply of cigarettes held out, and read. I'd made a number of bad decisions on the trip, there was no getting around it, and one of them concerned the reading matter I'd chosen to pack along: three back issues of *The Village Voice*, and

Joan Didion's latest novel, *A Book of Common Prayer*. The *Voice* was amusing enough—there on the icecap, the subject matter took on an edge, a certain sense of the absurd, from which the paper (through no fault of its own) benefited greatly—but in that tent, under those circumstances, Didion's necrotic take on the world hit a little too close to home.

Near the end of *Common Prayer*, one of Didion's characters says to another, "You don't get any real points for staying here, Charlotte." Charlotte replies, "I can't seem to tell what you do get real points for, so I guess I'll stick around here for awhile."

When I ran out of things to read, I was reduced to studying the ripstop pattern woven into the tent ceiling. This I did for hours on end, flat on my back, while engaging in an extended and very heated self-debate: Should I leave for the coast as soon as the weather broke, or stay put long enough to make another attempt on the mountain? In truth, my little escapade on the north face had left me badly shaken, and I didn't want to go up on the Thumb again at all. On the other hand, the thought of returning to Boulder in defeat—of parking the Pontiac behind the trailer, buckling on my tool belt, and going back to the same brain-dead drill I'd so triumphantly walked away from just a month before—that wasn't very appealing, either. Most of all, I couldn't stomach the thought of having to endure the smug expressions of condolence from all the chumps and nimrods who were certain I'd fail right from the get-go.

By the third afternoon of the storm I couldn't stand it any longer: the lumps of frozen snow poking me in the back, the clammy nylon walls brushing against my face, the incredible smell drifting up from the depths of my sleeping bag. I pawed through the mess at my feet until I located a small green stuff sack, in which there was a metal film can containing the makings of what I'd hoped would be a sort of victory cigar. I'd intended to save it for my return from the summit, but what the hey, it wasn't looking like I'd be visiting the top any time soon. I poured most of the can's contents into a leaf of cigarette paper, rolled it into a crooked, sorry looking joint, and promptly smoked it down to the roach.

The reefer, of course, only made the tent seem even more cramped, more suffocating, more impossible to bear. It also made me terribly hungry. I decided a little oatmeal would put things right. Making it, however, was a long, ridiculously involved process: a potful of snow had to be gathered outside in the tempest, the stove assembled and lit, the oatmeal and sugar located, the remnants of yesterday's dinner scraped from my bowl. I'd gotten the stove going and was melting the snow when I smelled something burning. A thorough check of the stove and its environs revealed nothing. Mystified, I was ready to chalk it up to my chemically enhanced imagination when I heard something crackle directly behind me.

I whirled around in time to see a bag of garbage, into which I'd tossed the match I'd used to light the stove, flare up into a conflagration. Beating on the fire with my hands, I had it out in a few seconds, but not before a large section of the tent's inner wall vaporized before my eyes. The tent's built-in rainfly escaped the flames, so the shelter was still more or less weatherproof; now, however, it was approximately thirty degrees cooler inside. My left palm began to sting. Examining it, I noticed the pink welt of a burn. What troubled me most, though, was that the tent wasn't even mine—I'd borrowed the shelter from my father. An expensive Early Winters Omnipo Tent, it had been brand new before my trip—the hang-tags were still attached—and had been loaned reluctantly. For several minutes I sat dumbstruck, staring at the wreckage of the shelter's once-graceful form amid the acrid scent of singed hair and melted nylon. You had to hand it to me, I thought: I had a real knack for living up to the old man's worst expectations.

The fire sent me into a funk that no drug known to man could have alleviated. By the time I'd finished cooking the oatmeal my mind was made up: the moment the storm was over, I was breaking camp and booking for Thomas Bay.

Twenty-four hours later, I was huddled inside a bivouac sack under the lip of the *bergschrund* on the Thumb's north face. The weather was as bad as I'd seen it. It was snowing hard, probably an inch every hour. Spindrift avalanches hissed down from the wall above and washed over me like surf, completely burying the sack every twenty minutes.

The day had begun well enough. When I emerged from the tent, clouds still clung to the ridge tops but the wind was down and the icecap was speckled with sunbreaks. A patch of sunlight, almost blinding in its brilliance, slid lazily over the camp. I put down a foam sleeping mat and sprawled on the glacier in my long johns. Wallowing in the radiant heat, I felt the gratitude of a prisoner whose sentence has just been commuted.

As I lay there, a narrow chimney that curved up the east half of the Thumb's north face, well to the left of the route I'd tried before the storm, caught my eye. I twisted a telephoto lens onto my camera. Through it I could make out a smear of shiny grey ice—solid, trustworthy, hard-frozen ice—plastered to the back of the cleft. The alignment of the chimney made it impossible to discern if the ice continued in an unbroken line from top to bottom. If it did, the chimney might well provide passage over the rime-covered slabs that had foiled my first attempt. Lying there in the sun, I began to think about how much I'd hate myself a month hence if I threw in the towel after a single try, if I scrapped the whole expedition on account of a little bad weather. Within the hour I had assembled my gear and was skiing toward the base of the wall.

The ice in the chimney did in fact prove to be continuous, but it was very, very thin—just a gossamer film of verglas. Additionally, the cleft was a natural funnel for any debris that happened to slough off the wall; as I scratched my way up the chimney I was hosed by a continuous stream of powder snow, ice chips, and small stones. One hundred twenty feet up the groove the last remnants of my composure flaked away like old plaster, and I turned around.

Instead of descending all the way to base camp, I decided to spend the night in the 'schrund beneath the chimney, on the off chance that my head would be more together the next morning. The fair skies that had ushered in the day, however, turned out to be but a momentary lull in a five-day gale. By midafternoon the storm was back in all its glory, and my bivouac site became a less than pleasant place to hang around. The ledge on which I crouched was continually swept by small spindrift avalanches. Five times my bivvy sack—a thin nylon envelope, shaped exactly like a Baggies brand sandwich bag, only bigger—was buried up to the level of the breathing slit. After digging myself out the fifth time, I decided I'd had enough. I threw all my gear in my pack and made a break for base camp.

The descent was terrifying. Between the clouds, the ground blizzard, and the flat, fading light, I couldn't tell snow from sky, nor whether a slope went up or down. I worried, with ample reason, that I might step blindly off the top of a serac and end up at the bottom of the Witches Cauldron, a half-mile below. When I finally arrived on the frozen plain of the icecap, I found that my tracks had long since drifted over. I didn't have a clue how to locate the tent on the featureless glacial plateau. I skied in circles for an hour or so, hoping I'd get lucky and stumble across camp, until I put a foot into a small crevasse and realized I was acting like an idiot—that I should hunker down right where I was and wait out the storm.

I dug a shallow hole, wrapped myself in the bivvy bag, and sat on my pack in the swirling snow. Drifts piled up around me. My feet became numb. A damp chill crept down my chest from the base of my neck, where spindrift had gotten inside my parka and soaked my shirt. If only I had a cigarette, I thought, a single cigarette, I could summon the strength of character to put a good face on this fucked-up situation, on the whole fucked-up trip. "If we had some ham, we could have ham and eggs, if we had some eggs." I remembered my friend Nate uttering that line in a similar storm, two years before, high on another Alaskan peak, the Mooses Tooth. It had struck me as hilarious at the time; I'd actually laughed out loud. Recalling the line now, it no longer seemed funny. I pulled the bivvy sack tighter around my shoulders. The wind ripped at my back. Beyond shame, I cradled my head in my arms and embarked on an orgy of self-pity.

I knew that people sometimes died climbing mountains. But at the age of twenty-three personal mortality—the idea of my own death—was still largely outside my conceptual grasp; it was as abstract a notion as non-Euclidian geometry or marriage. When I decamped from Boulder in April, 1977, my head swimming with visions of glory and redemption on the Devils Thumb, it didn't occur to me that I might be bound by the same cause-effect relationships that governed the actions of others. I'd never heard of hubris. Because I wanted to climb the mountain so badly, because I had thought about the Thumb so intensely for so long, it seemed beyond the realm of possibility that some minor obstacle like the weather or crevasses or rime-covered rock might ultimately thwart my will.

At sunset the wind died and the ceiling lifted a hundred fifty feet off the glacier, enabling me to locate base camp. I made it back to the tent intact, but it was no longer possible to ignore the fact that the Thumb had made hash of my plans. I was forced to acknowledge that volition alone, however powerful, was not going to get me up the north wall. I saw, finally, that nothing was.

There still existed an opportunity for salvaging the expedition, however. A week earlier I'd skied over to the southeast side of the mountain to take a look at the route Fred Beckey had pioneered in 1946—the route by which I'd intended to descend the peak after climbing the north wall. During that reconnaissance I'd noticed an obvious unclimbed line to the left of the Beckey route—a patchy network of ice angling across the southeast face—that struck me as a relatively easy way to achieve the summit. At the time, I'd considered this route unworthy of my attentions. Now, on the rebound from my calamitous entanglement with the nordwand, I was prepared to lower my sights.

On the afternoon of May 15, when the blizzard finally petered out, I returned to the southeast face and climbed to the top of a slender ridge that abutted the upper peak like a flying buttress on a gothic cathedral. I decided to spend the night there, on the airy, knife-edged ridge crest, sixteen hundred feet below the summit. The evening sky was cold and cloudless. I could see all the way to tidewater and beyond. At dusk I watched, transfixed, as the house lights of Petersburg blinked on in the west. The closest thing I'd had to human contact since the airdrop, the distant lights set off a flood of emotion that caught me completely off guard. I imagined people watching the Red Sox on the tube, eating fried chicken in brightly lit kitchens, drinking beer, making love. When I lay down to sleep I was overcome by a soul-wrenching loneliness. I'd never felt so alone, ever.

That night I had troubled dreams, of cops and vampires and a gangland-style execution. I heard someone whisper, "He's in there. As soon as he comes out, waste him." I sat bolt upright and opened my eyes. The sun was about to rise. The entire sky was scarlet. It was still clear, but wisps of high cirrus were streaming in from the southwest, and a dark line was visible just above the horizon. I pulled on my boots and hurriedly strapped on my crampons. Five minutes after waking up, I was front-pointing away from the bivouac.

I carried no rope, no tent or bivouac gear, no hardware save my ice axes. My plan was to go ultralight and ultrafast, to hit the summit and make it back down before the weather turned. Pushing myself, continually out of breath, I scurried up and to the left across small snowfields linked by narrow runnels of verglas and short rock bands. The climbing was almost fun—the rock was covered with large, in-cut holds, and the ice, though thin, never got steep enough to feel extreme—but I was anxious about the bands of clouds racing in from the Pacific, covering the sky.

In what seemed like no time (I didn't have a watch on the trip) I was on the distinctive final ice field. By now the sky was completely overcast. It looked easier to keep angling to the left, but quicker to go straight for the top. Paranoid about being caught by a storm high on the peak without any kind of shelter, I opted for the direct route. The ice steepened, then steepened some more, and as it did so it grew thin.

I swung my left ice axe and struck rock. I aimed for another spot, and once again it glanced off unyielding diorite with a dull, sickening clank. And again, and again: It was a reprise of my first attempt on the north face. Looking between my legs, I stole a glance at the glacier, more than two thousand feet below. My stomach churned. I felt my poise slipping way like smoke in the wind.

Forty-five feet above the wall eased back onto the sloping summit shoulder. Forty-five more feet, half the distance between third base and home plate, and the mountain would be mine. I clung stiffly to my axes, unmoving, paralyzed with fear and indecision. I looked down at the dizzying drop to the glacier again, then up, then scraped away the film of ice above my head. I hooked the pick of my left axe on a nickel-thin lip of rock, and weighted it. It held. I pulled my right axe from the ice, reached up, and twisted the pick into a crooked half-inch crack until it jammed. Barely breathing now, I moved my feet up, scrabbling my crampon points across the verglas. Reaching as high as I could with my left arm, I swung the axe gently at the shiny, opaque surface, not knowing what I'd hit beneath it. The pick went in with a heartening *THUNK!* A few minutes later I was standing on a broad, rounded ledge. The summit proper, a series of slender fins sprouting a grotesque meringue of atmospheric ice, stood twenty feet directly above.

The insubstantial frost feathers ensured that those last twenty feet reminded hard, scary, onerous. But then, suddenly, there was no place higher to go. It wasn't possible, I couldn't believe it. I felt my cracked lips stretch into a huge, painful grin. I was on top of the Devils Thumb.

Fittingly, the summit was a surreal, malevolent place, an improbably slender fan of rock and rime no wider than a filing cabinet. It did not encourage loitering. As I straddled the highest point, the north face fell away beneath my left boot for six thousand feet; beneath my right boot the south face dropped off for twenty-five hundred. I took some pictures to prove I'd been there, and spent a few minutes trying to straighten a bent pick. Then I stood up, carefully turned around, and headed for home.

Five days later I was camped in the rain beside the sea, marveling at the sight of moss, willows, mosquitoes. Two days after that, a small skiff motored into Thomas Bay and pulled up on the beach not far from my tent. The man driving the boat introduced himself as Jim Freeman, a timber faller from Petersburg. It was his day off, he said, and he'd made the trip to show his family the glacier, and to look for bears. He asked me if I'd "been huntin', or what?"

"No," I replied sheepishly. "Actually, I just climbed the Devils Thumb. I've been over here twenty days."

Freeman kept fiddling with a cleat on the boat, and didn't say anything for a while. Then he looked at me real hard and spat, "You wouldn't be givin' me double talk now, wouldja, friend?" Taken aback, I stammered out a denial. Freeman, it was obvious, didn't believe me for a minute. Nor did he seem wild about my snarled shoulder-length hair or the way I smelled. When I asked if he could give me a lift back to town, however, he offered a grudging, "I don't see why not."

The water was choppy, and the ride across Frederick Sound took two hours. The more we talked, the more Freeman warmed up. He still didn't believe I'd climbed the Thumb, but by the time he steered the skiff into Wrangell Narrows he pretended to. When we got off the boat, he insisted on buying me a cheeseburger. That night he even let me sleep in a derelict step-van parked in his backyard.

I lay down in the rear of the old truck for a while but couldn't sleep, so I got up and walked to a bar called Kito's Kave. The euphoria, the overwhelming sense of relief, that had initially accompanied my return to Petersburg faded, and an unexpected melancholy took its place. The people I chatted with in Kito's didn't seem to doubt that I'd been to the top of the Thumb, they just didn't much care. As the night wore on the place emptied except for me and an Indian at a back table. I drank alone, putting quarters in the jukebox, playing the same five songs over and over, until the barmaid yelled angrily, "Hey! Give it a fucking rest, kid! If I hear 'Fifty Ways to Lose Your Lover' one more time, I'm gonna be the one who loses it." I mumbled an apology, quickly headed for the door, and lurched back to Freeman's step-van. There, surrounded by the sweet scent of old motor oil, I lay down on the floorboards next to a gutted transmission and passed out.

It is easy, when you are young, to believe that what you desire is no less than what you deserve, to assume that if you want something badly enough it is your God-given right to have it. Less than a month after sitting on the summit of the Thumb I was back in Boulder, nailing up siding on the Spruce Street Townhouses, the same condos I'd been framing when I left for Alaska. I got a raise, to four dollars an hour, and at the end of the summer moved out of the job-site trailer to a studio apartment on West Pearl, but little else in my life seemed to change. Somehow, it didn't add up to the glorious transformation I'd imagined in April.

Climbing the Devils Thumb, however, had nudged me a little further away from the obdurate innocence of childhood. It taught me something about what mountains can and can't do, about the limits of dreams. I didn't recognize that at the time, of course, but I'm grateful for it now.

In the Shadow of Denali

Jonathan Waterman

The early people who lived around the mountain spoke in riddles (initiated by "Wait, I see something:") rich with metaphor. "Stars," for instance, also meant birds because both lived in the sky; great flocks of birds would perish after hitting the High One.

> Wait, I see something:
> The stars are rotting on my sides.
> Answer: Denali.
> —Early Athapaskan riddle

Herb Atwater was an Athapaskan who lived across the railroad tracks from the Talkeetna ranger station. His Fu Manchu mustache and his broad-cheeked face made him appear a lot older than his twenty-four years.

Herb and his father's father's fathers passed on oral stories about their beginnings, dating from the ancient "Distant Time," when "Raven" created the earth and all its beings. Rather than fictional legends or myths, Athapaskans consider the ancient stories to hold more evolutionary truth than, say, Darwin's *Origin of Species* and the Bible combined.

In the Distant Time, when all the humans died, they were transformed into the animals and plants of today. The respect that Herb Atwater felt, but could not articulate, explained his love of the wild game he shot, the salmon he hooked, and the beauty of the mountain.

245

In 1908, his people's story of Denali's creation was first documented by Jette, a Jesuit priest:

When Raven was a man he paddled across an expanse of water to marry a woman. When the woman refused his hand, Raven made her disappear, incurring the mother's wrath. Two brown bears were asked to drown Raven, but using his magic, he managed to calm a path through huge waves sent by the bears ripping up the shore.

Eventually Raven grew exhausted, threw a harpoon, and fainted. When he awoke, the waters had changed into a great forest; the wave that his harpoon stuck on had solidified into Denali.

Nowadays this tale has been forgotten and ignored, although Herb had heard it as a child. He was always curious about the mountain and asked many questions. Each time I took it to the next stage and hinted at inviting him on a ranger patrol, he begged off. Herb was clearly afraid of the mountain, and although he did not consciously admit that the mountain held great spiritual power, his blood coursed with the genes of respectful ancestors.

One morning during salmon season, I found a freshly caught coho salmon, still silver and untarnished from its long swim, mysteriously sprawled on the kitchen counter and waiting to be eaten. Athapaskans called coho or "silver" salmon *saan laagha* (summer swimmer), prized for its fat and richness. Herb was the only one who could have left it.

In the afternoons, Herb would wait quietly in the ranger station for the climbers to depart; then Scott and I fixed peanut butter sandwiches and a thermos of coffee and walked out with fishing rods. You had to run to keep up as Herb strode to Whiskey Slough; Denali stood fifty miles off like a brilliant and cloud-drenched sentinel. Herb would stop suddenly, pull off his ragged rucksack, and yank out a bag full of cured salmon eggs. Brandishing a gleaming six-inch knife, Herb deftly skewered the salmon roe, passed me a golf-ball-sized hunk with the tip of his blade, and silently directed me to bait my hook.

Herb smiled a lot when he was fishing and hunting. He never used any high-tech fishing accouterments—polarized glasses or hip waders or Gore-Tex raingear. Yet he always knew where to find the fish, and where he saw crimson, black-spotted underwater life, Scott and I saw only rocks or swirling patterns on the streambed.

In certain years, during the big spawns, the waters coursed with red, writhing fish. Or as an Athapaskan riddle goes:

Wait, I see something:
We come upstream in red canoes.
Answer: The migrating salmon.

After Herb pulled his salmon ashore, he killed them immediately by smashing his knife handle against their foreheads. He then pushed his blade into the fish vent and slit the belly up to the gills. If the fish was a female, Herb would cup one hand, pull out two coral-colored clusters of eggs, and carefully slide them into a canvas satchel. He popped stray eggs into his mouth like caviar.

There in the shadow of Denali, Herb taught me everything I know about salmon. He showed me how to cut the head off tight above the neck and tighter still with the fillet knife along the spines, wasting no meat and always flinging the innards back into the fast-moving river whence they came. At the time, I thought Herb was simply cleaning the house he lived in. But age-old traditions, instituted long before the modern environmental movement, mandated that all animals be treated with respect. Even after fish were killed, their remains had to be cared for properly. The spirits of animals could linger for days around their dead bodies.

Back at the Atwater house, we filleted the orange meat and hung the strips up in Herb's smoke shed, or cut the big fish crosswise, wrapped the steaks in newspapers, and set them gently into the six-foot-long freezer. Wild meat was never lacking here, and Herb's mother, Nellie, would grill us fresh salmon or moose steaks. As we drank cup after cup of acrid coffee, Herb shared his fantasy about moose hunting with his eight-inch handgun, or landing a salmon bigger than his 150 pounds.

In turn, Scott and I often spoke about our rescue work on Denali. Herb clearly preferred his ancestors' name for the mountain, and although he was too timorous to speak disdainfully of the white men who renamed the mountain McKinley in 1896, he sat up in his chair, put down his cigarette, and beamed when I first pronounced the Athapaskan name. While being up on Denali defined my own life, hunting and fishing defined Herb's. We tried hard to understand one another.

Herb had fished in the waters of Denali since he was a child, and he wasn't about to stop when the authorities closed the fishing. Once, while flying a helicopter up the mile-wide Susitna River, the fish and game cops spied Herb standing blithely up to his ankles in mud, dabbing his line in the tannin-colored waters of Birch Creek. Since the area was closed to fishing, the authorities immediately landed their Bell 101 helicopter between Athapaskan angler and birch forest. Herb, clutching his halibut fishing rod, jumped directly into the slough. As the "fish cops" screamed "Hey, you! Stop!" Herb surfaced beside a game trail into the thick alder on the opposite bank and disappeared as cleanly as a wolf.

He had been chased again by the fish cops, and he had been caught three times, but he refused to repent by informing on other illegal anglers—a common practice served upon Alaska's fishing criminals. When his license was revoked, Herb simply fished at night. He explained that you should never pay the fines because the fish belonged to everyone and as long as you respected and lived off whatever you killed, that was *real* law and order.

Herb would not talk about his work. Every fall, after he finished jarring salmon and butchering a moose, he traveled north to work at the Prudhoe Bay "oil patch," or south to an Anchorage construction site. He fit pipes and pounded nails for union wages that made our ranger salary appear a pittance; the rest of the year he collected fat unemployment checks. But Herb was diffident about money: It meant nothing to him. Nor was he meant to live in the modern working world. Herb was truly, as the cliché says, born a hundred years too late.

I always thought Herb wanted to come when we were called off on rescues. One Friday in August, we were asked to join a search for a missing hiker in Denali National Park; the Atwaters told us to be careful. Scott, Roger, Bob Seibert, Randy Waitman, and I immediately drove north to headquarters.

Gretta Berglund, twenty years old, had backpacked with her family in California and spent five weeks as a student in a wilderness educators' course in Wyoming. Although Gretta was one of a legion of wilderness connoisseurs who frequent the parklands, like most tourists she had more love for the out-of-doors than hands-on skill. Camping out in Wyoming under the tutelage of several instructors would provide most people with just enough knowledge to kill themselves in unforgiving Alaska.

My partners and I had learned that our backyard was vastly more rugged and unpredictable than that of the lower forty-eight. For instance, passing through a mile of dense alder and willow thickets can cost you five hours, and possibly a good mauling if you surprise a sleeping bruin.

Avoiding grizzly bears is sometimes feasible by day, but by night the bears often wreak havoc while you try to sleep. And while grizzlies might run off with all of your food or crack your skull like a walnut, a cloud of bloodthirsty buzzing mosquitoes can slowly drive you insane. I had witnessed otherwise gentle alpinists—people steeped in the art of suffering stoically—who stooped to petty vengeance by sitting behind tent bug screens for hours at a time, luring mosquitoes to the screen, then plucking out their tormentors' proboscises with tweezers. But Gretta came during a snowstorm that killed off the mosquitoes.

There was one more Alaskan difficulty about which Gretta had learned only the bare rudiments. When Gretta confronted a stream in the Wind River Mountains of Wyoming, she had simply grabbed a stout wading stick, pulled on a pair of sneakers, and unbuckled her pack waistbelt in case she fell in. She then waded up to her knees in crystalline water as fat trout flashed by. But in Denali National Park the glacial rivers are clouded with particles of rock called glacial till, preventing you from gauging either the next foothold or the depth of the water. Trout would perish here.

Most sensible backpackers consider Alaskan river crossings—in 36-degree-Fahrenheit, thigh-deep water—to be the most difficult part of every outing. By the time you arrive on the far shore, linked arm-in-arm with your companions, your body is clenched in a form of rigor mortis, your teeth are chattering like castanets, and your brain is locked in a severe ice cream headache.

Taking a solo trip into the Alaskan wilderness was something that my ranger colleagues and I had all undertaken once, but not twice. Clearly you needed a companion to share the route-finding decisions or to link arms with on river crossings. And stumbling too far into the wilderness of your own undiscovered psyche was dangerous stuff. As the northern lights lick the celestial palate above, the deafening silence of uninhabited open spaces preys on your mind with a ringing so loud that you feel compelled to scurry back for the trailhead—but here the only trails are meandering muddy ruts from flighty bands of caribou. As our backcountry ranger brethren were fond of saying, "Denali Park backpackers should be comfortable getting lost."

Gretta had chosen a solo overnight hike over to, then alongside the steep, three-mile Sanctuary River canyon. If you were accustomed to this kind of subarctic canyoneering, you could travel along the river by circumspect balance moves over polished river boulders, some short but technical scrambles over rotten cliffs, and hopping over metamorphosed scree that slides away beneath your feet.

When a ranger called the Berglund family in California to tell them that Gretta was overdue, Greg Berglund said that his sister was "high on life" when she left for Alaska. But he confessed that she had poor balance and a bad sense of direction and was overconfident from her Wyoming wilderness course.

Scott, Roger, Randy, and I spent the first two days beating the bushes while performing line searches: walking ten yards apart and canvassing less than a square mile per day for signs of Gretta. Snow frosted the ground, and at night we huddled around a campfire and watched our breath cloud the air. By the time Gretta's backpack washed up below the Sanctuary River canyon and a bloodhound had picked up her scent leading into the canyon, we all knew that we were wasting our time out in the forest. Gretta was in the canyon.

By Sunday morning we had become part of a fifty-five-member search team. Planes and helicopters shredded the air overhead. Wildlife had long since departed the area. Because the canyon was considered hazardous, and the mountaineering rangers were considered gullible, we four were assigned to comb the river canyon with grappling hooks and poles. Everyone else continued beating the bushes below the canyon.

At first the work was entertaining and we played like otters in the river, checked by our climbing ropes as we waded out into the torrent. We poked into backwaters and eddies with the poles, then dragged hard-to-reach pools with the hooks. Anything was better, we agreed, than monotonous line searches in tight willow and forest. Nonetheless, by midday our work turned repetitive and we grew chilled from wading chest deep in the glacial water.

Roger had become the self-appointed communications man. Whenever we rounded a bend in the river or checked out a new riffle, Roger excitedly plucked the radio out of his holster and barked out a progress report. Every rescue has its "radio rapper," and in a search this big, there were several other egomaniacs in the air above and combing the willows below. These men couldn't resist keying their radio every few minutes and proclaiming in long-winded ten-code lingo that they had heard Roger's message, as well as whatever else crossed their minds. "Ahh, ten-four [okay] on that, we're ten-eight [in service] and our ten-twenty [location] is about five miles east of the canyon, we're about to proceed with the next grid. We'll ten-five [relay] your message to base." Scott and Randy and I simply turned our radio volumes down and concentrated on the river, quickly losing patience with Roger and the radio rappers.

As Roger walked around a tower of crumbling basalt on the opposite side of the river, I found a leg bone stuck three feet under the water. I yanked it out, and after careful scrutiny, discovered that I was holding the decaying two-foot leg of a Dall sheep. By the time Roger reappeared on the opposite side, I lofted the bone, festooned with chunks of flesh, and yelled across the river, "Roger, look what we've found!" Roger's hand flashed to his hip, whipped out the radio, and he began shouting his discovery of Gretta's body; Scott keyed his transceiver button and blocked the call until Roger calmed down.

That evening, when the helicopter brought us back to our staging camp, Scott lifted his eight-foot pole toward the overhead rotor, and only the frantic gesturing of the pilot prevented that week's second mishap on the Sanctuary River. After that, the helicopter pilot treated us just like everyone else: turkeys looking for a decapitation.

As we changed into dry clothes, a support plane landed beside the river. When the blur at the nose of the plane reappeared as a propeller and the engine coughed shut, the pilot pitched out dozens of foam containers of freshly barbecued halibut and salmon. The pilot also handed out a discreetly wrapped package marked "Talkeetna Rangers." Once opened in the privacy of our tent, we found a bottle of whiskey wrapped in a note from our boss, Bob: "Find her *safely* you guys, then let's go home."

The night sky blushed deeper than ebony, and from somewhere far beyond, a wolf howled at our intrusion. Drizzle, then snow, pattered softly on the nylon walls. While Roger spoke of how much he missed his lovely wife, I thought how it would feel if I were Gretta. Even if you *knew* the backcountry here, a solo traverse of the canyon in flood conditions would offer all the edgy pleasure of a curfewed Zulu tiptoeing the midnight streets of Johannesburg.

Certainly, Gretta followed the correct river crossing protocol, unbuckling her waistbelt and wriggling out of her shoulder straps before getting pulled under. Although she somehow clambered out of the river, walking out must have been a futile act of desperation. She was soaking wet, shivering with cold, and her food, tent, and dry clothes had washed away. Her only chance was to try to hoof it upriver and out of the canyon. Somewhere, though, the river took her again.

Was she so cold that it didn't matter anymore, that everything became a blur? Or did she pray to see her new boyfriend and her family again? A starless night like this could last far longer than you planned, so my cohorts Scott and Randy and Roger and I drank the whiskey instead of talking about Gretta. We all knew that we would find her. By midnight we resorted to the mockery that substitutes for grown men expressing their love for one another:

"God, your boots are ripe."

"Move over, asshole, you're hogging the whole tent."

This banter mostly muted our fears about finding the body. But before falling to sleep, I promised myself not to look in Gretta's eyes when we found her.

Monday was our second full day probing the river canyon. Scott wore a neoprene wetsuit to insulate himself from the ice water, while the chief ranger lent me his windsurfing shell, more suited to the Caribbean than Alaska. Randy and Roger lowered us into the river, and each time we finished probing pools for a submerged body, we pulled up our legs and let the current sweep us back to shore. We moved quickly and efficiently, signaling by hand who would cover each section of river.

A surliness came over all of us as black clouds scudded past like warships in the vast sky above. Even Randy—who normally brightened our days with a disarming smile—frowned. And Roger stopped talking on his radio.

By five o'clock I was shivering and my lips were blue. After a long argument across the roaring, frothing waters with Scott—who would have searched all night—I convinced him I was hypothermic: I was shivering, my lips were blue, and I could barely bend my fingers. Scott argued that we had to be close.

Finally we agreed to call in our pickup and quit until tomorrow. Randy and I found a narrow spot where a running jump and a bit of a swim got us to Scott and Roger's side of the river. But as the chopper hovered in above a hillock, the search captain urged us back downhill by pointing urgently at the river. Twenty yards from where we had quit, an arm waved up and down in the current. Call it adrenaline or fear, but suddenly I stopped shivering.

Scott and I spent an hour up to our necks in icy water, trying to girth-hitch that waving arm. Her hand felt alive, and my heart galloped at the thought of the disembodied hand grabbing me back; mostly I wanted to get the job over with as quickly as possible. Every time I looped the webbing past the knuckles, the slippery, bloated flesh greased out of my own hands and back down into the depths. Through the murky waters I could make out a head of long, brown hair suspended in the current. Maybe I *was* hypothermic and tired, but there in that icy river there was the recurring impression that, if you got too close, this underwater Medusa would snatch you down and pull you under for company. Scott diagnosed, more rationally, that getting too close to the body would trap one of us—despite the roped belay—in the same rock crack that held Gretta fast.

Randy, his hair down to his waist, smiled like a knowing Buddhist and said, "Hey, she's dead, you guys, mellow out." So we threw the grappling hook. After snagging a leg and yanking, dreading that we might separate a limb, the body came free like a champagne cork and shot down the rapids. We ran pell-mell until the corpse finally caught on a shoal a hundred yards downstream.

Scott swam out with the rope and secured the body. When we pulled it ashore, I made the mistake of looking too long. Her hazel eyes leaked light, not water, and her pink face seemed frozen in a wan smile. Roger muttered that she still looked alive.

"She's too young," I said, "much, much too young."

Someone passed me the body bag, I looked away, and then it was done. No one spoke. We shivered beneath the rotor wash. My closest friends stood surrounding me, and I was thankful for that. We had enough respect not to try to lighten things with a joke. We all held hands over our ears, and the helicopter labored up the dark canyon. The orange body bag drew lazy, spinning circles against the sky.

On the bus back to headquarters I didn't know whether I was hot or cold. Fifty other rescuers sat jubilantly relieved. I put my pile jacket on, then took it off ten times before a woman across the aisle smiled. When she turned toward the front I thought for an instant that I was looking at Gretta. I closed my eyes and wiped my hands again and again and again on my pants legs.

At the rescue debriefing, I walked out because there was nothing to be learned. Moreover, one of the law enforcement rangers at headquarters had examined the naked body and made a lewd remark that left me and my partners filled with revulsion. I craved a hot shower.

While driving back to Talkeetna, we stared at pavement as dark as the night and discussed what kind of political pull the Berglund family had to put together a search that would cost the taxpayers more than $60,000. I tried to get our boss to stop for whiskey in Cantwell, but no one had any money. Bob drove all three hours, and no one spoke as water rinsed through the wheel wells like a broken washing machine. The mountain hid beneath the sorry black curtain that covered all of Alaska.

During that long, wordless drive, I realized that life beneath the mountain moved quicker than anywhere else, like a series of departures. Spring fell into summer, which bled into fall, but the darkened winter, as the joke goes, is the only true season in Alaska.

Finding tranquillity amid this landscape of perpetual change was tough. All was constant transition: Salmon were spawning and dying in the streams, wolves stalked the ungulates, and rivers flooded their banks. Life was short here. Although several climbers died every year up on the mountain, *off* the mountain, death seemed as constant as Denali, holding a dazzling white vigil above all of its dominion.

Back at our creaky-floored ranger station, home to a family of mice and colonies of mildew, we were all too tired to talk, so I walked to the back bedroom. I lay down on my bed and hoped the rain would stop by dawn. Sleep stole me away.

In the small hours of that morning, Gretta arrived outside and began scratching her fingernails against the window. I fought to wake up and end the nightmare, to no avail. So I forced myself to look in her wide hazel eyes again, and that placid pink face from the river was now a death mask of terror and unhappiness. If this was a dream, and if dreams can offer a glimmer of reality, Gretta Berglund was even more frightened than I because her destination was somewhere that no one should go until they're good and ready. Athapaskan stories tell of dead spirits walking down either an easy trail or a trail of suffering; Gretta's path was obvious.

When I finally forced myself awake and lunged for the window, she was gone. I sat up and turned on the light. During the long black hours before dawn the rain hammered the roof.

I lay awake thinking about Gretta. I was certain she had visited.

Although Gretta had now left the window, I could not put her out of my mind. Athapaskans also believe that spirits have a very long journey to make into their afterlife. Spirits were considered dangerous, and in the instance of violent death, they often lingered in the place where they had been killed; I was not anxious to return to the Sanctuary River. Spirits, the stories said, were most active at night.

Life around Denali seemed constantly shaded by such death. Perhaps I had just reached an age when everyone confronts these issues. Indeed, no one lives forever. My friends would die and I would die—perhaps even tomorrow.

While living elsewhere, it seemed a lot easier to "use your fun tickets" and become so preoccupied that you could avoid this nagging tug of mortality. But around the mountain the nature of rescue work—moreover, the immutable raw power of the primal landscape— left me with a new impression of how fragile life really is. Sooner or later, anyone living on the mountain or in its checkered shadow would be forced to confront the inexorable cycle of death.

The talk around town held that Herb had become a binge drinker. It had rained most of that summer, and locals wondered aloud if this was the year that Talkeetna—Athapaskan for "three rivers"—would flood.

Scott and I were ticketed at Montana Creek for fishing in a poorly signed closed area by a zealous fish and game cop. As he wrote us up, I entertained punting the potbellied, gun-slinging fish cop into the river, which Herb would have appreciated. Instead I let justice take its own slow course. The ticket read "fishing in a closed area"— which we thought was open—and we were to appear in court a month later.

Near the end of the salmon season, while fishing out on the Susitna River with Herb and Scott, I hooked a king salmon (*ggaal* in Athapaskan) that pulled like a whalish sixty-pounder. It exploded two feet out of the water as a blur of red-backed quicksilver, and after it splashed back into the milk-colored current, every angler on the shore pulled in their lines. The boat nearly tipped over when I stood up and "the king" surged downriver.

Of course, Herb, and even Scott, had landed the richest and biggest salmon. I had not. So it had become ritual for Scott to tease me that "I was not man enough" to bring in a king—naturally he was jesting, but Herb interpreted Scott's banter as condemnation; I didn't know why.

I had hooked kings before in this seven-mile-per-hour current, but they always turned downriver, and before Herb could pull the anchor and give chase, they broke my line. This time, though, Herb had changed my line to a sturdier ten-pound test, and I was playing the fish slowly, letting it run. Then winding it in slowly, letting it run, winding it in slowly.

I succeeded in coaxing the fish to the boat in fifteen minutes. As Scott reached toward it too quickly with the net, the king spooked and ran: My lightweight fiberglass pole snapped in two with the resounding crack of a sapling split by winter; now the king bolted downriver. Herb tried to smile. Scott laughed. I slammed the pole on the gunwale, then pulled the anchor. Nobody spoke as Herb yanked the engine to a roar and took us downriver, cupping his cigarette and steering the Envinrude tiller. He watched the ubiquitous and dazzling white mountain as if maybe fulfillment could be found up there in the clouds.

The next morning in the kitchen I found a brand-new, stout halibut fishing pole, guaranteed for hauling up hundred-pound monsters. The etiquette of lightweight fly rods did not impress Herb, and I would no sooner proselytize about sportsmanship in fishing than he would tell me how to climb Denali. Anyway, the rod was the same brand as Herb's, and it balanced on the counter where the salmon gifts had been placed. Herb was sitting on the couch drinking coffee—he clutched the cup tightly with both hands—nervously, it seemed, because he could not smoke in the ranger station. I picked up my gift carefully; tools of the hunt were infused with spiritual power and must be treated with respect. Herb flashed me that guileless smile of a man innocent of the complex world outside.

"That telephone pole," he said, "ain't gonna break. Let's get you a king."

Herb began his own passage toward the mountain during a rainy September night. In the middle of a dinner party at the ranger station, Nellie Atwater burst in and shouted, "Come quick, Herb's trying to kill his father!"

Scott and I sprinted across the railroad tracks and found Herb incoherent, his breath stinking sweeter than gin, his normally affable brown eyes filled with red rage at a world in which he could not belong, and inadvertently aimed at his father, Ted. When Ted's face appeared at the locked door, Herb bolted forward screaming murderous thoughts and threw his fist as Ted jumped away from the flying glass. Herb raked his arm back through the jagged shards of the door.

Blood covered his shirt. Scott and I tried to inspect his arm, but he pushed us off and warned us to leave as more blood spurted from his biceps. "You'll bleed out," Scott pleaded. "Let us help you!" But Herb only turned with slitted eyes toward the house, his blue jeans blackening with blood.

Scott's lips were clenched tightly, and we glanced at one another with eyes as wide as deer caught in headlights. I clenched my fist—never doubting my friendship with Herb—drew back my arm, and swung in an urgent, precise arc until my fist connected with the point of Herb's jaw. He dropped backward like a chainsawed tree. I jumped onto him and pinned his elbows with my knees while Scott held pressure on the three-inch laceration on the soft flesh of Herb's arm. Nellie called for an ambulance.

It was only an hour's ride to the Palmer hospital, but the oily, starless night stretched on and on as Herb struggled against the restraining straps, alternately whispering in my ear so his mother wouldn't hear, "Kill me, Jon, please kill me tonight, go ahead and do it, oh, please, kill me kill me kill me." I touched him softly on the shoulder, then clenched his hand as Nellie told him that we all loved him. At the hospital the doctor gave him a sedative, and everyone tried to erase the night from their memories.

A week later, Scott and I faced the judge. He announced to the courtroom of drunk drivers, bitter divorcees, and common criminals that we were federal rangers, no less, fishing in a closed area. We explained that the fine print on the fishing sign at Montana Creek was ambiguous, but the judge fined us each $100 anyway. Scott wrote out his check immediately so he would not jeopardize his ranger career; I just waved goodbye to the court clerk. If the bureaucrats who managed the Alaska Fish and Game Department ever issued a warrant for my arrest, I never knew about it.

At dawn of the first day of moose season, Herb took his fourteen-hundred-pound bull moose with the big pistol. Scott and I helped carry in the ribs, then the legs, then the haunches. It took all three of us to carry in the majestic antlered head. My pants were dappled with sticky blood; my back would ache for days.

Herb was sheepish at dinner, and although I whispered to him that nothing had changed for Scott or me, the smile had faded from Herb's face and his eyes lacked their usual luster. An unspoken shame wedged between father and son because Herb had not taken a career. He wanted to spend his time knocking the heads of grouse and stalking the waters for salmon and admiring moose prancing in the forest. He was an instinctive hunter and woodsman plunged into a world ignorant of the truth of the Distant Time. If the analogy of Raven holds true, Herb had also been turned down by a woman, but unlike Raven, Herb had no magic with which to calm the waters.

Nonetheless, the ritual of our moose feast made everyone light-hearted and happy. Instead of saying grace, Nellie passed the nostril (*bintsiyh*). It fell apart between my teeth like putrid gray gelatin, and I caught Herb smiling so beautifully from across the table that I laughed instead of gagging and thought that the taking of the moose had somehow restored my kindhearted friend. But I was wrong.

That winter Herb accepted a job pounding nails in Anchorage, far from the salmon streams that sustained him—Athapaskan legends tell of the salmon's ability to protect people from bad spirits. But Herb wore no dried salmon around his neck. And Herb had no one to marry, not even a girlfriend.

In the blackest part of winter, Herb began drinking again and concluded that he had no place in the modern world anymore. He had not fished for six months. His life seemed so distant from the wild country that made him whole that he unholstered his eight-inch pistol, lifted it deliberately to his head, and pulled the trigger.

> Wait, I see something:
> It is spreading softly on the surface of the water.
> Answer: Blood from the king salmon, clubbed in the water
> so it will not upset the canoe when it is pulled inside.

When Herb was alive, fishing and hunting sustained him just as Denali's glacial melt returned the salmon from the sea, just as the mountain's rich river sustained the moose.

On my wall there is a photograph of Herb, Scott, and me each holding up forty- to fifty-pound salmon. I had caught my first king all because of Herb. It was more than his kind patience and the "telephone pole"; it was his gift of intuition for the spirit of life that would make even sonar seem obsolete.

In the background of my photograph are a lush green meadow and thick leafy woods where a family of feral cats waited for scraps. Scott and I jostled one another about whose fish was bigger; Herb stood just beside us so serene with his broad cheekbones, holding the most silver-skinned fish of them all.

I do not know if he went down the trail of suffering or the easy trail. I am sure that either way, like Gretta, he haunts his river.

Now I know that "to hunt" literally translated from the Athapaskan tongue means "to be a man." And I will never forget that Herb and his father's father's fathers named the mountain Denali.

$\mathscr{F}$ROM THE $\mathscr{F}$ARAWAY $\mathscr{N}$EARBY

John A. Murray

The dangers of life are infinite, and safety is among them.

—Goethe

I. In late August, 1992, Duane Crawford and I flew in a twin-engine Beechcraft from Fairbanks, Alaska, where we lived and worked, 150 miles north to Fort Yukon. From there we were flown, one at a time, in a Piper Supercub 75 miles into the Brooks Range, where we established a camp and hunted caribou for a week.

What follows is an account of that trip.

Those who have heard the chronicle have often urged me to make a written version, and so here it is, such as it is, a narrative that has heretofore been available only as a campfire tale, a fugitive artifact of the backwoods, as, they say, the story of the Laestrygonians was once, or any of those anecdotes regarding Odin and Ymir the frost giant, or, for that matter, the Wife of Bath's tale.

II. The story begins with a phone call. Summer term was over and I was grading English papers in my windowless office—a converted music practice room—in the basement of the fine-arts complex at the University of Alaska. On the phone was Duane Crawford, a former student, saying that his brother-in-law was too sick to accompany him on a caribou hunt and that he needed a replacement. He had to find this replacement by the end of the day, and I was the only person he knew outside of work. In retrospect, I should have realized that Duane's brother-in-law was too sick of *Duane* to come on the hunt. In

259

any event, I was, at least then, always willing to render assistance to anyone in need, and so I told Duane, sure, man, I just happen to have a spare week before fall semester, I'll help bail you out of this little situation, yes, yes, of course I understand. Don't worry about a thing. I'll be at the south end of the airport tomorrow morning. Right, 6:00 sharp. Alright, then, 5:30.

The garage turned upside down, all manner of outdoor gear spread across the living room floor, driving around town for supplies, grades handed into the Dean's office, little if any sleep.

Disarry and uncertainty, the parents of every disaster.

On the flight over to Fort Yukon I spent most of my time admiring the White Mountains, a wild glaciated range Alfred Bierstadt would have loved. Duane sat across the aisle reading the morning paper, telling me, among other things, that the latest polls showed his man Bush handily defeating the Arkansas governor. To which I decided the best response was silence. Once past the White Mountains the country flattened into a basin that stretched to the horizons—brown muskeg and green patches of spruce, shallow lakes and ponds, peat bogs and horsetail fens, occasionally the odd hill, aspen or birch covered. We flew across the Yukon Flats on a line as straight as the mark a jeweler cuts on a diamond, and after awhile I saw the big brown river ahead, low and muscular and slow, winding its way across that province of the world as it had been doing since the beginning of time.

The airport was located in a birch forest south of town, which in turn was downstream from the confluence with the Porcupine River. As we made our approach Fort Yukon sprawled below: a community building, the Alaska Commercial Company general store, a busy waterfront, a school with a baseball field, several churches, a couple of log-hewn lodges, and the scattered homes of the 600 souls who called this place home. The pilot circled once, losing altitude, and then lined up with the runway—cabins and outbuildings below, people in flannel shirts cutting wood and working in vegetable gardens, woodsmoke puffing from stovepipes.

Mornings are cold in the valley, even in late August.

After we landed and pulled the gear from the belly of the beast, Duane led the way across the runway to Elden Morris's maroon-and-white Supercub, tied down beside a 500-gallon aviation fuel tank. The depot served as the international headquarters for Elden's one plane operation, Sheenjek Air. It was an old plane—six years older than me—but Duane said it was a sound machine and that its pilot was not as bad as some. The passenger seat was positioned behind the pilot's seat, and both sat beneath the oversized wing. Behind the passenger seat was enough room for one seabag, a backpack, and a rifle. The plane looked as though it would fly, through no fault of its own.

As we stood there waiting, two Kutchin men drove up on a four-wheeler to say that Elden was on his way. They were his neighbors, Sam and Charlie, and appeared to be brothers. Duane showed them his rifle, a .375 H and H magnum. A man lies in direct proportion to the size of the rifle in his hands—consider that an axiom.

A little while later Elden roared up on a motorcycle with his terrier, Hayduke, and I was introduced to both man and dog. Hayduke would be accompanying us on the trip, Elden announced, because he had proven himself to be a "good-luck charm." Elden was a gentle giant, half Kutchin and half Canadian, and was thick-necked and big-shouldered as all firewood cutters are. He wore a faded "Midnight Sun Fun Run" T-shirt and a Sourdough Roadhouse baseball hat. His jeans were stained with the recent blood of moose and salmon. On his feet were well-worn surplus army boots, the sort girlfriends are always trying to throw away but wives do not mind so much. In the village he was famous among schoolchildren for owning the only Harley-Davidson north of the Arctic Circle.

Elden told us that he had been having minor engine problems all week but that he believed everything would be alright today, or at least he sincerely hoped that would be the case.

Duane, who had previously insisted that he go first, now generously suggested that I have the privilege, and so we loaded the plane with my gear and some of his. After waving goodbye to Duane and the men still admiring his howitzer, I squeezed into the seat behind Elden with Hayduke on my lap, careful not to disturb the cables on the floor that controlled the rudder and flaps in the tail.

Elden started the engine, which smoked at first from a "bad gasket—nothing to worry about," and we idled to the main runway, stopped on the numbers, received clearance from the tower, and proceeded to take off. Or tried to. A couple of hundred yards down the runway, at an altitude of 10 or 12 feet, the engine sputtered, stalled, started up again, and then completely conked out. After losing power we dropped back heavily and unevenly onto the runway, first on the right wheel and then on the left, and then back again, careened toward the edge of the pavement, and then braked so abruptly that Hayduke cut his lip on the back of Elden's seat.

Both pilot and passenger climbed out and pushed the plane into the grass so that Elden could install new spark plugs. I was assigned the task of hammering the right wheel support, now partially bent, into a straight position. The support had been previously repaired with a section of hollow plumbing pipe and so I had to be careful with the framing hammer.

While we were working on the plane a military transport touched down—a C-130 Hercules—and it was exhilarating to stand a few yards from a landing aircraft. Crew members stared incredulously from cockpit windows. The dog was transported into a state of religious ecstasy by the experience, barking so energetically his feet left the ground.

Forty-five minutes after the aborted liftoff we attempted to become airborne again—and this time actually made it.

Shortly we were flying over the Yukon Flats, the quiet village and the broad muddy river behind us.

From the air we saw the north country as the white-fronted goose or the black plover sees it. And it was a beautiful country, far more so from 500 than from 5,000 feet. The wild grasses were dry and hay-colored with winter approaching and the birch groves and aspen parks held the last of their gold to the sun. In every low place there was water. Around every lake, and there were thousands of old sloughs and stranded oxbows and dead muskeg ponds, you could see the trails of moose. They led through the smoky yellow willows into the forests where the moose slept, heavy and dark and still as the centuries. A rock was a rarity. Anything stationary soon disappeared into the mouldering green moss. From the sphagnum grew many things, but the tallest and most striking were the spruce. They were as numberless as the quills on a porcupine and they came in two varieties: thin and very thin. Across the whole landscape there was not one sign of the human race. Not one cabin. Not one boat dock. Not one smoke plume from one campfire. Here was the New World before the cross-bearing conquistadors, before the slave plantations, before Wounded Knee and the Dust Bowl and the Trinity Site. Here was the beginning and the end.

"You know," Elden said through the headsets, "I was the first person to land on this mountain."

"When was that?"

"About two weeks ago."

Elden spoke in a soft, restrained voice, as if superstitious that raising his voice or speaking disrespectfully about anything would bring him bad luck. I adjusted the earphones and tried to move my knees into a more comfortable position. The dog was staring out the window as intently as a person.

"How do you know you were the first?"

"No wind sock. First thing a pilot does is put down his flag. Country's big enough we don't bother each other. At least most of us don't. Nobody in Yuk knows about this mountain, and I plan to keep it that way. Do you see that lake coming up on the right?"

I told him I did.

"That's Kwittevunkud. My middle son Ronnie killed his first bull moose on the lake a year ago."

"How old is he?"

"Thirteen next month."

I spotted a lanky black bear eating blueberries on the shore of the lake, and Elden said if the bear didn't put on more weight it wouldn't survive the winter.

"You see them sometimes," he continued, "in the middle of the winter. They come out on the ridges, covered with frost. They don't last long at fifty below. A week later you see where the wolves have found them."

I asked him how he found the mountain, and he said that he was taking a shortcut home from a Dall sheep camp on the Wind River, dropped through a hole in the clouds, and "there it was." He spotted a pair of shed moose antlers and landed on the tundra to pick them up.

"What do you do with them?"

"I just like to have them around the yard."

I knew that wasn't true, but didn't say anything.

I asked him if we could see the mountain yet and he said no, we were still too far away, but that after awhile it would appear dead ahead. I peered over his shoulder and past the vibrating gauges and through the blur of the propeller at the foothills of the Brooks Range, about 70 miles away. Behind the foothills were the clear sharp peaks of the Arctic Divide. Above the Arctic Divide were clouds, high and brilliant white with summits trailing plumes and plunging misty canyons—the cumulus clouds of summer still.

Elden told me about the country as we flew north, about how the Brooks Range was the northernmost mountain range on the planet and was home to everything from polar bears to flying squirrels; and how each November he counted moose for the state in aerial surveys; and how the perpetually burning summer fires caused the broad sweeping patterns of dead and living forests we were seeing. He pointed to Burnt Mountain, a vast unfinished pyramid of a mountain to the northeast, and said the government built a remote seismic detector there to listen for Soviet nuclear tests at Novaya Zemlya. Burnt Mountain was, Elden claimed, the quietest seismic location on earth. In bad weather he often landed just below the summit to wait for blue skies, and sometimes poked around the "top-secret" strontium-90 generators that every ten-year-old child in Fort Yukon knew about. I asked him about his family, and he told me about his Kutchin wife Monica, a nurse in the village, and his three children, and how this bushpiloting was sure better than anything he had done before, fighting fires for the BLM, or trapping lynx with his brother from homemade dogsleds (snowmobiles being unreliable in the deep cold of January) on the Coleen River, or working as a deckhand on a Yukon freighter barge.

Suddenly the plane lurched into a steep left-hand bank and I felt a stab of adrenaline. Even without looking I knew the cause. Before departing Fort Yukon, Duane—worried he had too much gear for the second trip—had insisted that we take along his empty backpack. The only place for it had been tied loosely to the left wing strut, which angles from the bottom of the plane to the center of the wing and holds the wing in place. Because Duane had tied the pack the wrong way, the main bag had blown open in the airflow and was dragging us down. Elden worked the plane back to our cruising altitude of 500 feet and was now constantly fighting the plane's tendency to bank in the direction of the resistance.

It took awhile, but our hearts finally slowed from a gallop to a canter.

"Boy," Elden said, his neck muscles bulging as he grasped the yoke, his voice now strained, "I just wish there was some way I could climb out there and cut it loose. That thing could make landing tricky. And if it blows off and hits the tail . . ."

His voice trailed into silence.

I pictured a sudden wind gust on final approach, the left wing dropping sharply, the plane cartwheeling across the steppes.

After a few minutes of battling the yoke, Elden said, "Do you think—"

I finished the sentence. "Yeah, I can do it."

"How?"

I explained my proposal and asked if he could safely reduce airspeed a little to make it easier, and he said yes.

"Elden, do you by any chance have any rope under your seat? I've got some in the pack but it's hard to reach."

"I've got plenty of rope."

"Good. Give me as much as you can."

Elden reached under his seat, one hand on the yoke, and handed me a coil of blood-stained half-inch rope over his shoulder.

"Don't forget to take your glasses off," he said.

"Right."

I placed my glasses in my baseball hat and laid it under the seat. I could feel Elden throttle back. I didn't like the sluggish feel of the plane at lower speed, and we were already losing what little altitude we had, but it would hopefully only take a minute.

"Everything okay up there?"

"No problem."

"Alright, here goes."

I unfolded my skinning knife and laid it beside me on the seat, unsnapped the safety belt, put Hayduke on the floor, took off my headsets, and lowered the window. Loose items began flying around the cabin immediately—an aerial map, a paper cup, the page from a mail-order catalog—and were promptly sucked out the window into the maelstrom. I squeezed my head, arms, and torso through the window, leaned into the airflow—which was like leaning into the side of a tornado—and tied one end of the rope to the top of the pack frame, with three half-hitches behind the knot to hold it secure. When that was done I slid back in and tied the other end of the rope to the crossbar under the bottom of the seat, tightly. I then reentered the wind tunnel with knife in hand and began cutting away the quarter-inch nylon rope that held the pack to the wing strut.

When every inch of Duane's rope was five miles behind us I wrestled the pack through the window—it just fit, at the widest angle and with considerable wrenching and pulling. Once the pack was inside—temporarily pinning Hayduke to the floor, but he seemed to understand the importance of being still just then—I raised the window and locked it tight.

"Everything secure?" Elden asked, looking over his shoulder. I didn't have my headsets on yet, and so it was hard to hear him over the engine.

"Yeah," I said.

I snapped my seatbelt and put the headsets on. My whole body was numb, my right ear felt strange, and my eyes hurt. The headsets had become unplugged, and so I had to search for the plug until I finally found it above me. Once I was settled in, Hayduke crawled into my lap and began smelling the pack. It was a nuisance there between me and the left side of the plane, and so I worked the pack between the back of Elden's seat and my knees—a tight squeeze but better than having it on the strut.

The knife was on the seat beside me. I snapped it shut and put it back in my pocket. After that I put my glasses and baseball hat back on.

The plane was gaining speed—and altitude.

"I can feel the difference already," said Elden.

"Me, too."

"I'll never do that again," said Elden. "I tie antlers to the struts all the time. But I had no idea how dangerous a pack could be."

The plane was flying straight and normally now.

Elden studied the wing for awhile and then, as if guilty for something he was thinking, said, "Still, Duane's a good guy. Don't tell him this, but I'd fly him up here for free I like him so much."

I knew the only reason Elden said that was because Duane's agency—the Bureau of Reclamation—was a major source of his income.

"Yeah, he's an interesting person," I said.

"How'd you two meet?"

"He was a student of mine."

Duane had dropped out after a month. The reason for his enrolling in the night class, a writing seminar, was never clear, perhaps related to work.

As we talked I scanned the terrain. The level earth stretched out evenly toward every horizon, with mountains rising at a distance in all directions. The mountains to the north were considerably closer than the others. Soon we would be over the foothills. Everywhere I looked there were places I had never seen, places I would never go. I was so happy I wanted to shout for joy, or cut loose with a rebel yell, but restrained myself with the microphone.

"Are we in the Arctic Refuge yet?"

"Just crossed the southern boundary."

"Man, this is beautiful."

"Oh yeah."

We were in the mountains now, a tumbled hill and valley country with the gentle contours and rounded knolls of the oldest grounds. The fall colors, the reds and oranges and yellows, were like an oriental tapestry, and there were caribou moving across the tundra domes. Down below, in the wide timbered valleys, beaver ponds backed the clear cold water up into grassy swales and cattail marshes and moose thickets, and from the sheer number of ponds I would have guessed that no one had trapped this country in about 10,000 years. We were flying low enough to see the Arctic grayling in schools just beneath the surface of the ponds, and once I spotted a pair of trumpeter swans and pointed them out to Elden, who nodded and said they would be turning south to Oregon soon. Far to the east a flock of white cranes the size of a jumbo jet fluttered south, and I watched them until they vanished. It was the finest country I'd ever seen. In my life I had never been so many hundreds of miles from a road, and I probably never would be farther, and so I scanned the whole country in every direction several times to get a complete sense of its scope. Wherever I looked there were mountains in every size and shape, as if this was the warehouse where God came when he was building a new range and needed a mountain.

To the east twenty miles was the wide cut of the Sheenjek River, and I marked its drainage carefully, for the Sheenjek is where, Elden was saying, we would have to hike if anything happened to him and the plane. "Just follow any drainage east and you'll wind up on a gravel bar beside the Sheenjek. Build three smoky fires and wait."

Ahead of us and beyond the foothills was the cordillera of the Brooks Range, which looked like the Rocky Mountains west of Denver, and I asked if we would be flying much closer to the high peaks.

"Not today. And I'm glad. You can't tell from here, but the wind is blowing through those passes like a hurricane right now."

A minute later Elden motioned to a prominent mountain underneath the left wing and told me not to talk anymore, that he needed to concentrate on the landing. From the air the mountain resembled an enormous island rising from a sea of forest. The greater length of the mountain measured about five miles, and two side ridges extended a mile or so from the central mass. Elden pointed with his finger to the compass on the instrument panel, and I saw that the needle was spinning wildly, as if we were flying over a magnet. As we neared the mountain I could feel its power. The midday thermals buffeted the wings like the first punches of a boxer early in the round. The plane banked abruptly and then made a sharper turn and began losing altitude rapidly as Elden lined up with some point I could not see.

All the time we were bucking regularly and things were falling down—Elden's spiral-bound logbook lodged between the instrument panel and the windshield, the small pair of binoculars stored in the net bag over his seat. My head was banging against the top of the plane, and I held on to the bottom of the seat and kept an arm around Hayduke. I studied the main ridge closely, rising ahead of us like the back of a moose, and wondered where a plane could possibly land. Every instinct in my body told me there was no place to land a fixed-wing aircraft, and I wanted to suggest that we pull up while there was still time and fly elsewhere, but Elden had asked me not to speak and he was sitting in the pilot's seat. Before I knew it we were over the trees. I could not believe we were that low, with nothing resembling a safe landing place ahead, and that we hadn't hit a tree yet. If I had been sitting on the wheel brace my feet would have been dragging on the tops of the spruce trees. I put my head down so that I would not see what was about to happen, and then, not able to resist, I looked up. As we came in a bit too fast, with the wings pivoting back and forth on the ground winds and the rubber tires a few feet over the last trees and the engine throttled just above stall and nothing ahead but reindeer moss and rocks and a scattering flock of ptarmigan, I was fairly certain it would be a fatal crash.

But we didn't crash and the 45-year-old plane bounced and braked to a quick stop on the gravelly slope near Elden's wind sock, which was a blaze orange scarf tied to a dead white spruce.

Elden said it was okay to get out, and so I removed the earphones, opened the door, and jumped down after Hayduke. It was good to be on the ground again—real good. Elden followed, relieved himself on the dead spruce with Hayduke, helped unload the gear, looked over the plane, then stood with his hands on his hips, surveying the landscape as if he were the owner, which in a way he was.

"This is the country, eh?" he said.

That it was—in every direction, a place so stunning it would be a national park anywhere else in the world.

"You know, people live their entire lives and never see anything like this. Just think of all the people right now in the Lower 48 who would kill to be where we are."

I agreed.

"I never forget how special the Arctic is," he said. "Even a bad day here is better than the best day any place else. Still—." He paused, a flock of chickadees chirping by on a gust of wind without a care in the world. "I don't want to be doing this forever. Not with kids to raise."

Elden then mentioned there was no water on top of the mountain and that we would have to hike to the bottom of yonder valley for water. No big deal, we both agreed, although it looked to be a four-mile round trip.

"Just out of curiosity," I asked, "how close is the nearest person?"

"That would be Arctic Village—60 miles in that direction."

He pointed to the northwest.

I remembered all the crowded places I'd been, the tedious lost years in cities and suburbs and even small forgotten towns that were bustling centers of humanity compared to the absolute solitude of the bush, and I felt fortunate.

As Elden and Hayduke got back into the Supercub, a sort of time machine if you thought about it, he turned and said, "Remember everything I said and have a good hunt."

He gave me a little salute and I returned it. And then the door closed and he was gone, the little red-and-white plane bouncing down the slope and off into the big blue, and I was more alone than I had ever been in my life, with the pale sky curving away deep and far and empty. The air was more clean than anything I'd ever breathed. It was an extraordinary air born on the northern ice and washed by the swells of the Arctic Ocean and scrubbed by the glacial peaks and freshened by a million square miles of open tundra. It reminded me of ocean air, only it was better, for it carried with it the scent of snow and winter and, somewhere nearby, caribou. It smelled of distance, of space that had never known a surveyor's transit or a township line, and never would.

I stood there for quite some time just taking it in, feeling a great sense of relief, as an ailing patient does when finally placed in the hands of a competent physician.

After awhile I carried my gear down the hill to timberline and made camp. I found a perfect place, a dry terrace surrounded by blueberry bushes, facing east and out of the wind. There were even a few spruce trees to give the place a little more life and comfort.

I then returned to the top of the mountain.

The views were immense—in every direction. To the north and west were tundra highlands—low massive hills, grassy swales, isolated granite tors. South of the mountain the country sloped off through wooded foothills toward the Yukon Flats, and to the east was the Sheenjek Valley—heavily forested, cut north to south by the river, with treeless uplands on the far side.

In all the sky there was not one cloud.

It was a clear warm day. There was a soft autumnal light over the hills, as in those Winslow Homer paintings of Newfoundland, and the sky was flawless in its clarity. It was the sort of day when a sound, however small, carries a long way—the cry of a raven, the chatter of a pine squirrel, a spruce half-fallen and creaking against another. The landscape was filled with color, though in the subtle tones of the spent earth: the rusted stalks of fireweed, the salmon-hued clumps of blueberry, the dull orange streaks of dwarf birch, and, under it all, the grayish cream of reindeer moss.

I looked at my feet and saw many old friends—cotton grass, cranberry, crowberry, cloudberry, moss campion. Because of the rainy summer, the blueberries were thick. Some were dangling from twigs and others were lost in the leaves. Most were sweet, but a few, touched by frost, were tart. All showed variations on the color blue—from Prussian blue to pinkish blue and everything in between. Among the blueberries were a few late bloomers: yellow dryas, white bistort, and bright red shooting stars, each deeply bedded in the mat of reindeer moss and heather.

I walked a mile west across the ridge, to where it joined the main ridge, and stopped where the trees ended. I had forgotten—always do—how hard it is to walk on tundra, which more or less levitates over the permafrost. There was grizzly scat on the ground in several places, filled with berries, and I took note of the fact that the bears had passed through earlier that day, an adult and her nearly full-grown cubs. At the edge of the trees, half buried in the moss, was the lichen-covered skull of a bull caribou. The lichens were orange and ochre and olive and resembled the encrustations of coral on a reef, colonizing dead matter with the bright colors of the sea. One painted antler protruded upward, the other was covered with moss and fallen willow leaves. The antler that stuck up had been gnawed on by a porcupine on its furthest tines. Down lower the size of the teeth marks indicated something smaller—a boreal mouse or red-backed vole. Tilting the skull upward from its resting place, I saw that the bone was stained green and black where it touched the ground—the earth had begun to reclaim its loan.

What else?

A spider had occupied one eye socket for the short summer—bits of web and a few ant carapaces remained in the cavern.

The single protruding antler resembled a hunting bow in the grace of its curve, and I saw how easy it would be to fashion a bow from the antler, with the proper tools. Even sharp stones would do, and for a bow string perhaps fibers twisted from the thin supple roots of spruce.

And what of those cliffs over there—couldn't caribou be driven over them? What a treasure trove could be obtained, and so easily. And there would be furbearers drawn by the scent—wolf, wolverine, lynx, fox—and they could be snared, their fur the difference between life and death when the cold of outer space came to earth.

The mind considers such things, alone and in a wild place.

Old memories, strange but familiar, return from the past.

Suddenly a keen chill flowed across the land—a bitter western wind—and I heard the persistent annoying buzz of an airplane.

III. It was evening now and Duane sat across the fire against a stump, a steel cup of tea in his hands. We'd already burned one timberline tree, and had started another. I hated to burn those beautiful dead trees—it was like destroying works of art—but the fire felt good against the Arctic cold. Behind Duane was what looked like the Ur-backpacking tent from the 1960s. The zipper had long ago been torn off, and the front flaps were held together with a dozen safety pins. It was the first time I had ever really looked at Duane. He was a big man, with a rising tide of gray in his mustache and thick eyebrows and shaggy hair, and the widening paunch of a man approaching 50 who has spent too much time behind a desk. His eyes were set back under a prominent bony arch, and so he looked out at the world as from a cavern. The right eye squinted frequently, as if he knew that one bad thing you did once. The only other notable feature on his face was a red spot on his cheek where the frost had paid a visit—a not uncommon feature to those who have wintered in the Arctic.

The western sky held its violet-cobalt blue light until past seven, and then slowly darkened through a Phoenician purple to an ivory black, revealing stars and northern lights. The moon was low in the east and so the sky was fine for northern lights. The auroras were like self-contained theatrical events, beginning in the north with a minor rustling of green or red, then building to a whirling crescendo at the zenith and finally playing out toward the south. I never tired of watching them—wave after wave they came on, some as delicate as the light reflected on the ceiling of a grotto, others the visual equivalent of a Jimi Hendrix guitar solo.

As I sat there carving on a piece of wood, and occasionally looking up to admire the northern lights, Duane was pretty much holding court, and I was letting him run with himself, curious to see where it led. Unfortunately, as the evening progressed and he revealed more about himself ("Pardon my profanity but this is the way I talk"), I began to realize the grotesque nature of my plight. The man across the fire, whom I'd known only casually in town and consequently made many false assumptions about, was my polar opposite. In fact it was worse than that. Duane was of the nature of an evil twin or anti-self, an antipodal character such as populate the works of Joseph "The Secret Sharer" Conrad. In story after story, one disturbing revelation after another surfaced from his murky depths. First was the incident from Vietnam, which involved the killing of a civilian in retaliation for a series of casualties suffered by his unit, and with no remorse on his part. Next was the elaborate fiction concerning a self-inflicted wound in his foot that brought him, a troubled draftee, back home six months early. Then came a rambling piece of vitriol concerning the various races, Duane unaware that my first wife was Jewish, my second wife was Japanese, my sister-in-law was black, and so on. The whole thing reminded me of the "Star Trek" episode in which Captain Kirk and his nemesis the reptile captain were marooned on a desert planet by invisible superbeings as part of some sort of interstellar behavioral experiment.

Indeed.

What happened?

After an hour, tired and disgusted, I got up, and, despite the inconvenience, moved my tent and gear under the stars to the far side of the mountain, the bright side of the planet, and a quarter of a mile from Duane. I told him that I could not tolerate one thing in this world and that was racism. I also told him I had seen my share of the human condition in the service, but that nothing in that experience quite compared with what I had just heard. I told him that we were stuck together in this place for the week and I would be polite and make the best of it, but that I preferred some distance between us.

I had lived long enough to know there was little point in trying to reform a person over the age of 40, particularly one whose vulgarity ran in such a deep fissure from circumference to center.

As I left, Duane, surprised someone had finally stood up to him, mumbled something about it being better to camp together because of the bears.

That was the first night, before things got really bad.

In the morning the clouds had moved in from the west and low-ered over the top of the mountain and fog was running everywhere, thick and cool and translucent, through the green forest and across the red and orange meadows, creating an optical effect such as you see in a coral reef when a storm has roiled the sand and reduced visibility. Everything was covered with a fine mist, as if the world had just been born and was covered with afterbirth. As I was putting on my rain pants and my rain jacket, which would be worn continuously for the next week, Duane walked over, ready to hunt. He seemed to have for-gotten about the previous night entirely, or at least was trying to make it appear so.

Even as I stood there trying to decide what to do with him, the fog was dissipating, the drizzle gathering strength.

I walked west on the whale-backed ridge toward the last stand of spruce, Duane following. Beyond that was a country of rolling tundra. Along the way I noted fresh caribou tracks pressed into the wet ground. Duane straggled behind, explaining how the storm was the remnant of Typhoon Iniki, which had leveled the Hawaiian Islands earlier in the week. He said there would be snow soon, as the first bliz-zard of the season rolled in from Siberia.

The man was a perpetual font of good news and cheer.

At the juncture of the ridges Duane spotted two, then three, bull caribou on a hill to the south. He told me to stand aside and watch the master as he killed them in succession from right to left (the legal limit being four per day). Duane emptied his cannon—five rounds, and each one painfully loud in the gallerylike silence—and never came close.

He then blamed me for not spotting the shots.

Repelled by the entire spectacle, I parted company with him, saying I wold spend the rest of the day exploring to the north, away from the trees, and out on the open tundra.

"Good luck," he exclaimed sarcastically.

Fifty yards later he called out and said that all kidding aside he would really appreciate it if I killed one for him, because there might be something wrong with his scope and his wife would make his life miserable if he spent all that money and returned with no meat.

Something wrong with his rifle scope? I wanted to say there might be something wrong with his head.

It was good to be away from that maniac, and after awhile I slowed my pace and enjoyed my surroundings. It was, after all, a new and good country.

I hiked for several hours at a very slow pace, not so much hunting as exploring. The going was slow on the muskeg, with the grassy mounds and tangles of heather, and with each step I became increasingly wet. Water was everywhere—at one point I sank to my thighs in a hidden baptismal pool. Near noon I came to a hill topped with granite tors, each 12 or 15 feet tall, grouped by nature in such a way as to evoke Stonehenge. Beyond the tors was a hummocky region of *baydzheraki,* or Siberian cemetery mounds—soft green remnants left behind when ice wedges melt. It would be a quagmire in that region, and so I decided to rest awhile and have lunch among the druid stones. After eating I lay down, spread the poncho over me like a tent, and fell asleep.

Hours later I awakened. The rain was drizzling steadily on the poncho, and the light told me it was much later in the day.

Ptarmigan were clucking all around.

I sat up. The flock of ptarmigan fluttered off, their wing and chest feathers already winter white, the rest of the plumage still summer brown. Nothing had changed. In all directions, fog and rain and lovely bleak tundra.

I was happy to be far from civilization and its discontents, and far from my companion, the reincarnation of Captain Ahab, and, not wanting to turn back to camp just yet, I decided to hike another mile and see what happened.

I crossed the Siberian cemetery, climbed another Labrador tea hill, crossed another peat bog, and then something far ahead made me stop. I had no binoculars or telescopic sight, and so all I could do was squint. There, at the edge of vision, was movement. I tilted my glasses to make the lenses stronger and saw there were a couple of caribou perhaps 300 yards ahead, feeding away from me, heads down. When they raised their heads I could see they were mature bulls with heavy necks and racks. I dropped my survival pack, marked the location—a lone spruce with a split main branch due east—and ran to an exposed grassy point 200 yards ahead, hidden from view by an intervening ridge.

Once there, on top of the knoll, the length of a football field from the animals, I sat down, placed my elbows on my knees, and centered the iron post on the shoulder of the nearest one. At that exact moment the caribou stopped feeding and looked around, sensing some disturbance, but the wind was in my face. I held my breath, squeezed the trigger, felt the recoil, and watched the near caribou drop. There was a second shot as he struggled, as all life does, with the strange new freedom of death.

The other caribou, including three I had not seen, ran for the horizon, every horizon, including mine—one passed at a distance of 20 feet, unaware in his panic of my presence.

When I reached the bull he was dead, sprawled out in the grass, the light gone from his amber eyes, and, as always, I was appalled at what I had done. I felt particularly bad when I noted the condition of his hooves—torn, cracked, frostbitten—and couldn't escape the sense that I had committed a crime for which I would one day be held accountable. Regret attends every death inflicted by a hunter, but on that occasion, in those surroundings, the act of sport hunting seemed particularly absurd. Even though I had hunted since I was 19, and had worked my way through college partly as a hunting guide, I resolved that I would never kill another animal again, unless personal survival was involved. He was—or rather had been—a beautiful animal, the size of a bull elk, with antlers still in velvet. He had a long-muzzled, square-nosed face, a glistening white neck, and a dense white mane. The whiteness spread over the shoulder and down the back, which was as gray as the Arctic twilight. His hooves were flat and rounded, perfect for the tundra. I touched a long blade of grass to the eye several times to make certain he was dead, and then I put my rifle down, unfolded my knife, and opened the body from the pelvis to the sternum. After that I rolled up my sleeves, pulled loose the viscera, and reached past the diaphragm for the lungs and finally the heart.

All this was done in twilight, largely by feel, and in the rain, and with fresh grizzly sign on the nearest hill. I worked quickly and carefully and finished in 20 minutes, and then I set back for camp through the fog and darkness, retrieving my pack along the way, hoping the rough compass heading I had followed on the way out was correct in reverse.

Sometime after nine o'clock, moving in the darkness at the speed of a 90-year-old on the way to the day room, I spotted Duane's distant fire and veered toward his campsite.

I told him about the caribou, and that he could have some of the meat, and then retired to my campsite over the hill, crawled into the tent, and slept among the dead.

In the morning, quite early and in the continual presence of our faithful companion the freezing rain, we hiked the three miles to the carcass and deboned the meat, Duane to have whatever he could carry. During this process Duane nearly cut his left thumb off, exposing the flesh to the bone from the first joint to the knuckle. It was a deep ugly wound, but he bandaged it and kept working on his end of the caribou. With perhaps 200 pounds of meat divided between us on our pack frames, we trudged back, me in front and him behind, with our rifles at port arms and stopping periodically to scan behind us. During the last mile we had to stop every 50 yards, Duane's bad foot having been wrenched in the tussocks.

That night we established a truce—Duane's self-inflicted injuries were forming a pattern—and I joined him at his fire and listened to the extended version of his life story. It was a century-long saga involving a German immigrant turned pioneering Oklahoma sodbuster, a prosperous ranching clan that lost everything in the Great Depression, a forced exodus to the city and the purgatory of urban wage-labor, and then a concluding chapter about his now-stalled-before-retirement career with the agency. The story of his loveless marriage, senile live-in mother-in-law, and ungrateful children could have been written by Dickens.

Before I departed for my camp that night, Duane began shifting around uncomfortably, and then awkwardly announced he had something to say. He cleared his throat and, staring at the fire, said he was sorry for "carrying on like I did the other night." The apology was accepted, but with the knowledge that the statement was not made from any fundamental change in character.

The next morning we hiked over for the rest of the meat, but three grizzlies were feeding on the remains, accompanied by a gathering of ravens. The bears had heavy square heads and contoured shoulder humps and each time they moved the silver fur rippled over their bodies. Occasionally the younger ones stared at us, but the mother fed without distraction, apparently confident we would not approach any closer. She may have never seen a human before—certainly she had never been shot at, or she would have run at first sight. Duane wanted to kill the sow, which was legal because the cubs were almost as large as the mother, but I prevailed upon him to spare the animal. As we sat there and watched the grizzlies crack the bones in their teeth and use their claws to retrieve the marrow, I told Duane about the past five summers I'd spent in Denali observing grizzlies and the book I was writing about them. For all its reputation, "the American Serengeti"—with its sightseeing buses, helicopter tours, and citation-writing rangers— now seemed about as wild as Central Park, compared to the far north.

We then returned to camp, both feeling as though the hunting part of the trip was over. For one thing, Duane's thumb was a mess, and his foot was too stiff to walk for more than a few miles. For another, a storm was on its way, and packing meat through snow would give new meaning to the word *travail*.

And so we organized our gear at our separate camps and began to disengage ourselves from the trip and prepare to return to civilization. The trip was already receding into the past, to an extent, and to become part of that dust cloud that forever drifts behind us on the road.

Or so we mistakenly thought, unaware that the real adventure, the life and death struggle that is always just a moment away in the wilderness, was about to begin.

That afternoon I hauled my gear to the top of the mountain and walked over to Duane's camp. Elden was scheduled to stop by and fly out any meat, and so around one o'clock Duane placed his radio among the branches of the tallest spruce, uncoiled the 50-foot wire antenna, draped it around the neighboring trees, and found the frequency used by local pilots from Fort Yukon and Arctic Village.

After several minutes of white noise we heard the following transmission: "Sheenjek Air. Mayday, mayday. Engine fire. Going down south of KV."

Five or six seconds later we heard an ominous crackle of static, followed by repeated unanswered calls to Sheenjek Air from the tower at Fort Yukon.

At which point Duane turned off the radio to save the batteries. We sat down by the fire and considered the situation. It was not as bad as it could be, nor was it as good as it had been. This much was certain: The only person who knew where we were had just crashed near Kwittevunkud Lake 40 miles to the south and was possibly dead, the season's first major snowstorm would soon arrive and we had no snow gear, we were 20 miles from the nearest regular route of travel for local pilots, current food supplies would not last indefinitely, and Duane had a hand injury and could not hike any distance on his foot.

For quite some time we didn't say much, mostly stared at the fire, somewhat in a state of disbelief, almost expecting Elden to arrive as planned. The crash, in those circumstances, seemed to belong to that category of events one reads about now and then in the Fairbanks newspaper, that occur to the friend of a passing acquaintance, or to the cousin of someone at the other end of the street, or to a high school classmate of the office secretary, but never to anyone close to you. For years, life goes on like that, the comfortable illusion that nothing bad happens inside the circle of family and friends, and then one day, in an instant, everything changes, and suddenly you are confronted once again with one of the many unpleasant facts of this small world—that, for example, worn oil gaskets fail and hot engines catch fire and smoking planes fall from the sky.

Nothing had changed in the landscape around us—the Bohemian waxwings still fed among the blueberries up the hill and the ravens still talked back and forth in their ancient corvid dialect—and so the event we had just overheard seemed unreal, part of another universe, both related and not related to us.

I tried to inject a sense of humor, as usual, even a bit of gallows humor (such as the fact that, on the bright side, if no one came for us at least we wouldn't have to go to work anymore; or that we could now live out every man's dream and spend the rest of our days hunting, fishing, and trapping in the wilderness). Duane, however, good old migraine-headache Duane, thought the situation was too serious for humor. My philosophy is the reverse—the more serious the situation, the more essential the need for humor—but of course he could not be persuaded to join the revolution.

His answer to the situation was to tell the story about the wildlife photographer. Apparently a few years earlier a *cheechako*, or inexperienced newcomer from the Lower 48, had been dropped off in the Brooks Range by an unreliable pilot with a drinking problem. The pilot returned to his cabin near Fort Yukon, settled into his usual routine, and proceeded to forget about his client, completely. The body was found about a week too late—the photographer had already shot himself, thinking he would never be rescued and not wanting to die from starvation and exposure.

As I say, Duane was a missionary in rags for the creed of optimism, a student by candlelight of the works of Aristophanes, high priest for the Cult of Perpetual Happiness, perennial poster boy for the Royal Good Fellow Society, and the actual person on whom producers based the cartoon character "Chuckles, the Happy Clown."

And so on.

At around three o'clock a 747 passed overhead—several made the high-altitude transit every afternoon, en route from Heathrow to Narita—and Duane went into his tent and pulled out a small two-way radio he had not told me about that enabled him to communicate with the pilot on an emergency frequency. His transmission went like this: "Ground party in Arctic Refuge to passing transpolar jetliner. We are in urgent need of assistance. Please respond, over." Unfortunately the pilot, flying for the Hong Kong–based carrier Tiger Air, was Chinese and spoke only enough English to land at airports. He had no idea what Duane was saying. Even if the pilot had been more fluent, Kutchin words such as Kwittevunkud or Sheenjek would not have meant much to someone whose native language was Mandarin. Another complication was that we only had a couple of minutes before the plane passed out of antenna range. The *coup de grace* was that the batteries went dead in the middle of the brief conversation, Duane having forgotten to recharge them after his last trip.

Duane proceeded to throw an "all hope is lost" fit, and I suggested that he try to adapt the batteries from the other radio. He worked on that project, like Dr. Spock in the Edith Keiller episode (Captain Kirk and company stranded on 20th-century Earth, with Joan Collins as the doomed Edith Keiller fighting the fascists), for the rest of the afternoon without any success.

The diversion, though, enabled me to finalize my plan, and over dinner I told Duane I would hike out the 20 miles to the Sheenjek and build the three signal fires, as Elden had instructed.

Duane asked if I could actually complete a cross-country trek without a map or trails, and I told him it would be no problem, providing it didn't snow. I would simply follow the streams to the river. Twenty miles is, after all, not that far. In the Marines we hiked 20 miles before noon. In Denali I day-hiked that far all the time, and never with the luxury of a trail. It would be no problem.

Duane gave me a look. I knew he thought I couldn't make it, and that was all I needed to make it.

So that settled the matter—one of us would go out "there"—*into that howling wilderness beyond their lonely outpost* (as Jack London might have phrased it)—and *that unfortunate man never heard from again* would be me.

Duane was in considerable pain from the thumb, which had begun to change color, and after dinner I convinced him to cauterize the thumb with boiling water, which was a screaming but necessary ordeal. I then tried to suture the wound with a sterilized needle and thread from his medical kit, but after the first shallow stitch Duane started throwing up. After that he took some heavy-duty prescription painkillers and passed out. He had previously declared that if necessary he would consume the entire bottle, which he carried for this sort of contingency.

And so in the pages of my journal I quietly bestowed upon him, as has long been the custom on the American Frontier, the honor of a nickname, a phrase that would capture his essence for posterity, an appellation such as was given to Francis "The Swamp Fox" Marion, or "Honest" Abe Lincoln, or "Grizzly" Adams, or "Buffalo Bill" Cody, or "Cactus Ed" Abbey.

The name I chose for Duane was "Mister Sunshine."

And what of myself? Well, by then I had more than earned the sobriquet of "The Idiot" for having been so foolish as to go on a wilderness excursion with someone I barely knew.

We waited one more day, just to make certain no one was coming, and then decided, from the condition of the sky and the lowering temperatures, there could be no further delays.

IV. The following morning I departed at first light, my frame pack stripped to the essentials. The sky was overcast and the wind was blowing from the west. Once off the tundra and in the woods, I felt more relief than concern. It was good to be moving, especially with the snow coming and the understanding of what that would mean. And it was good to be among trees—a more protected and congenial realm than the alpine. Whatever lay ahead, at least we had a better chance with one of us going for help. It was also nice to finally be away from Duane, and that dismal place he lived in.

For the first mile, the woods were open and parklike and there wasn't much brush or deadfall. I soon began to feel warm from the exertion and unzipped the rain jacket, opened my coat, and pushed my hat back on my head. I didn't want to become overheated so early in the day. The pack was heavy, and so was the ten-pound rifle in the bend of my arm, and I had to pace myself, find a comfortable rhythm, and stay to it.

There was not a sound in the woods, and the air was still. The songbirds of summer had long since departed. It would be a quiet trip, but at least there would be no mosquitoes. At its far end the main ridge diverged into two ridges. The northern ridge dropped steeply over a layer of exposed shale into a side drainage. The eastern ridge extended in the proper direction, but then descended into a forested plateau that appeared to be an excellent place to become lost. I decided, at the risk of alder, to follow the water.

And so I hiked downhill a mile into the basin and stayed parallel to the stream, following the trails of the moose.

Thank God for the moose. In Africa, the trailblazers are the elephants. In Alaska, the pioneers are the moose, boldly leading the way—impassable thickets, tangled stretches of black timber, godforsaken mountain ranges—in their determined quest for food.

The only problem was that moose don't mind wet hooves, and sometimes I had to climb a hill or detour through a woods to avoid a marshy area.

But steady progress was being made, about a mile an hour, and at that rate I would reach the Sheenjek by the next day, hopefully in advance of the snow.

I had just made that calculation when it began to snow. Not a lot, but enough to hurry the general pace.

About an hour later, as I was hiking along absorbed in these thoughts, I entered a clearing and a covey of spruce grouse, feeding on cranberries, exploded in front of me.

Nearly producing a cardiac event.

But mostly it was quiet in the woods, deadly quiet. Old spiderwebs in the grass, shed moose antlers, sun-bleached bone yards, dry fallen leaves rustling crisply underfoot, the patient cheerful trickle of water in the stream.

And all the while a steady dusting of fine snow, as when a teacher knocks the accumulated chalk powder from two erasers.

Left, right, left—your military left you at the end of first squad.

Hour after hour.

As I hiked along I saw once again how a forest is composed of different neighborhoods. Here was an old burn rich in firewood, and here a dry slope poor in blueberries. Here was an aspen grove with a bird nest in nearly every tree, and here a sedimentary outcrop where the fossil hunting would be good. This spot would be ideal for a little cabin, and that spring up the hill could provide a reliable source of water.

At the end of a long day—four-thirty and dead-tired—I reached an exposed rocky point that overlooked the country I would traverse the next day. I had come perhaps 10 miles. Perhaps a little more, perhaps a little less. But around that, around halfway. The point offered a commanding view—ahead were creeks, ridges, divides, low passes, and timber domes, all sloping toward the river. Across the Sheenjek, which was running dark and unfrozen at the bottom of the valley, was more hilly country, topped with treeless tundra. Upriver the back range had come partially into view—eroded crags with vertical head-walls, hanging glaciers, and soaring pinnacles. All views to the south were blocked by intervening ridges.

A decent place to camp.

For half an hour I dragged dead trees in from the forest and then, using one of the lantern candles, built a bonfire that could be seen from the space shuttle—there is nothing like a fire at such a time.

I pitched the tent beside a shelf of rock, so that the heat of the fire would be reflected back—it would be nice and warm through the night.

Dinner consisted of freeze-dried chili with chunks of caribou tenderloin. The more I ate the better it tasted. "Hunger is a good sauce," as Captain Bourke wrote toward the end of his dusty career on the Mexican border. Bloody good tucker, mates. And all that. By fire-light I wrote in my journal in the manner of the lifelong naturalist—that, for example, I was camped beside a blocky tor of horizontally fo-liated metamorphic rock and that down the slope was a broken scarp of the same material. The rock was porphyritic granite, I wrote, iden-tical to that I'd found on Primrose Ridge in the Alaska Range and on Wickersham Dome in the White Mountains.

That was the last thing I wrote before sleep.

V. The first vague morning light showed about three inches of fresh snow had fallen during the dark hours and more was falling. The ther-mometer on the pack registered 24° F. It felt colder, but it naturally tends to in a situation like that—200 miles from the nearest road. I didn't restoke the fire, only nibbled on some cookies for breakfast, and then quickly packed up and set off.

Mount up and move out, Bravo One.

Not 50 yards from my camp, a moose had bedded down for the night. The snow was melted and glassy from his body heat, and nearby was a pile of black pellets, not yet frozen. His antlers had left impres-sions in the snow and the blades of grass near the front of the bed were still frosted from his breath. Perhaps he felt safer near the fire, sensing wolves wouldn't come near, or perhaps that was one of his customary bedding locations.

As I hiked along I could see where he had fed on twigs, branches, bark, leaves—anything green.

There were a lot of moose in the valley. The rut would begin soon, and they were drifting in from the hills. Tracks were everywhere—herd bulls and upstart bulls, barren old cows and fertile young ones, abandoned yearling calves and those fortunate ones still with their mothers, all about to commence with the moose version of the Mardi Gras.

The valley woods were not as lifeless as the highlands. Down lower, there was considerably more activity, and I frequently had company: a red fox eating rose hips that was startled, perhaps even embarrassed, when I walked by and said hello; a troupe of black-beaked magpies playing in a thicket, the young ones almost as large as their parents, seven in all, clamoring about like busy happy families everywhere; a cow moose plodding along through the snow, head lifted, completely ignoring me, late, it would seem, for an important appointment.

It was a gentle familiar woods, the woods of home.

Late in the morning I came upon the scene of a wolf attack, the evidence no more than a few hours old. I saw in the snow where the wolves had brought a moose to bay and torn a piece of its hindquarters off. The moose ran for 100 yards through the snow, trailing spots of blood, and the tangle commenced again. It became a prolonged engagement that went on for half a mile along my route of travel. In the end, the moose ran for the safety of an alder thicket, where it could cut its tormentors to pieces with those sharp hooves, and the wolves, two adults and two young of the year, trotted over the side of the hill into another valley—they would return after a day or two, in the hour before dawn, the killing hour.

I followed neither trail, but remained on the high ground.

At midafternoon I stopped for 10 minutes and ate the last of my cookies. After that, it would be blueberries pulled from the branch.

Hour after hour, striding along, avoiding deadfalls and thickets, checking my compass, my breath in a ghostly plume behind me, always the soft crunch of the snow beneath the felt-lined paks.

The storm began to taper in the afternoon. As it did, the clouds lifted and the light was beautiful—a rose-gray glow to the southwest casting subtle shadows over the land, and in the east a venous blue edging into violet, which gave the sky in that quarter the appearance of a healing bruise.

At three o'clock, hiking down the last side valley, I was joined by a raven, who chattered incessantly in that peculiarly human voice of ravens, and followed me through the woods as if he was the local real estate agent. I was near the floodplain of the Sheenjek now and the snow was abating and my pace was slowing—the end was near. I enjoyed the antics of my new friend the raven—they are among the most intelligent birds, with over 100 sounds in their language After awhile the moose trail we were following led off into a basin of beaver ponds—heaven to a moose, hell to a man—and so I climbed a hill to avoid becoming soaked and then cut back through the woods toward the sound of the river.

As I was walking through the woods I saw the raven sitting on an oddly angled object in the trees. I stopped and stared at the raven. Something about the scene was not quite right—an unexpected mass, an unnatural angle—and so I made a detour.

The object that did not fit into its surroundings turned out to be the collapsed remnants of an antique cabin and a tipped-over meat cache of the same vintage. The ruins had been there for quite some time, judging from the lichens. Near the cabin was a large crystalline ridge that ran above ground for hundreds of yards. Resting on the side of this ridge was a rusted pick, the wooden handle long ago devoured by porcupines. I took off my pack, for I was very tired, and slowly walked up and down the ledge, trying to figure out what it was. The wall appeared to be a nearly pure vein of milky quartz, and on closer inspection the rock was marked with the cobalt blue of copper, the corroded gray of silver, and the bright unmistakable flecks of gold. I found a piece that filled my gloved hand and put it in the pack.

The river was calling and so I resumed the march. A quarter of a mile later, there she was—the river Sheenjek, running bank full—and what a welcome sight. I set up my orange tent on a gravel bar beside the river. It would be cold there, but at least the tent would be visible from the air.

VI. And I didn't have to wait long. Early the next morning, tending my three fires in what had become a driving blizzard, I heard human voices. Shortly, two 14-foot flatboats, their engines out of the water and drifting with the current, came into view. I waved and shouted and they pulled over. The occupants were Dorothy and Leo Peters, Kutchin residents of Fort Yukon, their teenage son Richard, and a gregarious wolf hybrid named Hooch that liked to lick your face. Dorothy and Leo were physically as different as two people could be—Leo short and small-boned, Dorothy, in a word, massive. Richard appeared more related to his mother than his father but still had his father's strong chin and thick eyebrows. All three wore rubber hip boots and parkas.

They were in a hurry because the river was dropping and they had to get through something called "Peel Canyon" before nightfall, and so after explaining my situation they said I could ride in the boat with their son and his dog but that we must leave now. What about my companion? I asked. "God help him if he's up there in this blizzard," answered Dorothy. "Now hurry up and get in, or stay, it's up to you."

I stuffed my gear in the pack, took one final look at Fort Necessity, Population 1, and stepped into the boat with Richard.

My job was to man one of the 10-foot aspen poles and help steer the craft, something I'd never done before but would now have the opportunity to learn.

It was cold on the river, even with seven layers of clothing, and I shivered a lot. They told me that they had never been that far up before—nobody had—but the record rains had enabled them to explore farther than in past years. I asked if they were hunting moose, and the mother laughed—she was the boss and did all the talking—and said nobody in their right mind would hunt moose this far from Yuk. No, she said, look under the tarp.

Under the canvas tarp was the tusk of a mammoth, six or seven feet long and mottled green and dark tan and light gray. It was as big around as my thigh.

"How much does this thing weigh?"

"About as much as the gasoline it took to get here," said Dorothy, with a smile.

She said they found the tusk in a cutbank a few miles above my camp. They spotted another but couldn't dig it out because of the ice and with the dropping water decided to come back some other year if the water ever got this high again.

We had just drifted by an eagle nest in a cottonwood tree, and I was trying to estimate the diameter of the nest (10 feet? 12 feet?)—when I heard a roaring downstream. I turned toward the other boat to ask what was happening and was immediately instructed to pull up the pole—it would be useless in the rapids—and find a safe place to sit in the middle of the boat.

Rapids?

"Look alive, man," the father sternly warned, the first words he had spoken. "We're gonna run the canyon. Richard knows what he's doing. Keep your weight in the center and don't move around."

By now the rock walls had risen on either side of the river and the current was accelerating and the roar of the rapids was tremendous. A huge volume of water was compressed between the rocks and there were white-crested waves everywhere. The sounds were amazing—midtones and overtones and under it all something like a big bass drum banging away, throbbing, resonant. The acoustics were superb—it was a place to sing "Shenandoah" at the top of your lungs. Or a place to die, in an instant.

Up and down we went, over churning waves and into sucking troughs.

There were stumps and whole trees riding by on the current, and Richard deflected them with his oar. Sometimes he was only partly successful, and they collided with the boat, branches reaching. They were half-submerged from their own sodden weight and turned slowly in the current, like drowning people lifting an arm before going under.

And all the time it snowed—unrelenting, the end of the world, All Souls' Day, the sky falling.

Just when I thought we were free—cliffs lowering, gorge widening—the river grabbed the paddle from Richard's hands—it was gone in the time it takes to read this aside—and he turned to his parents and shouted something. I looked toward the other boat. Leo was yelling, but we couldn't hear him.

I was sitting in the back of the boat and Richard was telling me to turn on the engine, turn on the engine. I looked for a cord, didn't find one, turned to ask Richard where it was and saw a rock in the middle of the river. Rock? It was the size of a Ryder truck and it divided the river in two, one side half as wide as the other. There was a white mist hanging around the rock, and I realized there was a whirlpool beyond it and that we must somehow go through the wider of the two channels.

But it was too late.

We could not stop and in a few moments hit the rock to one side, crunching the side in, and I felt the water lift us up, as if the river was studying us for a moment, and then we plunged through the wrong gap, sideways, and were spinning around and around in circles and I thought for sure the boat was going to turn over and spill us out but then we were suddenly in the next stretch, floating backward in the wide, deep, and quiet water, everything calm.

It happened that quickly.

Richard stepped over Hooch and started the engine as you do a lawnmower, with a pull cord on the outboard side. In a moment Dorothy and Leo came through the gap.

Dorothy was laughing.

Leo smiled, the spaces in his teeth showing, and called over the water: "Rivers are like the government—they can't be trusted."

He started the engine on his boat and we cruised together down the lovely empty river through the snow.

We covered 45 miles that day, according to Dorothy, and the farther we went the more the river began to meander, like a string a cat has been playing with on the carpet. There were side streams and islands, logjams and floating trees, sweepers and unexpected rocks, and on either side, always, the snow-covered spruce forest, fronted with willows and alders.

We saw one beaver that day, and nothing else, and it never stopped snowing.

We camped above the confluence of the Sheenjek and the Porcupine, about 60 miles from Fort Yukon. It was a level spot in the spruce where river travelers have probably camped for 10,000 years. Leo set up a canvas tarp between two trees in such a way as to make a three-sided tent. Dorothy built a fire in front of it and inside the tent it was as warm and dry as inside a cabin—we laid out our sleeping bags and made it quite comfortable.

Dinner consisted of the last of my caribou meat mixed in with macaroni and cheese and eaten from a large suet-covered steel pot, all of us gathered round with forks in one hand and bread in the other.

At some point after dinner I asked what the land status of the area was—whether we were on federal land, or not.

That was a big mistake. Dorothy's face flushed and she started in on a long tirade about the federal government—"How would you feel if someone came in and took over your country and stole your land and then made you pay taxes on top of that?"

Leo made a face that said, "You don't want to get her started."

Richard got up to take a walk, even though it was nearly dark.

"I hate those people," Dorothy continued. "They come into the village and don't try to get to know anybody. They just start ordering us around like we're children."

Leo started telling jokes, trying to mollify his wife. Such as,

"Why is the fed standing with his hand on the lightbulb?"

"He's waiting for his three assistants to spin him around."

And,

"How do you know the feds have been in the village?"

"The dogs are pregnant and the trash cans are empty."

She finally smiled, a little.

Later that night, when I was looking for my toothbrush, I found the piece of milky quartz in my pack and showed it to them.

"You guys ever see anything like this before?"

Leo took the rock, his eyes a few inches from it. He handed it to his wife. She held the crystal toward the campfire and traced her fingers over the planar faces, the light of the flames passing through the quartz and onto her face.

"Where'd you find this?" she asked.

"In the hills behind where I was camped."

"What was it like where you found it?"

I described the wall of milky quartz and the cabin.

They spoke back and forth excitedly in their language.

"What are you saying?" I asked.

Dorothy proceeded to relate the story of Robert Hess, a Canadian who wandered into Fort Yukon in the summer of 1909 or 1910, purchased a riverboat and supplies, and then disappeared into the wilderness for two years. When he returned to Fort Yukon he claimed to have discovered gold on the upper Sheenjek and had a bag of gold to prove it. No one knew exactly where the mine was—he kept the location secret, but he did mention an exposed quartz ridge. Over the next four years he brought in $20,000 worth of gold, just working by himself and sometimes with his brother Lancaster. After the war started, the Hess brothers went down to Vancouver and enlisted in the British Army. They promised to return and take a company of men upriver to work the mine, but both were killed when a German submarine sank their transport in the North Atlantic. The location of the mine died with them. After years of futile searching everyone forgot about the Hess Mine, except the old people, who kept the legend alive during the winter nights—it was their north-country version of the Lost Dutchman Mine, for whosoever found the Lost Hess Mine would be forever transported from the realm of earthly cares, the gold both an element on the periodic chart and a metaphor for some sort of paradise the human race hasn't known since Mesopotamia.

There followed a lively discussion, in which I played little part, about whether the site was in fact the Hess Mine and, if it was, what should be done. Leo wanted to file a claim and tell the world. Dorothy insisted the discovery be kept secret and that only a small amount of ore be removed every now and then, very discreetly. That way they wouldn't have to deal with the dreaded "feds."

When asked my preference, I replied that I had no interest in the subject. The information was theirs to do with as they wished. They could even keep the rock. I had no desire to ever return to the place.

You have never seen three more surprised people.

When I turned in that night they were still talking around the fire in their language, which reminded me of Navajo. It is a musical language, beautiful in its phrasing and intonations, and is pleasant and relaxing on the ear.

The next day it snowed much harder, big flakes. Snowing, snowing, the river hissing against the bottom of the boat, Hooch sleeping soundly on top of the trophy bone he had dragged in from the field, which would make him king of all the dogs back in Fort Yukon.

We stopped once—to ask to use a camp radio—but the radio was broken and everyone was drunk. "You don't want to stop at some of these camps," Dorothy warned. She believed there was a difference between people who lived in the villages and those who did not, who maintained small cabins along the back sloughs and lived strange impoverished lives.

The confluence with the Porcupine was amazing—like motoring out on a lake, compared to the narrow Sheenjek. It was a wide slow-moving river, with the greenish color of an aquarium that has not been cleaned in six months, and we roared along, watching always for snags and sandbars, whirlpools and riffles, and seeing only the occasional flight of mergansers or buffleheads waiting out the storm.

Approaching Fort Yukon by flatboat was like paddling a canoe toward St. Louis in the year 1820—a crowded, perpetually busy waterfront, a modest supply post of a village in the woods beyond, the immense river in front serving as the sole highway into a vast unsettled territory. Here was the last stop before the "last great wilderness on earth," the muddy portals to the primeval, the wormhole entrance to that other, older universe, and on the well-worn banks were all variety of frontier folk, most with the bark still on them. I imagine the end of the world to be such a place, a final cluttered weigh station before eternity, an unadorned aperture into the unknown, a glimpse across the waters to a place that will be both the same and different for each traveler.

After we dragged the flatboats from the water and unloaded the gear and the giant tusk into a caravan of four-wheelers, I presented Dorothy with my rifle in gratitude for the passage (the gun quickly handed to a beaming Richard), wished them well, and asked directions to the troopers' office.

At the top of the hill I found the local office in the same building as the clinic. I kicked the snow from my paks, stepped in, dropped my pack, and identified myself to the officer on duty, who was putting on his down coat and was about to leave. On the wall behind him was a topographic map of Alaska, including the Aleutians, divided by state trooper districts, and a framed painting of Alexander Murray, who founded Fort Yukon in 1847.

"What happened to Duane?" I asked.

"He was picked up the day after you left. He's at Fairbanks Memorial."

"Infected thumb?"

"No, he walked into the airplane wing and cut his head open."

"Weren't you guys going to look for me?"

"Sure, once the storm cleared. But we can't launch an aerial search in a blizzard. Not without a beacon locator or anything. We knew your general route. We would have started tomorrow."

I asked him if I could use the phone to call Fairbanks, but he said the lines were down, a now deceased porcupine having chewed through the cable to the Alascom satellite dish. He then headed for the back door and told me to lock the front door on the way out.

There are two lodges in Fort Yukon, one run by the Kutchin and the other not, and I walked over to the first to rent a cabin for the night—Dorothy and Leo had politely invited me to spend the night at their place, but I didn't want to impose any further. As I was registering at the counter of the Gwitchyaa Zhee Lodge a man closely resembling Elden Morris walked in, a man in fact who appeared to be Elden Morris.

I blinked at the sight, not trusting my senses, and then glanced at the woman across the counter, to see if she, too, saw the visage. She did.

"I thought you were dead," the figure said, stepping closer and punching my shoulder.

"I thought *you* were dead," I said, realizing it was indeed Elden and shaking his hand in both of mine.

"Dorothy briefed me," he said, motioning toward the street.

In a moment, everything was explained. Earlier that month a pilot named Trent Collier had started flying side jobs for Elden and using his call sign, Sheenjek Air. Elden had been en route to our camp when Trent, in an overloaded Cessna, went down. Elden turned back, landed near the crash site, pulled the most critically injured hunter out, and flew him to Fort Yukon. The rest of the day was involved with the crash. The following day Elden had to fly to Beaver to pick up a woman in labor. The day after that he put skis on his plane and flew to our camp, but by the time he arrived I was miles away and the snow had begun to fall.

We shook hands again and said goodbye and I walked to a table, ordered the beef stew dinner, talked with the waitress for awhile, and read a three-day-old newspaper. After awhile a couple of children came in and played with their toys by the fireplace. I ate dinner and watched the evening news—another Republican member of Congress indicted on some minor felony, rumors that the Democratic presidential candidate was given to a loose interpretation of the seventh commandment, my favorite football team already a long shot for the playoffs.

America.

The high point of the day was having hot apple pie and vanilla ice cream with the waitress and then going for a ride through the woods on her snowmobile, something, over four Alaskan winters, I'd never done.

By the time I reached the cabin I was so tired I didn't build a fire. I dumped my pack on the floor, spread the sleeping bag on top of the bed, and collapsed. Outside the dogs were barking and howling at something. Inside a mouse was already scratching around the pack. Suddenly the light of the moon streamed through the window. The storm had finally blown off to the east.

And then there was a knock on the door—an armful of kindling for the fire.

A deep cold settled over the land that night, and stayed for eight months.

VII. The walk, the weather, the sky, the solitude, the river—they would become sweeter over time. It is well sometimes to see a country as it was before we were here. To recall freedoms lost and gained, and to understand where we may be on the more extended journey, and to gaze through our longest lens, which is the past, into the future. To remember the world as it was in the beginning, and to listen again to a harmony that expresses itself in silence.

Down from the hills I had traveled, and I would never regard wilderness, civilization, or myself in the same way. I saw that what we call civilization is more wild than that which is commonly given the name, and that the gulf between who we are and what we are is as great as the span between the cry of a newborn baby and a handful of ash in an urn.

In after-years memories return: of vast steppes lying desolate under clear skies, of a mighty river making its way to a distant Arctic sea, of a snowy forest where the only darkness was the eye of a raven, of a place so immense and still that I can hold it close whenever I feel myself at turmoil, and instantly be at peace. The generations that follow should always allow for such places to endure, places where the wild animals roam freely and the storms last for weeks, places where time is measured in the melting ice and shooting stars blossom in the moss, places that the human race leaves undisturbed as we leave undisturbed the hearts in our chests that beat and give us life.

Notes on Contributors

Rick Bass is one of our nation's most distinguished writers of prose. Among his many works are *The Lost Grizzlies, Ninemile Wolves,* and *Where the Sea Used to Be*. He lives in Troy, Montana, with his wife Elizabeth and their two daughters.

Carol Ann Bassett is a professor of journalism at the University of Oregon, Eugene. Her work has been published widely in newspapers and magazines, including the *New York Times* and *Newsweek*.

William Bartram, son of colonial botanist John Bartram, undertook a pioneering survey of the Southeast in the late eighteenth century. His account of the expedition is one of the earliest nature books in American literature.

Isabella Byrd is one of the most influential women nature writers of the nineteenth century. A true pioneer as a woman and as an author, her book *A Lady's Life in the Rocky Mountains* is now considered a classic of the genre.

William Byrd was dispatched to settle a border dispute in the Carolinas in the years before the Revolutionary War. His journal chronicles a lost eastern wilderness—bison, elk, passenger pigeons, and Native Americans living in harmony with the landscape.

Lisa Couturier lives with her husband Kirk and daughter Madeleine in Bethesda, Maryland. Her writings have been widely published, most recently in the *American Nature Writing* series and in *Heart of a Nation* (National Geographic Books, 2000).

William O. Douglas served as an associate justice of the Supreme Court after a brilliant career as a law professor at Yale University and as chairman of the Securities and Exchange Commission. An active environmentalist, he authored several wonderful nature books, including *My Wilderness*.

Aliette Frank is a recent graduate in environmental science from Dartmouth University. Her writing has appeared in the *American Nature Writing* series and in *Sports Afield* magazine. Her travels to date have taken her to Uganda, Costa Rica, Jamaica, and Alaska.

A. B. Guthrie is best known for authoring *The Way West*, a novel that was awarded the Pulitzer prize. His screenplay for the classic western film *Shane* was nominated for an Academy Award.

Jon Krakauer is known throughout the world for his experience on Mount Everest, a climbing trip he wrote about in *Into Thin Air*, which was later made into a television movie.

Barbara Kingsolver is one of our country's most beloved writers. The selection is taken from one of her most popular books, *High Tide in Tucson*.

Aldo Leopold wrote only two small books, *A Sand County Almanac* and *Round River*, but has had a profound influence on environmental philosophy. For many years he worked as a professor of biology at the University of Wisconsin, Madison, before being felled by a fatal heart attack while fighting a fire near his beloved "Shack."

Sue Marsh has worked for many years as a wilderness ranger for the Teton National Forest in Jackson, Wyoming. Her writing has appeared in the *American Nature Writing* series and several journals, including *Orion*.

Debbie Miller worked with her husband for several years as a schoolteacher in Arctic Village, Alaska, which is located deep in the Brooks Range. Her book *Midnight Wilderness* is a moving tribute to the wild region.

John Muir, a native of Scotland, immigrated from Wisconsin to California in his twenties, and was forever transformed by the beauty and power of the Sierra Range. Few people have had such a profound influence on the relationship between human culture and nature. His books and essays remain widely in print today, nearly a century after his death.

David Petersen is the author of over a dozen books and is also known as the editor of Edward Abbey's journals, *Confessions of a Barbarian*. He and wife Carolyn live in a remote area of the San Juan Mountains in southwestern Colorado.

Rob Schultheis was trained as an anthropologist at the University of Colorado, Boulder, and later traveled widely across the American West and the world. His book *The Hidden West* is now considered a classic of the genre.

Henry David Thoreau is best known for his year-and-a-half stay at a small cabin near Walden Pond in eastern Massachusetts. His book, *Walden*, made a permanent contribution to world literature. His political writings, most notably the essay on civil disobedience, transformed passive resistance movements in the twentieth century.

David Rains Wallace has authored over a dozen works of natural history, in-cluding *Idle Weeds* and *The Dark Range*. He lives in Berkeley, California, with his wife.

Jon Waterman is one of our finest mountain climbing writers. His celebrated book *Eiger Dreams* takes us to the ends of the world—Denali, K2, and Everest.

$\mathscr{A}$CKNOWLEDGMENTS

Rick Bass: "Magic at Ruth Lake" from *Wild to the Heart*. Copyright 1989 by Rick Bass. Reprinted with permission of the author.

Carol Ann Bassett: "Mountain Mazama: The Realm of Becoming." Copyright 2000 by Carol Ann Bassett. Reprinted with permission of the author.

Lisa Couturier: "A Clandestine Freedom." Copyright 2000 by Lisa Couturier. Reprinted with permission of the author.

William O. Douglas: "White Mountains" from *My Wilderness*. Copyright 1960 by William O. Douglas. Reprinted with permission of Doubleday.

Aliette Frank: "Crevasse." Copyright 2000 by Aliette Frank. Reprinted with permission of the author.

A. B. Guthrie: "The Rocky Mountain Front." Copyright 1990 by Northland Publishing. Reprinted with permission of the publisher.

Jon Krakauer: "The Devils Thumb" from *Eiger Dreams*. Copyright 1990 by Jon Krakauer. Reprinted with permission of The Lyons Press.

Barbara Kingsolver: "Infernal Paradise" from *High Tide in Tucson*. Copyright 1996 by Barbara Kingsolver. Reprinted with permission of Harper-Collins.

Aldo Leopold: "Thinking Like a Mountain" from *Round River*. Copyright 1949 by Oxford University Press. Reprinted with permission of the publisher.

Sue Marsh: "Belly of the Indian." Copyright 2000 by Sue Marsh. Reprinted with permission of the author.

Debbie Miller: "A Mystery Solved" from *Midnight Wilderness*. Copyright 1989 by Sierra Club Books. Reprinted with permission of the publisher.

John A. Murray: "From the Faraway Nearby" from *American Nature Writing: 1998*. Copyright 1998 by John A. Murray. Reprinted with permission of the author.

Acknowledgments

David Petersen: "Baboquivari!" from *The Nearby Faraway*. Copyright 1998 by David Petersen. Reprinted with permission of the author.

Rob Schulheis: "Navaho Mountain" from *The Hidden West*. Copyright 1983 by Rob Schulteis. Reprinted with permission of The Lyons Press.

David Rains Wallace: "Volcanoes" from *The Monkey's Bridge*. Copyright 1998 by David Rains Wallace. Reprinted with permission of Sierra Club Books.

Jon Waterman: from *In the Shadow of Denali*. Copyright 1998 by Jon Waterman. Reprinted with permission of The Lyons Press.